Jewel Tea Grocery Products

C.L. Miller

Schiffer Publishing Ltd
77 Lower Valley Road, Atglen, PA 19310

Library of Congress Cataloging-in-Publication Data

Miller, C.L. (Charles L.), 1941-
Jewel Tea grocery products/C. L. Miller.
p. cm.
Includes bibliographical references and index.
ISBN 0-88740-984-9
1. Jewel Tea Company--Collectibles--Catalogs. 2.Grocery trade--Collectibles--United States--Catalogs. I. Title.
NK808.M565 1996
683'.8'0973075--dc20 96-6042
CIP

Printed in China
ISBN: 0-88740-984-9
Book Design by Audrey L. Whiteside

Published by Schiffer Publishing, Ltd.
77 Lower Valley Road
Atglen, PA 19310
Please write for a free catalog.
This book may be purchased from the publisher.
Please include $2.95 for shipping.
Try your bookstore first.

We are interested in hearing from authors
with book ideas on related subjects.

DEDICATION

To the women of the Jewel Test Kitchen:
Mary Reed (Mary Dunbar) Hartson, Ruth Leone Rutledge Carroll, Julia Goddard, Marian Kessel, Mavis Galloway, and Mrs. Bierman.

This is the Jewel Homemakers' test kitchen in Barrington, Illinois, where ingredients were tested and recipes developed. Ruth Leone Rutledge Carroll is shown on the left with two Jewel employees. Note the Jewel Peanut Butter and Jewel Vanilla Bottles on the counter and the various Jewel premiums in the background. The visible premiums include a two-quart salad bowl, 5-1/2 pint capacity ice lip beverage pitcher, gravy boat, sugar and creamer, various plates, Model J-1 electric coffee granulator, and a set of nested bowls. It is evident that an examination is being conducted in this historical 1940s photograph. This photograph is similar to a historical photograph appearing later in this publication.

ACKNOWLEDGMENTS

I can never fully express my appreciation for the support, encouragement, and help I received from each collector, during the development of this, my latest book, on this historical company. Without their knowledge, persistence, inspiration, and collections, this book would never have been possible. My sincere thanks goes out to each of you: Al Barnes, Dan W. Andrews, Richard Berres, Jean Boelter, Shelley Boelter, Neal and Patti Byerly, Dan and Char Casey, Ruby Cochran, John Crouse, Douglas B. Dupler, Larry Edelman, Gary and Carol Eisnaugle, Richard G. and Helen T. Fair, Aileen Ferriera, Ann Griffen, Myrtle Gutwein, Bill and NanSue Hamilton, Bill and Dee Hedges, Scot L. Heimann, Mary Ann Housel, Lon and Lynda Lemons, Charles and Mildred Lombard, Ralph and Linda Miller, Jim and Tommi Orr, Jim Parshall, Art and Barbara J. Randall, Dick and Sandra Spayde, Clinton Steelman, Randy and Marsha Vogel, Joel Wilson, Virginia Lee Wilson, and finally to my family and friends for their faith in me. If I have overlooked anyone I apologize at this time.

Ruth Leone Rutledge Carroll appears in this historical photograph. Mrs. Carroll became the most famous Mary Dunbar in Jewel's history, replacing her predecessor, Mary Reed Hartson (a.k.a. Mary Dunbar), in 1926. Mrs. Carroll had a 17-year association with the Jewel Tea Company and became the first woman in Jewel's history to become an executive. Ruth Leone Rutledge Carroll died in September of 1975.

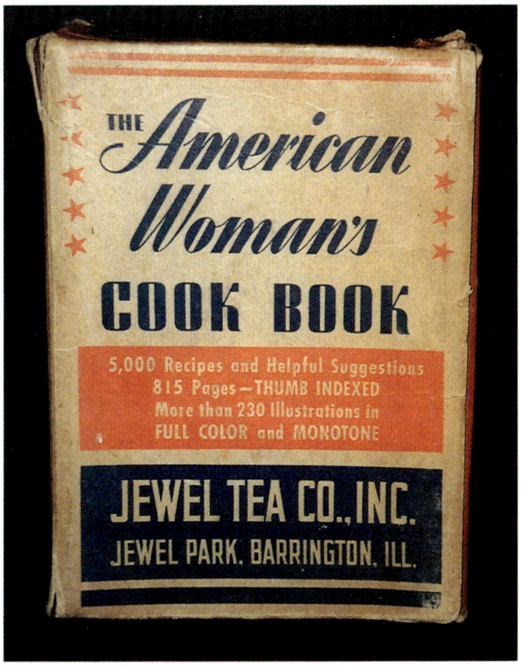

This cardboard carton is marked "JEWEL TEA CO., INC., JEWEL PARK, BARRINGTON, ILL." Enclosed is an 815 page copy of "The American Woman's Cook Book." No indication of association with the Jewel Tea Company appears in this cook book. The book is hard bound with 5,000 recipes and "Helpful Suggestions" and included 230 illustrations in full color and monotone. The American Woman's Cook Book in the original carton was discovered in an attic. *Fair Collection.*

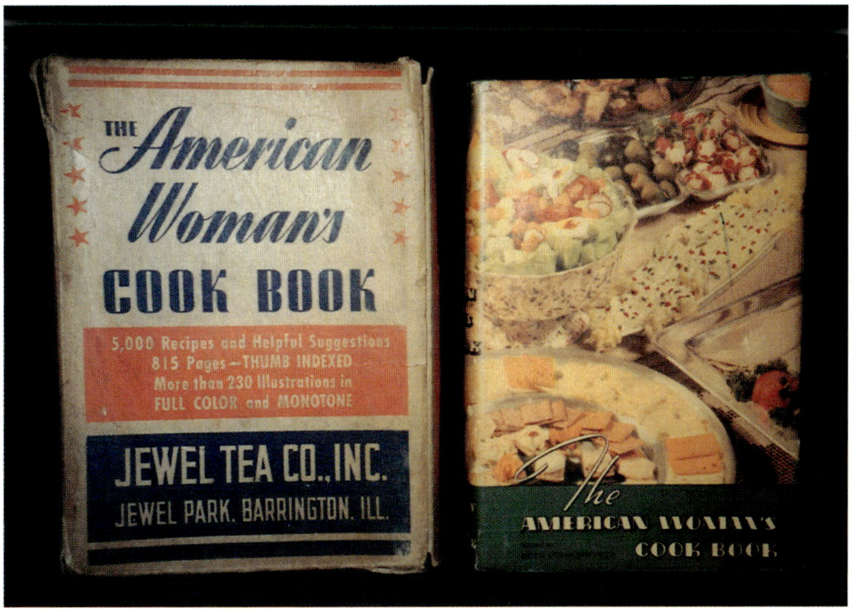

FOREWORD

After the publication of my first two Jewel books — *The Jewel Tea Company. Its History and Products* (1994) and *Jewel Tea. Sales and Houşeware Collectibles* (1995) — many collectors wrote or phoned me, directly asking for a Jewel grocery products book. I was very reluctant to begin another Jewel book as I had started documenting another historical company. When the calls continued and the mail piled up inquiring about a Jewel grocery product publication, I changed my mind. I compiled an outline, spoke with Schiffer Publishing Ltd., and this book was launched.

Throughout this publication an array of Jewel grocery products will appear, as well as original advertisements that once appeared in monthly issues of the Jewel News. However, many dates are not certain in this publication, as every Jewel publication was not available for my research. If I misled anyone or have made mistakes, I apologize for it at this time. If you should have Jewel grocery products in your collection that are not shown in this publication, I would appreciate hearing from you.

I have also included clippings from original 1970s Jewel Stock Cards. Jewel Stock Cards, measuring approximately 14" long by 10-1/4" wide, were used to promote various Jewel grocery products. Many items appear either in color or black and white. Various Stock Cards can be found with free samples attached, i.e. spatulas, dish clothes, or finger nail clippers. Presently JEWEL STOCK CARDS are modestly priced and provide good reference.

Much has been written about the Jewel Tea Company; therefore, in this publication I am providing only "A Brief History." We shall examine "The Jewel Way," understand the "Merchandising Principles," and discover what was "Influencing the Housewife." How a Jewel product received the "Seal of Approval" and the "Condition Factor" of historical products.

As stated above, the name "Mrs. Brown" was a general title given by the Jewel Tea organization and their salesmen when they referred to Jewel's women customers in general. Before the introduction of "Mrs. Brown" as a general title for a female customer, Jewel referred to such a customer as "Mrs. White." This can be seen in numerous Jewel reference materials.

Today the title of Mrs. Brown still belongs to those dedicated women who shopped "the Jewel way." Many collector's owe Mrs. Brown their gratitude for keeping all those items, that are now so collectible, available to them.

It is impossible to list or photograph every Jewel grocery item that was available to Mrs. Brown. Many items were lost to time. Only those survivors made available to the author are shown. As you read this book and examine the products, it would be wise to remember that products bearing the phrase "Distributed by" were manufactured by someone, whereas "Manufactured by" indicates that the product was produced by Jewel.

It is also wise to study each product carefully. Examine every item and learn to recognize the various logos. Remember that Jewel moved into their Barrington headquarters in 1930. If a Jewel product is marked "Jewel Park" this indicates a date after 1930. Many logos overlap, as Jewel used up older products before issuing new.

A five digit zip code number was put into use by the United States Post Office in 1959. Zip codes appearing on any product indicates a date after 1959.

Finally, as you make your way through this publication, savor the aroma of "Jewel Coffee, Tea and Cocoa Products," inhale the pungent smell of "Jewel Spices, Extracts and Dressings." Distinguish the difference in "Jewel Breakfast Products" and behold the fragrance of "Jewel Soaps and Cleaning Products."

Sample "Jewel Candy" and "Jewel-Jell." Try Jewel Peanut Butter, Crackers, Desert Products, Macaroni, Noodles, and Spaghetti as well.

Learn about "Victory," one of the most sought after products in today's market. In the "Beware" Chapter, also learn about "Condition Factor and Caring for Your Products" and what lives within those cartons.

CONTENTS

The Jewel Tea Company's Barrington, Illinois home office and principal manufacturing plant. If a grocery product is marked Jewel Park, this indicates a date after 1930 when Jewel moved into their Barrington, Jewel Park, Illinois headquarters. *Boelter Collection.*

INTRODUCTION

The Jewel Tea Company, Inc.

Do you find yourself driven to collect advertising tins? If so, you are not alone. It is estimated that over 800,000 collectors across the United States maintain a collection of advertising tins and historical products in one form or another. An average collector has approximately 150 - 300 grocery advertising products in their collection. It is impossible to provide a complete listing of the collectible tins available in the secondary market today from the Jewel Tea Company, or from any other source.

There are many excellent publications on various advertising tins available to the collector. It is wise to seek publications from your local library or to check with various book dealers that specialize in collectors' books. Most antique shows and flea markets have book dealers selling a wide variety of collectors' books.

What would Frank V. Skiff and Frank P. Ross, founders of the Jewel Tea Company, think if they knew that the grocery products they delivered, and those which followed from the enterprise they created, were yielding high prices in the collecting world today? When a Jewel customer (known to the Jewel sales force generically as "Mrs. Brown") purchased her weekly supply of coffee, teas, spices, and groceries supplies, she had no idea those simple containers she acquired from her Jewel man would one day be sought by a generation of collectors across the United States. Those common grocery tins kept in a kitchen pantry — containing Jewel spices, teas, and coffee — provided not the slightest intimation that a younger generation would later seek them out.

Jewel grocery products, either tins, cardboard containers, or bottles and jars, have recently escalated in both price and demand. Within the last fifteen years collectors from both the National Autumn Leaf Collectors Club (N.A.L.C.C.) and from China Specialties (along with advertisement collectors and collectors in general) have taken notice of the grocery line from this historical company. Many grocery products bring higher prices today than some of the famous Hall Jewel Autumn Leaf China wares offered by this company as premiums in the secondary market.

The Jewel Tea Company often advertised, "Give Jewel premiums as presents. Let your grocery purchases pay for them." According to Jewel publications, when Mrs. Brown started to trade with the Jewel Tea Company, she paid the Company and its groceries a compliment. The honor Mrs. Brown gave Jewel resulted in an obligation by the Company to please and satisfy her and to hold her trade. Jewel premiums were considered one way of holding that trade.

In 1926 and early 1927 Jewel salesmen, carrying "only the purest and finest quality Jewel grocery products," reached over 2,500,000 customers. Along with over fifty food, laundry, and toilet products, nearly one hundred premiums were available to their customers.

Jewel President M.N. Karker once said, "We (Jewel) use the possessive form in speaking of 'our' customers because we are proud of them, because they are the source for all things good for us, and because their buying is the final seal of approval on all our work. If we had no customers, there would be no sales — no job — no Jewel."

Jewel was a merchandising business and they were aware of the facts that sales made jobs and that the real job was in the hands of the Jewel salesmen. To the Jewel salesman, selling was an obsession, a dedication. It was the salesman's mission to bring Jewel customers better food at less cost, thus saving them money, time, and energy. The Jewel salesmen tried to help Mrs. Brown make her grocery money go further and, if he succeeded, the results to both were satisfaction.

For the American housewife, Jewel proclaimed that their groceries "did a better job than any other brand in the World." For it was Jewel's selling job to keep each Mrs. Brown convinced that this was true. Throughout this book, you will become familiar with many of those products that convinced Mrs. Brown to trade the Jewel way. You will see numerous examples of those that have survived.

When Frank V. Skiff, the son of a Newton, Iowa grocer, joined force with his brother-in-law, Frank P. Ross, in the city of Chicago, they brought one new and revolutionary idea into the industry. That idea was to advance the customer's first premium with the delivery of her first grocery order.

This is how the premium system worked. With every Jewel product that was purchased, Jewel gave a substantial discount in the form of a Profit Sharing Credit (or P.S.C.). Mrs. Brown selected a premium she wanted and then used the profit sharing credits she obtained with all of her Jewel grocery products to pay for the premium without any cash outlay. The first premium was advanced to her with her very first order of "Jewel Best" coffee or other products.

Jewel did not advertise for new customers through public media. When additional customers were needed, Jewel felt that it was necessary that new customers should be only in certain neighborhoods or even on a certain street. If Jewel advertised — there would be no control as to where the response would come from. Jewel would receive requests from areas where Jewel service was not available and then many people would be disappointed. Instead, Jewel sales representatives worked in areas where they knew there was a need and where regular service could be provided.

The premium plan was another reason why Jewel did not advertise. It was a known fact that other companies spent twelve to fifteen per cent of their budgets promoting products through advertising. Jewel took the same amount and spent it on premium merchandise.

In 1916, the term "Inc." began to appear on Jewel products. The Jewel Tea Company was incorporated on January 26, 1916.

Years later, in 1932, Jewel entered the food store business, when 77 "Chicagoland" stores owned by the Loblaw

There is no indication of the Jewel salesman's name or the date on this historical photograph. Note the "Bar 'n Circle" logo on the side of wagon; this logo is believed to be the oldest and dates products between 1903 to approximately 1910. *Boelter Collection.*

Groceterians, Inc., and four stores of another chain, were leased. By 1966 there were over 250 Jewel Food Stores in the Chicago area.

All Jewel grocery products were produced to exact specifications set up by the Jewel Tea Company and were subject to extensive quality testing. To earn the Homemakers' Seal of Approval, a product had to pass five tests. Only if all five were passed was a product awarded the seal: TESTED AND APPROVED BY MARY DUNBAR JEWEL HOMEMAKERS INSTITUTE.

Jewel grocery products were backed by Jewel's unlimited guarantee — satisfaction or your money back. If a dissatisfied customer returned any products, either credit was given to her for the return amount of the purchase, her money was refunded, the item was exchanged, or the price of the product was applied toward another purchase. All records of purchases and returns were recorded on the customer's house card.

By 1928, the acceptance of this method of merchandising was shown by the facts that over 775,000 homes in America was served by Jewel and that over 3,000,000 customers were satisfied by Jewel grocery products. Jewel's merchandising system, with their lower prices and door-to-door service, provided the customer with a money saving plan for meeting her table and household needs. Jewel's business grew to a mammoth size because it could render a service that made Mrs. Brown's life easier.

Hired in 1923 to head a quality control staff, Mary Reed (Mary Dunbar) Hartson later created a column called "The Idea Exchange." Referring to this column, collectors can discover what caused many grocery products to survive with punched holes and why many grocery tins where located in a damp basement, an out building, or in grandmother's pantry.

In 1957, Eisner Food Store, headquartered in Champaign, Illinois joined Jewel. In 1961, a self service drug store named Osco Drug (originally called PayLess Drug) merged with Jewel. The first Jewel-Osco unit was opened in Chicago, Illinois in 1961. By 1977, Osco Drug stores were the largest of Jewel's general merchandise retail businesses and achieved record high sales and earnings.

In 1962, the first Turn-Style, a self service department store, was opened with the Jewel Food Stores in Racine, Wisconsin. On March 7, 1978 an announcement was made that Jewel and The May Department Stores Company had reached an agreement in principle under which all of the assets of Jewel's twenty-two Turn-Style stores would be sold for cash to May effective no later than June 1, 1978.

The May Company assumed lease obligations for nineteen stores, while Jewel Company maintained leases on two locations in Chicago which were being converted to other Jewel uses. The other location was disposed of later on.

A Jewel Company since 1964, the Star Market served the New England states. The Star Market began when the Mugar family's father and son started a partnership and purchased a store in 1917 in Watertown, Massachusetts.

It is believed Jewel acquired Brigham's Ice Cream in 1964. Brigham's had a 60-year old reputation for quality ice cream, candy, bakery, and food service in the Boston Metropolitan area.

In 1965, Jewel began franchising convenience food stores called White Hen Pantries to independent operators in the Chicagoland marketing area.

In 1966, the Jewel Tea Company, Inc., became known as Jewel Companies, Inc. Products marked "Jewel Companies, Inc.," indicate a date after 1966.

On June 15, 1966, Buttery Foods, Inc. merged with Jewel Companies Inc., in connection with which 430,171 shares of Jewel common stock were exchanged for all of the outstanding common stock of Buttery. In 1974 the newest Jewel Company was a high quality food retailer with stores located in Montana, Idaho and Utah.

Also in 1966, the Jewel Home Shopping Service moved its mail-order operation into a newly leased 120,000 square foot facilities in Elgin, Illinois were over 2-1/2 million orders were processed in 1967-68.

In 1976, over 200 companies bought products made at Jewel's Barrington, Illinois plant.

These men were "The most progressive branch in the most progressive district — Dallas 1938." Front Row — Left to Right: J.L. Turley, J.O. Davis, R.L. Hunter, J.E. Koonce, H.F. Cope, home office Vice President C.W. Kaylor, Charles Rinehart, Nathaniel Erwin, W.B. Wood, N.V. Hamrick, R.L. Dawson, E.W. Freiner, H.A. Barnard, W.M. Barry, C.G. Mash, R.J. Sitton and A.M. Sherbet. Top Row — Left to Right: G.B. Smith, E.L. Barham, J.G. Perkins, D.K. Wood, R.M. Gage, R.L. Upton, B.C. Barclay, D.C. Bussey, M.B. George, S.L. Elliott, H.W. Spradley, F.B. Lewis, C.G. White, K.V. Townsend, W.C. Stinecipher, A.E. Johnson, K.D. Fowler, W.E. Cook, D.F. Albright and S.K. Lester. *Eisnaugle Collection.*

CHAPTER 1
A BRIEF HISTORY

In 1899, with a horse, wagon, and $700 dollars in cash, Frank V. Skiff decided to venture into his own business in Chicago, Illinois by buying up supplies of coffees, teas, spices, and extracts to sell door-to-door. Skiff was boarding in a house at 403 S. Drexel at the time.

In 1901 Skiff's brother-in-law Frank P. Ross, a traveling freight agent who had met and married Frank V. Skiff's sister Blanche Skiff in Iowa on February 7, 1889, resigned from the Minneapolis & St. Louis Railway Company in Newton, Iowa. He and his wife Blanche then embarked on a trip to Chicago, where he took residence up at 221 S. Wabash Avenue.

Skiff and Ross soon formed a partnership. This partnership may have been the reason Frank P. Ross left his job with the railroad.

On the south side of Chicago, Frank V. Skiff and Frank P. Ross rented a small store and the Jewel Tea Company was started. By 1903, the first routes outside of Chicago were begun. In 1906, Jewel acquired property at the intersection of Randolph and May streets in Chicago and began manufacturing Jewel Baking Powder along with their other products.

As the company expanded, a need for larger accommodations became apparent. By 1908 they built a new modern structure at Washington and Ada streets in Chicago.

In the year 1916, the business was established on a nationwide basis. At this time the company continued to steadily grow and was successful enough to engage eastern investment bankers in a plan of reorganization. The banker purchased both preferred stock and part of the common stock of the company. Skiff and Ross continued in the management of the business until 1919 when they relinquished control to the bankers and turned over the active management of the company to them.

To head the quality control staff for the Home Service Division, Mary Reed Hartson was hired in 1923. She had

"Serving American Homemakers since 1899." This illustration appeared on the cover of a 1960s Jewel publication.

college training in home economics and was therefore sound in her theories of foods and nutrition. Her years in the world of business gave her a practical insight into the field of Home Service as it existed between Jewel and Jewel customers.

A decision was made in 1924 to expand and improve Jewel service by establishing the Jewel Homemakers' Institute. Mrs. Mary Hartson was designated "The Jewel Lady" and through the Jewel News, a bi-weekly publication distributed to customers, she shared recipes and household suggestions and invited correspondence, doing it with dignity, tact, and understanding.

Jewel management soon realized that "The Jewel Lady" needed a name, the personal touch was lacking. An old issue of the Jewel News, describes how it came about: "Mrs. Hartson said, 'Why not use a real name — not a coined one. Use Mary Dunbar, which is my maiden name. I will present it to the Jewel Tea Co., Inc. and renounce all future claims to its public uses.'"

In March 1926, "The Jewel Lady," after two years of serving Jewel customers, revealed herself. Thus began an era.

Her influence was felt in every department of the Jewel business, for she and her staff were constantly at work to insure the quality of Jewel Products and Premiums.

Mary Reed Hartson (Mary Dunbar) resigned because of health reasons later in 1926. Presently I am unable to trace records of her later years after she left Jewel. If you should have information about Mary Reed Hartson, I would appreciate hearing from you.

In 1926, Mrs. Leone Rutledge Carroll joined Jewel (1926-1943) to assume the directorship of the Jewel Homemakers' Institute and by far became the best-known Mary Dunbar. Her national reputation in the field of nutrition, her degrees in chemistry and home economics, and her teaching experience were just the background Jewel was looking for. She became Jewel's first woman executive.

One of Mary Dunbar's most famous efforts was *Mary Dunbar's Cookbook,* first published in 1927. Delivered personally to Jewel customers by route salesmen, the free cookbook proved so popular that several editions were printed. The last edition, published in 1943, went to 800,000 homes.

The tradition of Mary Dunbar and the Homemaker's Institute — of testing grocery and household articles for purity, durability, and serviceability before offering them for sale — was carried on throughout the life of the company.

For further information on Mary Reed Hartson (The Jewel Lady)(Mary Dunbar), and Leone Rutledge Carroll, see *The Jewel Tea Company. Its History and Products,* Schiffer Publishing, 1994 and Chapters 4, 5, and 6 in *Jewel Tea. Sales and Houseware Collectibles,* Schiffer Publishing, 1995.

30 YEARS AGO

BARRINGTON Jewels have been asking for pictures displayed on the 30th Anniversary (April 1) in the 1st floor lobby, on the 5th floor bulletin board, and on the bulletin boards in the Plant.

As this issue of The JEWEL contains a story of that 30th anniversary (pages 6 and 7) this insert supplements that story and will serve as a souvenir.

Housewarming in 1930 attracted more than 2,500.

PACKAGING equipment was of the latest design. Jewel Toothpaste was a big seller in 1930 also.

VANILLA line -- Frank Farwell, Foreman, Adeline Korbel, E. Meister, V. Benson, M. Sutfin.

LOADING platform in 1930 -- looks different now. (Foreman Bill Conrad, Sr., with Hobart Swan.)

Building basement - pillars rise through 4th floor.

Flowers filled Office on Opening Day, April 1.

TRAFFIC Section grew since 1930. Above are Helen Ketter, Anna Flood, Florence Doris, Tom Philbin, E. Brinckman, M. Olson, H.N. Williams.

HOMEMAKERS' Kitchen was the latest thing in 1930. Changes through the years keep it modern.

JIM O'CONNOR and Art Hedley (both retired) inspect new coffee equipment on 5th floor in 1930.

Nestled among thousands of beautiful trees, present 4 buildings attract many visitors each year.

These historical photographs were part of an insert supplement in "The JEWEL." These photographs are from Jewel's Thirtieth anniversary. This insert supplement was purchased at a flea market in Atlanta, Georgia.

By 1936 the Jewel Tea Company had grown to a fleet of 1,500 delivery cars serving a million customers living in 12,000 communities across America. Jewel's trained salesmen called on each customer every two weeks — on the same day of the week and at the same hour — delivering the groceries ordered two weeks before and taking orders for groceries to be delivered at the next regular call. Selling groceries directly to American homes, the Jewel Tea Company, Inc. also provided a method of merchandising unheard of at the time — the sharing of profits through an advance premium plan.

THE JEWEL WAY

Jewel was more than a big business, it was a "Service," giving its patrons four worth-while services for the price of one — to the American housewife it became known as "The Jewel Way."

Jewel's "Quality Groceries" — Coffees, teas, a variety of food products, laundry products, and toilet articles — were considered to be Jewel's first service to Mrs. Brown.

The company proclaimed that Jewel groceries were always uniform and good, they were prepared with care, and that "quality was put into them." Mrs. Brown paid no more for Jewel groceries than she paid for the same elsewhere.

"Quality Premiums" was second in Jewel's four services to Mrs. Brown. These premiums were things she needed and which were made to please and satisfy her. With every package of Jewel groceries the customer received a credit which she applied toward payment for the household article of her choice, thereby paying for it without additional cash outlay. This credit allowance did not increase the price she paid for her groceries.

Third, Jewel listed "Quality Personal Service." Jewel brought the markets of the world direct to their customers. Jewel gave them the advantage of buying at home, where Jewel salesmen served them intelligently, respectfully, and regularly.

The Jewel salesman's watchword was "Service," for satisfying Mrs. Brown was his primary goal. The Jewel business was built on the regular patronage of satisfied customers.

Jewel vehicles such as this provided "Service" to every Jewel customer in 1938. *Eisnaugle Collection.*

The fourth service of the Jewel Way was the "Unlimited Guarantee." Jewel stood behind their groceries, with an "Unlimited Guarantee" for its household articles and personal service, with an absolute satisfaction or money-refund guarantee.

Grocery products were all pure and of the highest quality, meeting requirements of all Pure Food Laws of the day, and going beyond the law. Jewel household articles were also guaranteed to be of the highest quality. Jewel's salesmen were even guaranteed, guaranteed to be courteous, honest, and regular.

If Mrs. Brown, at any time, was not fully satisfied, her money was refunded promptly and Jewel guaranteed to make satisfactory any part of its service that she was not pleased with.

Because of its nation-wide business, serving over two million people during the 1930s, Jewel was able to buy in immense quantities from original sources and to manufacture its own products on a large scale.

Bringing Jewel products direct to the front door from its factors saved them the wasteful expense and profits of all middlemen. Jewel believed this to be a short cut in distribution.

Jewel spent no large sums for advertising. Money allocated for that purpose went back to its customers in the form of premiums, quality, and "Service."

The company stated, however, that "Jewel never once claimed to give something for nothing — Mrs. Brown paid for what she got, but when buying from Jewel she received more than when she traded with others sources."

The fundamental principles of all effective Jewel sales talks were basically the same, although details varied with different circumstances. Jewel instructed their salesmen to fit any premium into their introduction of Jewel service to Mrs. Brown. The points needed for each premium and a display of the premiums were all that was needed when the salesman introduced the premiums to Mrs. Brown.

MERCHANDISING PRINCIPLES

> Jewel's principles of merchandising were simple: "Distribution was direct to the consumer's home, Groceries sold only for cash, Advertising with premiums, Delivery of the premiums in advance, Best of quality — always and everything — groceries, premiums and service were guaranteed." *How To Get New Customers,* 1936.

The most distinctive feature of the company's method of merchandising was the aforementioned advance premium plan. The amount of profit sharing credit offered to the customer varied according to the product. The premium was the service which Jewel felt first interested and attracted their customers. Jewel believed in premiums enthusiastically, but the premiums and their distribution were strictly governed by five rules of honest merchandising.

1) The premium must be useful — have a genuine utility or add to the beauty of the customer's home.
2) Something she needs — something which will please and satisfy her.
3) It must represent the highest quality obtainable.
4) It must be honestly priced — worth to the customer what she is asked to pay for it.
5) It must be sold to her frankly on its merit, without any misrepresentation whatever as to its quality, its price, or terms of sale and settlement.

Jewel proclaimed that the high quality of their products, whether groceries or premiums, was rigidly maintained. Jewel Coffees were to be selected, roasted, and blended to a uniformly high taste standard which never varied. All merchandise was purchased, manufactured, and packaged with the utmost care. Items which were not manufactured by the company were carefully inspected to see that they were up to Jewel's specifications.

Notwithstanding Jewel's nation-wide distribution in 1936, a large number of homemakers scattered throughout forty-six states were not experiencing the benefits of buying from Jewel and knew nothing about Jewel groceries and premiums.

The duty of extending that knowledge, those benefits, and of adding new customers to Jewel's "rapidly growing family" was divided between two distinct groups of Jewel employees. It was the duty of the route manager, the salesman who regularly served each territory, to maintain and increase the list of customers by daily solicitation of selected prospects who lived within the territory of the routes he served. But his duties in calling promptly upon his regular customers and serving them required the major portion of his time. When it was necessary to add an unusually large number of new customers to any set of routes, or when new routes were added, the services of specially trained men devoting all of their time to securing new customers were called upon.

This group of trained, advanced sales personnel was an important unit in the Jewel system of selling and service. Its members were essential to the program of steady and continuous increase in the number of routes served by Jewel route managers, and, from time-to-time, in the rebuilding of established routes. This program of measured expansion had been consistently maintained for some sixteen years, from 1920-1936. Each year, including those of the Depression, had seen more families being served by Jewel, more routes established, and more employees on Jewel payrolls.

Jewel's plan was to build new routes, in new territories, and in communities the company was not currently serving. Customers for these new routes were obtained entirely through the efforts of the advance sales organization. "The field was broad and fertile, its opportunities were practically without limit."

The work was profitable and enjoyable for one who mastered its simple technique — who learned how to tell the Jewel story in a convincing way and who worked consistently and steadily. Reasonable success ensured a livelihood and the security of a permanent income for a Jewel salesman.

The advanced sales person would go into a given territory in advance of the route manager, give his pitch to the housewives within the territory who were not already trading with Jewel, and take the customer's initial order which was delivered later by the route manager assigned to that territory.

The advanced salesman did not make deliveries, collect money, or fill out company reports. However, for every customer secured, to whom the route manager delivered an order, the advance salesman was paid a commission.

The sales approach was straightforward and simple, and the material contained in his booklet was drawn from the experience of more than thirty-six years of Jewel selling.

INFLUENCING THE HOUSEWIFE

Learning the wants and needs of the Jewel customer and supplying these requirements was "Good Merchandising." The Jewel Tea Company, Inc. was constantly in touch with the needs and requirements of the housewife and prospective customers, for packaged groceries and premiums carried in the Jewel line and in the Jewel Salesman's carrying basket. Jewel interviewed 3,000 housewives in one of their representative branch cities, seeking opinions about their company and answers about the products they sold. An outside firm engaged in this type of operation conducted the survey. The gathered information was then passed on to the company sales force, helping them to build sales volume and increased earnings.

According to Jewel, "The survey results found the Jewel Tea Co., Inc. stood high in the estimation of the public, the quality of Jewel merchandise was outstanding, Jewel expected these kinds of results, for they had always known this!" *The Jewel Way,* 1936.

Housewives liked the personal qualities and sales methods used by the salesmen. They liked a salesman who was dependable, respected their time, and kept his promises. A salesman who knew about the merchandise and made suggestions was preferred.

They liked a salesman who kept accurate records, was neat in appearance, pleasant, cheerful, and who had complete knowledge of his products. These facts were learned through customer interviews.

After obtaining this valuable information, Jewel presented it in various sales courses. In order for the salesman to receive full benefit from his course in "What Influences the Housewife to Buy from the Jewel Salesman" and to fully apply it, Jewel prepared the material in a permanent form for insertion into their manuals.

Information was based on factors pointed out in surveys. When Jewel salesmen used the material made available to them, they found themselves building more good will on their routes, more enjoyment from their work, and their earnings increased proportionately.

Jewel maintained that if a salesman knew his groceries and premiums this was a great influence on a housewife. Knowing their grocery and premiums meant knowing "The outstanding Sales Feature of Each Product and Premium," "The Uses in the Home," "Competition," "Jewel Quality and How It's Maintained," "The Right Use of the Guarantee," and "Where to Get the Information." Knowing these helped the salesman and resulted in new customers, increased capital, and deliveries.

Knowing and filling customers needs, a salesman had first to learn the size of the family he was serving — things they liked and used. He observed the customer in her home and gave her tips about her needs. He taught customers to look over supplies available, to take notes, and refer to them when taking future orders. In filling customer's needs he informed the customer what Jewel groceries and premiums would do for her, he displayed his items, suggested additional items, and made other suggestions. He described Jewel recipes using the groceries, the use of Jewel premiums, and extended an invitation to her to use the "Home

Service," Jewel's door-to-door delivery service. The salesman provided the customer with a copy of *The Jewel News* and pointed out the various household hints, how to prepare more appetizing dishes, saving money, lightening housework, saving kitchen expense, and beautifying the home.

By knowing and filling his customers needs, a salesman saved the customer time and money and increased his own commissions. Building customer good-will increased customer appreciation of Jewel service.

SEAL OF APPROVAL

Gaining the "Seal of Approval" required that all of a grocery products' ingredients be checked in the Barrington laboratory prior to their introduction as new product lines. This "Seal of Approval" was much different than what Jewel President M.N. Karker once referred to when he said Jewel customer buying was the final "Seal of Approval."

Meeting quality specifications, all perishable ingredients were rechecked when they were ready to be mixed to ensure those ingredients had retained their "highest purity and freshness."

Two samples were tested from the same batch before they were packaged. Examination of one sample was made for flavor, color, texture, and body in the Jewel test kitchen. The second sample was tested in a Jewel laboratory.

Only after the product was thoroughly examined, in five tests process, was packaging started. Occasionally packages were removed from the production line and retested by the Jewel homemakers.

Each Jewel package was checked for proper weight and double sealed to retain freshness. Jewel rejected a box or an entire batch if it failed any one of the five tests before awarding the seal.

A 1940s historical photograph, Jewel grocery products are undergoing testing in the Jewel test kitchen in Barrington, Illinois. Leone Rutledge (Mary Dunbar) Carroll center, shown with three Jewel employees. It is believed the lady seated is the secretary to Mrs. Carroll. The lady to the left (Mrs. Bierman) is testing Jewel Biscuit Flour, as another staff member (name unknown) prepares another test in the back. Also, note the Jewel Peanut Butter and Jewel Vanilla bottles on the counter. On the far left is the Jewel Biscuit Flour.

In this historical photograph, Leone Rutledge (Mary Dunbar) Carroll "Home Economics Consultant" and a Jewel kitchen assistant (either Marian Kessel or Mavis Galloway), inspect the Hall Autumn Leaf oval covered vegetable dish (a dish offered by Jewel from 1940-1976). Note closely the Jewel grocery products in glass front cabinets, i.e. Jewel Pepper, Extracts, Dessert mix, Cinnamon, Cocoa, and a variety of Jewel-Jell. In the cabinet behind Mary Dunbar can be seen Jewel Noodles, a variety of Jewel Teas, Peanut-Butter, and other Jewel grocery products. Also note various pieces of Hall Autumn Leaf china in this photograph dated 1940s.

In 1966, the Jewel Tea Company, Inc. became known as Jewel Companies Inc. The change meant more than just a switch in corporate titles; it was a change in management philosophy, under which each Jewel company was operated as a separate company, with the freedom to adapt to change and to move rapidly to respond to new opportunities. Each Jewel operating company was charged with managing its financial resources to generate the return required for Jewel Companies Inc., to succeed, and to grow profitably.

In 1974, the original Jewel company marked its 75th anniversary. Called the Direct Marketing Division, it was symbolized to generations of Americans from coast to coast by the Jewel Tea routeman ... or woman. In 1974, 22 of the Jewel routes were operated by women. The routes were distinguished in 1975 by their 54th consecutive year of earnings.

On March 24, 1981, the dealer-owned cooperative IHSS (In-Home Shopping Service, Division of Jewel Companies, Inc.) was incorporated. On May 23, 1981, IHSS, Inc. acquired certain assets of the "Jewel Home Shopping Service Division" of Jewel Companies, Inc. To develop an identity of their own, one of the conditions of the purchase was that the name Jewel be phased out over a three year period. Thus it became "J.T.'s General Store." On October 3, 1994, J.T.'s General Store was sold to employees and the new name became "JT Dealer Sales and Services Corp."

The "America's Groceryman" appeared as the back cover of "JEWEL Home Shopping Service Spring and Summer 1952" catalog. Using a magnify glass may help in dating many of your products to this era. Since many of these products appear throughout this publication, it is wise to use this photograph as your reference.

CHAPTER 2
COFFEE, TEA AND COCOA PRODUCTS

"From the Plantation to the customers door."

According to the company, "Jewel Coffee was the most economical a customer could buy in 1923. Every pound conformed to Jewel's most rigid standard quality — delicious flavor, wholesome strength, and rich aroma. Jewel coffee experts devoted all their time to testing and blending in order that only the highest standard could be maintained. The roasting of Jewel Coffee was done in the largest and most modern coffee roasting equipment in the world."

COFFEE

"Where there's life — there's coffee! And where there's coffee — Jewel is tops!" *Jewel News,* 1937.

Jewel was a leading manufacture of coffee and this advertising slogan shown directly above appeared in numerous publications promoting coffee. Jewel told their salesmen, "Where there's enthusiasm for coffees there also will be increased sales and an increase in the fine reputation Jewel enjoys." The reputation of Jewel was never at stake and there was never any doubt about the coffee they provided their customers.

"There was no other coffee in the world that excelled Jewel Coffees." Jewel based this statement on the most exacting standards and care given when buying green coffee and in preparing it for the consumer. Very seldom did a publication from Jewel not mention "Coffee."

Jewel coffees were purchased, processed, tested, packaged, and delivered with the most exacting standards and under the most modern conditions. "Only from Jewel could American housewives buy coffee that was so rich in flavor, pure, uniform, an so fresh." *Jewel News,* 1937.

Two different methods were used in preparing coffee for market, the "Dry method" and the more modern "Wet method."

DRY METHOD: the berries where spread on the drying ground very thinly and remained exposed to the sun and wind for approximately three weeks, allowing the berries to thoroughly dry.

WET METHOD: was a method used for a better grade of bean known as "washed coffee," which demanded a higher price than the "Dry method." The "Wet method" was generally prepared on larger plantations that had a sufficient supply of water and the required machinery.

Jewel coffee is being tested in a Jewel laboratory. The coffee expert is unknown. No coffee was ever sold by the Jewel Tea Company, Inc., without first undergoing testing. No Jewel blend coffee changed, because Jewel blended to a taste standard.

Jewel had three blends of coffee, "one that suited every taste." Jewel coffees remained uniform, even though different crops of the same growth of green coffee varied in cup quality, because Jewel coffee was blend to a "taste standard."

The Jewel experts seated themselves before a round revolving top table to perform a "cup test." Located on the edge of this table were various cups with the ground coffee in each. Behind the cups, two trays containing green beans were located, as well as roasted beans. Both samples were from the same chop (the term "chop" applied to all bags in the same lot from the same plantation).

Depicted here is Chief Coffee Roaster A.J. (Art) Hedley with an unknown Jewel employee. Hedley joined the Jewel staff in 1908, he supervised the roasting of millions of pounds of Jewel produced coffee, he oversaw the shipment of 80-pound, hand sewn bags to branches, and the installation of Jewel's first roasting machine in Barrington. Hedley retired after 30 years with the company on October 18, 1938.

Art Hedley, Chief Coffee Roaster, operating the "Ro-Tap" in the Barrington, Illinois plant. Mr. Hedley took a one pound sample of Jewel Coffee twice a day and placed it in the Ro-Tap machine he is shown with. This machine shook the ground coffee through five screens, one on the top of another. Each screen retained part of the coffee. When the machine came to a complete stop, Hedley measured the amount on each screen on a scale, visible on the left in this photograph.

In a special storage unit in the company's plant at Hoboken, New Jersey, green coffees that had satisfactorily passed Jewel tests were stored. These were sorted according to their chop mark. As it was needed, coffee was taken from storage to fill branch requisitions.

In the packaging department, automatic packaging machines "Triple-sealed" Jewel coffee immediately after is was ground. Jewel's package had three separate and distinct seals, which were considered ideal for keeping coffee fresh. This package was essentially airtight and moisture-proof, yet avoided damaging the coffee with the high pressures and extreme changes typical of vacuum packing.

No order was ever made up that was not based on a branch requisition. Orders were shipped only in refrigerator cars because merchandise was packed better in them with less damage.

This procedure was done in percentages, if any variation from Jewel's standard grind was shown, the rollers in the granulators were then immediately adjusted.

Located in Hoboken, New Jersey was a twelve story building of concrete, fireproof construction that contained 273,000 square feet (six acres) of floor space. The coffee was roasted and prepared for the consumer in this location. On the river, the Hoboken Jewel plant had its own wharfage so vessels could unload the green coffee right at the Jewel plant location. At a location on the other side of the plant was a railroad siding, so roasted coffee for shipment to company branches could be loaded directly onto cars with minimal expense and delay.

The New Jersey plant was equipped for the milling, blending, roasting, grinding and packaging of Jewel coffee. The operation of this plant was automated. From the time the bags of green coffee are first opened, the beans themselves were never touched by human hands.

Twelve roasters, with a capacity of 120,000 pounds per day, were power heated by gas. After roasting, the coffee was dumped into a large wire-bottomed box referred to as a cooler. From the cooler, coffee dropped approximately ten feet through a chute onto a sieve or stoner. After the last process, the coffee was carried directly to the packaging machines and/or the grinders. Various chutes were used for coffee that was being packaged in whole bean and for coffee that was being ground before packaging. Located in the plant were 48 power-driven grinders, each having a 300 pound-per-hour capacity.

Conveyors moved the ground coffee to large "Tru-flow" mixing bins, which were connected the automatic weighing machines, that filled the cartons into which the coffee was packaged. This process was also performed by automatic machines. First in line was a carton feeder, where the flat carton was shaped and then moved to the next machine where glue was placed on the bottom flaps and forced them together to form the bottom of the carton. A parchment paper container was then formed and deposited inside the pasteboard carton. The coffee was weighed and deposited into the appropriate carton; the weight was then checked again by another machine. Those cartons with incorrect weight were removed. As the coffee cartons moved on to another machine, the top of the parchment liner and the top flaps of the pasteboard carton were sealed. The final operation was the application of the colored lithographed wrapper that covered the carton; this final operation also sealed the wrapper on the side, top, and bottom. Wrapped cartons of coffee were then placed in corrugated shipping containers and were ready for shipment to Jewel branches.

Jewel salesmen took coffee orders from their customers and turned these orders over to their branch managers. These orders were then submitted to the Hoboken plant for processing. No roasted coffee was kept on hand at the Hoboken, New Jersey plant.

This operation, as described, was carried on through the late 1920s. Coffee was roasted every day, only in the quantities needed, and shipped the same day it was roasted, or never later than the following morning. Branches stocked only very small amounts of coffee. The Hoboken plant was constantly shipping coffee from its location to each branch.

Four weeks from the date of roasting, Jewel coffee was delivered to the customers. Each individual package was code marked with the date of roasting before it left the Hoboken plant. This allowed the Jewel branch manager and salesman to determine the exact age of the coffee at the time of delivery.

Coffee Dissatisfaction

An independent organization, which provided the public with advice about many products, conducted a survey in 1937 about the coffee industry and supplied a report that included "Even coffee which meets all specifications can be ruined completely, if it is improperly prepared." This supported what Jewel, Mary Dunbar, and her staff had been teaching for years. Jewel therefore believed that any dissatisfaction with Jewel Coffee was caused by the way the customer made her coffee.

Jewel boasted of another slogan, "The Most Complete Coffee Service in America." Every salesman had to do three things: 1) sell his customers good coffee-making equipment; 2) see that his customers knew how to make coffee properly; 3) keep his customers supplied with fresh coffee by selling a canister in every home, especially in homes buying ground rather than whole bean coffee.

Jewel did everything possible to supply only fresh coffee using a correct grind and a triple-seal package through their fast delivery system. But it was up to the salesman alone to see to it that the customer kept the coffee as fresh as possible.

During the mid-1930s Jewel customers were introduced to the metal Autumn Leaf motif canister. Jewel believed every coffee user should included this reliable canister in her kitchen.

Jewel provided a list of four methods of coffee-making and urged customer to study them. Jewel pointed out that the pot method of coffee-making rated "good" on only one factor, that of cleaning the vessel. The percolator method was better, but boiling the coffee ruins the flavor, because there were no controls. The Silex maker rated poor on control, cleaning, ruggedness and only fair on brewing. (See the "Victory Silex" page 69 in *JEWEL TEA Sales and Houseware Collectibles.*) The drip method rated "good" on every factor.

During the mid-1930s, Jewel's goal was to put a Jewel Coffee Maker using the drip method into every coffee-drinking American home which it served. In 1936 they sold approximately 113,000 drips, in 1937 — 148,000, and in 1938 — 232,000 drips were sold. Records for 1939 were unavailable.

Jewel suggested that every Jewel salesman have a Coffee Maker in his car at all times, and that he use it to sell more drips, answer coffee complaints, and provide a demonstration that Jewel Coffee was delicious if only made "RIGHT."

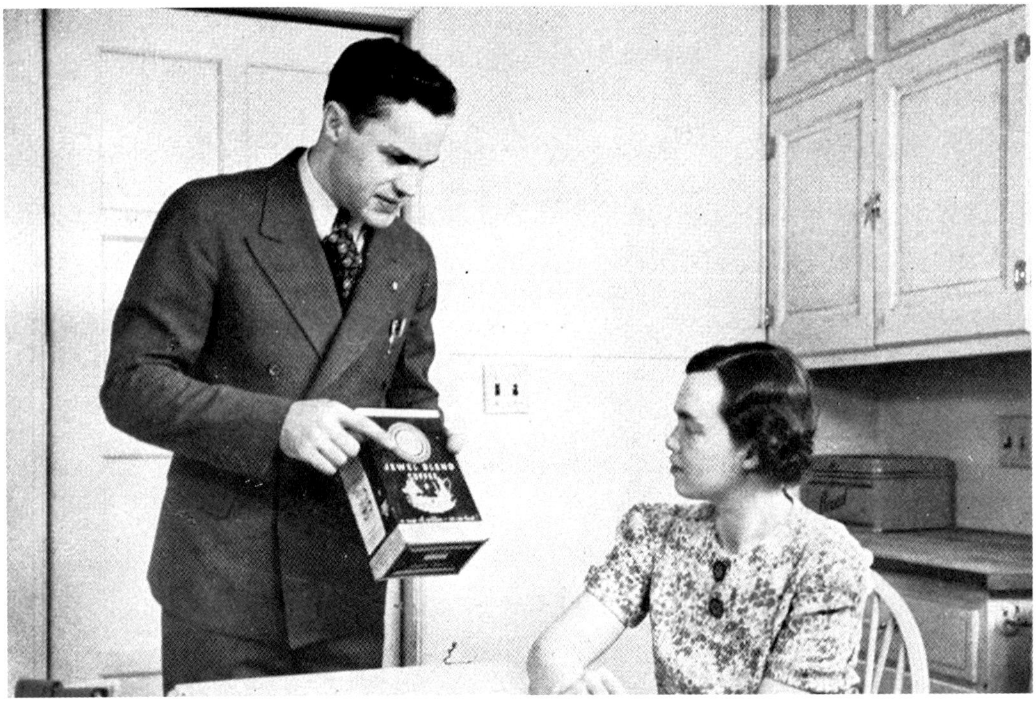

A final decision is made concerning "Jewel Blend Coffee" in the test kitchen of The Jewel Tea Co. Inc., Barrington, Illinois. Shown in this mid-1930s photograph, Leone Rutledge (Mary Dunbar) Carroll and a Jewel employee.

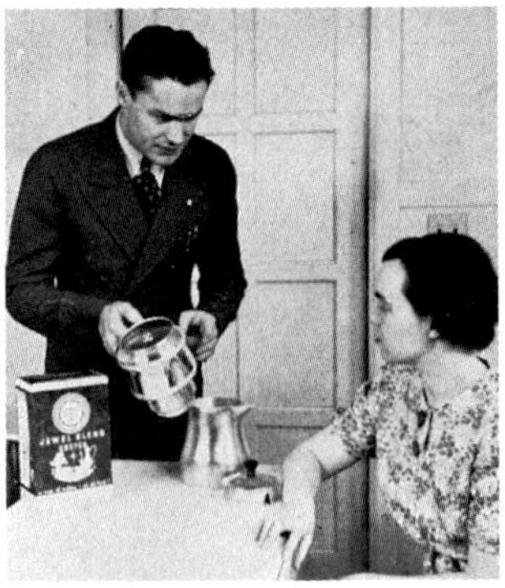

Shown in this series of photographs, Leone Rutledge (Mary Dunbar) Carroll and an unknown Jewel employee discuss "How To Make Good Coffee." Top to bottom 1) Use fresh cold water 2) Start with good coffee and proper equipment. 3) Accurately measure coffee, a shake-level measure per cup. 4) Bring water to a good rolling boil. 5) Pour water in maker to proper level.

While the company served more than 775,000 customers in 1927, Jewel resisted producing cheaper coffees, stating that their customers expected more. In providing a desirable coffee, Jewel asserted that they bought only the best grades obtainable. Jewel experts reviewed every single detail to ensure quality coffee that would satisfy the consumer. Every pound sold also carried with it the company's unqualified guarantee in giving complete satisfaction or refunding the full price paid.

This photograph appeared in a 1932 Jewel News, promoting Jewel coffee with "There is no finer beverage than good coffee. ... The excellence of Jewel coffee is winning more friends for it every day." Note the aluminum coffee maker.

In 1932, Jewel used this promotion in an issue of the Jewel News. "Use your favorite blend, JB, JS, or JC, for preparing that most delicious beverage — coffee ... steaming hot or icy cold. Perhaps you think you would not care for coffee iced if you have never tried it, but with plenty of cream and sugar you will find its smooth flavor coolness most satisfying. Jewel coffees are all of excellent quality and blended to suit three distinct individual tastes. 10¢ credit on your premium with a 2 lb. package. 15¢ credit on your premium with a 3 lb. package."

In 1932 Jewel promoted this coffee maker as making "Coffee the Modern Method." This was a nine cup, aluminum, easy to use, and easy to clean modern drip coffee maker "that ensured excellent coffee every time." Jewel listed this maker as Item No. 63 and priced it at $2.25.

Millionaire Brand Coffee

Shown here is one of the most sought after coffee tins available from the Jewel Tea Company. The "Millionaire Brand Coffee" tin sold for 80¢ and has the slanted "Bar 'n Circle" Jewel logo that indicates it was produced around 1909. This is a metal tin with a paper label. *Orr Collection.*

This ground coffee was "Imported Roasted Packed and Sold Direct To The Consumer By JEWEL TEA CO. HEADQUARTERS WASHINGTON BOUL. AND ADA ST. CHICAGO." Even in this condition, this coffee tin is highly sought by collectors. *Hamilton Collection.*

If you closely examine these illustrations of the "Millionaire Brand Coffee" tin, you can see the new section. On the bottom below the "Directions" appears the slanted "Bar 'n Circle" Jewel logo. Directions provided, included "For every large cup of Coffee wanted use one tablespoonful of fine ground Coffee. Scald the Coffee pot before putting the Coffee into it. Do not use a pot with inside enamel broken. Be sure the water is boiling; measure the number of cups wanted, and pour on the Coffee and let it come to a boil. Set back on the stove and keep very hot for ten minutes, but do not allow to boil, then clear with a dash of cold water. The mixing of the ground coffee with white of egg before the water is poured on, ensures a clear Coffee without the cold water and adds to its richness. To make good drip Coffee, use one heaping tablespoonful for every cup wanted. Be sure the water is boiling before using and measure each cup. It is absolutely necessary to scald the coffee pot before using." *Hamilton Collection.*

The paper label on this "Millionaire Brand Coffee" tin shows an illustration of the Washington Boulevard and Ada Street headquarters. Jewel moved into these new quarters in 1908. On close examination of this illustration we can see the new addition that was later added to the original structure. *Hamilton Collection.*

The "Bar 'n Circle" logo appears on the lid. This coffee was sold only in 2 lb. cans, either whole, ground, or pulverized. This tin can be dated to 1909, before Jewel was incorporated. *Hamilton Collection.*

Jewel Brand Coffee

The slanted "Bar 'n Circle" Jewel logo appears on the lid. A later tin can be found with the addition to the Washington Boulevard and Ada Street location. This tin, with the new addition, can be dated to approximately 1915. On January 26, 1916, Jewel was incorporated and began using the term "Inc." *Hamilton Collection.*

This "JEWEL BRAND COFFEE" can be dated to approximately 1909. Priced at $1.00, this is a 3 lb. tin measuring approximately 9-1/4" tall and 5-1/4" in diameter. This tin pictures the headquarters on Washington Boulevard and Ada Street, Chicago, Illinois and has the "Bar 'n Circle" Jewel logo. *Hamilton Collection.*

A side view of "JEWEL BRAND COFFEE." "This Coffee is sold only in 3 lb. cans, either whole, ground, or pulverized. It is packed fresh from the roasters in sealed cans. It is always uniform in quality and skillfully blended to suit critical coffee drinkers and is guaranteed by the Jewel Tea Co. The Largest Exclusive Retail TEA and COFFEE HOUSE in the World. First hands to Consumer and Middleman's Profit." *Hamilton Collection.*

Jewel Cup Coffee

In 1926, JEWEL Cup Coffee was promoted. JEWEL Cup had been called the popular blend because it was so universally accepted as a quality coffee, and because it was reasonably priced. It was touted as "always uniform, fresh, and delightful." JEWEL Cup was ground and available in either 2 or 3-lb. packages.

The 2 lb. net weight JEWEL Cup dates post-1930. This package is marked "JEWEL TEA CO. INC., JEWEL PARK BARRINGTON, ILL." *Ferriera Collection.*

Special Blend

The 3 lb. package of "SPECIAL BLEND COFFEE" was "Roasted and Package by JEWEL TEA CO. INC., JEWEL PARK BARRINGTON, ILL." This product post-dates 1930. Jewel moved into their headquarters in Barrington in 1930. *Randall Collection.*

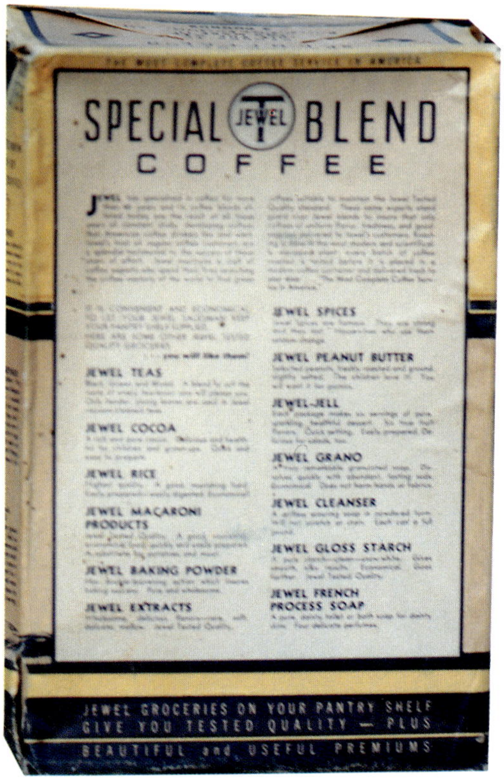

Various Jewel products were promoted on the reverse side of the "SPECIAL BLEND COFFEE." *Randall Collection.*

Mary Dunbar

Key-Wind coffee tins are highly sought by coffee collectors. This pound container of "MARY DUNBAR COFFEE" was "Distributed by Jewel Food Stores Chicago, a Department of Jewel Tea Co., Inc., Barrington, Ill." See other Key-Wind Coffee tin's in this section. *Hamilton Collection.*

The lid to the "REGULAR GRIND MARY DUNBAR COFFEE." This Key-wind tin has the number 2263 imprinted on the lid. This may indicate the year "1963," as Jewel was using the "DUNBAR" name during this period. *Hamilton Collection.*

Plastic Snap On Lids

The 2 lb. "JEWEL SPECIAL BLEND COFFEE" has a plastic snap on lid. Very common even in today's market, this lid kept the contents fresh. Note the 1960 - 1966 "Block Jewel" logo. *Lemons Collection.*

Two containers of "JEWEL SPECIAL BLEND COFFEE." Note the "Scripted Jewel" logo on the left. This logo was popular during the 1950s - 1960s. The "Block Jewel" logo appears on the container on the right. Each container held 3 lb. of coffee. *Vogel Collection.*

The front and reverse side of the 3 lb. "JEWEL SPECIAL BLEND COFFEE," the coffee was "Roasted and Packaged by JEWEL TEA CO., INC., BARRINGTON, ILLINOIS." *Vogel Collection.*

Note the slight difference in height of these two "JEWEL BLEND COFFEE." This does not effect the price or demand of this 3 lb. container. *Byerly Collection.*

"Roasted and Packaged by JEWEL TEA CO., INC., BARRINGTON, ILLINOIS." This 3 lb. "JEWEL BLEND COFFEE" container is commonly found. In 1975 this all-purpose grind coffee appeared in a Jewel grocery stock card; this item was listed as No. 001-0025. *Hedges Collection.*

"JEWEL BLEND COFFEE" in a 3 lb. and a 2 lb. container. The 3 lb. container is marked "Roasted and Packaged by JEWEL COMPANIES INC., BARRINGTON, ILLINOIS 60010." The 2 lb. is marked "Roasted and Packed by JEWEL TEA CO., INC., BARRINGTON, ILLINOIS." It is not uncommon for collectors to search for both containers. Examine the container before you buy to determine if it's a 3 lb. or 2 lb. Prices may vary! *Vogel Collection.*

The front of this "JEWEL BLEND COFFEE," is very colorful. *Casey Collection.*

The coffee was "Approved by Mary Dunbar," note the seal on the side of this container. *Casey Collection.*

This 2 lb. "JEWEL BLEND COFFEE" has a plastic snap on the lid and the container itself is cardboard. *Vogel Collection.*

The reverse side of the cardboard "JEWEL BLEND COFFEE." This coffee was "Roasted and Packaged by JEWEL COMPANIES, INC., BARRINGTON, ILLINOIS 60010." *Vogel Collection.*

The label of this 13 oz. "HERITAGE BLEND decaffeinated coffee" shows an Autumn Leaf "Breakfast Cup and Saucer" introduced in 1936 — do not date this coffee in that era. "HERITAGE BLEND" decaffeinated coffee" was "Distributed by JT's GENERAL STORE JT MERCHANDISE SERVICES, INC., Barrington, Illinois 60010." This was an All Purpose Grind Coffee and dates after 1981. *Byerly Collection.*

A metal 2 lb. "JEWEL COUNTRY KITCHEN COFFEE" container with a plastic lid. *Vogel Collection.*

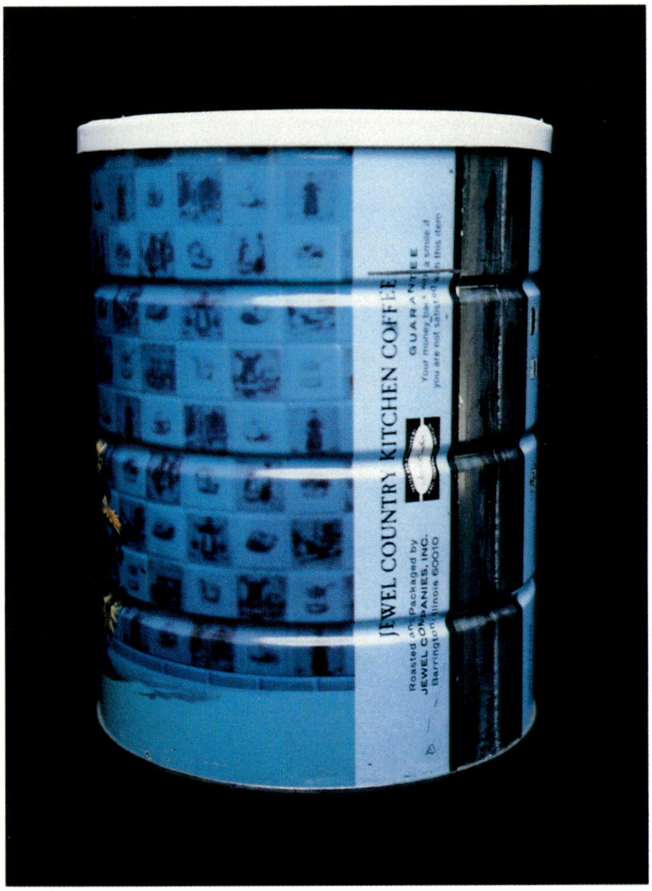

"Roasted and Packaged by JEWEL COMPANIES, INC., Barrington, Illinois," this 2 lb. "JEWEL COUNTRY KITCHEN COFFEE" was "Approved by Mary Dunbar." *Vogel Collection.*

Cardboard Containers

It is not uncommon for collectors to wrap products in a clear wrapping as shown here. These two containers of "CUP BLEND COFFEE" held 3 lbs. of coffee each. Marked "JEWEL TEA CO. INC., JEWEL PARK BARRINGTON, ILL." *Hamilton Collection.*

Note the Jewel logo on this exceptional Jewel Coffee carton. This container is marked "JEWEL TEA CO., INC., NEW YORK — CHICAGO."

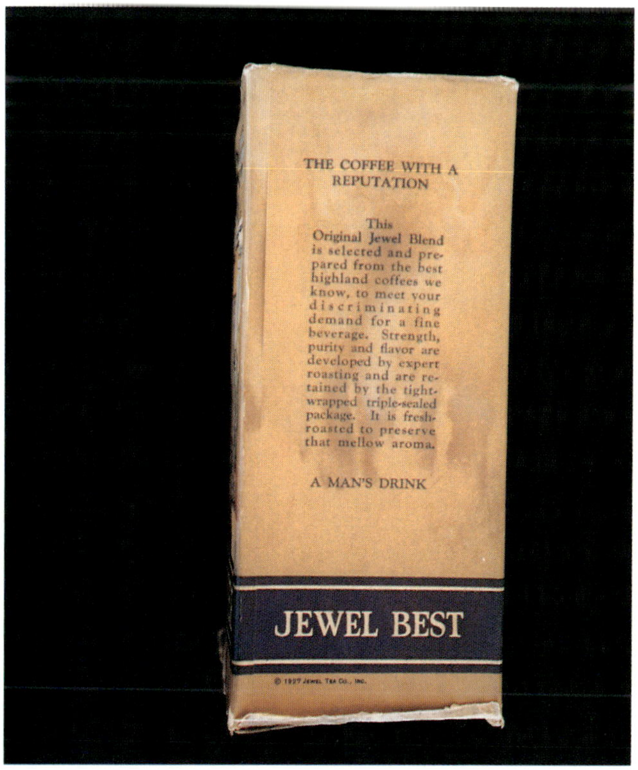

On the side panel "©1927 JEWEL TEA CO., INC." appears. This coffee appeared in the Jewel News Vol. 2 No. 2 1924 and other publications. *Hamilton Collection.*

A 2 lb. cardboard container of "Jewel Blend Coffee, Makes The Whole Meal Better, Roasted and Packaged by JEWEL TEA CO. INC., BARRINGTON, ILL. —ANAHEIM, CAL." At the time of this writing I could not locate information on the Anaheim, California plant. *Byerly Collection.*

The reverse side of the "Jewel Blend Coffee." This coffee was "Approved by Mary Dunbar." Note advertisement on the side panel for "Jewel Instant Coffee." *Byerly Collection.*

The "Jewel Blend Coffee" container is full. The opposite panel reads: "Jewel Home Shopping Service Taste Blended to insure delicious flavor in every cup! Double Sealed for Freshness — When you buy Jewel Coffee you can be certain it's ground FRESH! roasted FRESH! delivered FRESH!" *Byerly Collection.*

The 2 lb. "JEWEL BLEND COFFEE" is marked "ROASTED AND PACKAGED BY JEWEL TEA CO. INC., JEWEL PARK BARRINGTON, ILL." Someone has penciled the date of April 9, 1944 across the top of this cardboard carton. *Vogel Collection.*

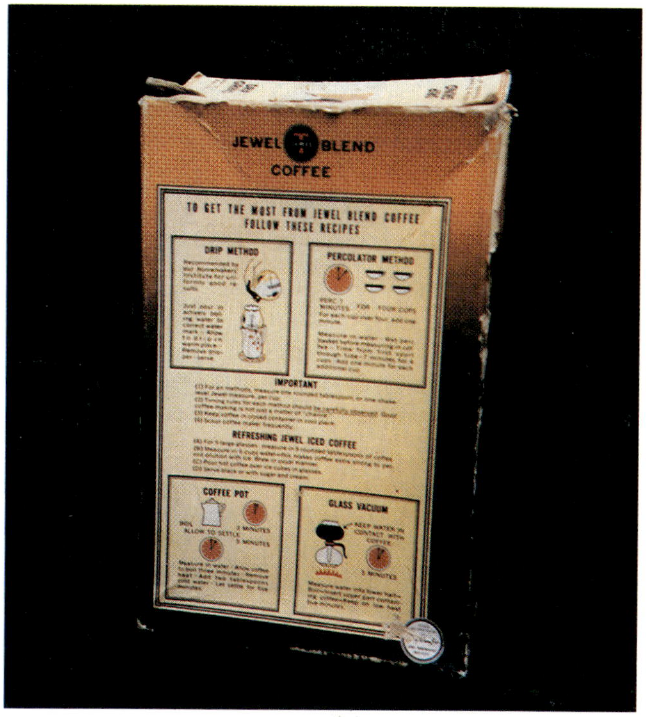

The reverse side of "JEWEL BLEND COFFEE." Recipes were provided to get the most from "JEWEL BLEND COFFEE." *Vogel Collection.*

Jewel had various large organizations as customers. A 3 lb. cardboard container of "SPECIAL HOTEL AND RESTAURANT COFFEE." "ROASTED AND PACKED BY JEWEL TEA CO. INC., JEWEL PARK BARRINGTON, ILL." *Hamilton Collection.*

"SPECIAL HOTEL AND RESTAURANT COFFEE" packaging provided "Directions for Glass Coffee Makers" on a side panel as shown. *Hamilton Collection.*

West Coast Coffee

"West Coast Jewel Blend Coffee" was "Roasted and Packed by Jewel Tea Co., Inc., Los Angeles, Cal." During the mid-1960s the Los Angeles plant closed. Note the seal in upper left-hand corner, this indicated a "valuable coupon" was inside. Saving these coupons a customer could redeem them for flatware. This is a Key-Wind container. *Lemons Collection.*

A "valuable coupon" was enclosed in this Key-wind "West Coast Blend Coffee." "Roasted and Packed by Jewel Tea Co., Inc., Los Angeles, Cal." Note these two containers are slightly different. One is referred to as "Jewel Blend" and the other "Blend." Collectors search for both containers. *Lemons Collection.*

A different labeling appears on the "West Coast Blend Coffee" 2 lb. container. Marked "JEWEL TEA CO. INC., LOS ANGELES, CALIFORNIA." *Lemons Collection.*

This "West Coast Blend Coffee" appears under a completely different label. "ROASTED AND PACKED BY JEWEL TEA CO. INC., LOS ANGELES, CAL." Note the difference in the bells and logo. *Lemons Collection.*

Even though part of the paper label is missing from this 1 lb. "WEST COAST BLEND COFFEE," it is still highly sought by collectors. This missing label affects the selling price! This coffee was roasted daily in California. *Lemons Collection.*

Two identical containers of "WEST COAST BLEND COFFEE" in paper packaging. *Hamilton Collection.*

A front view and a side view of "WEST COAST BLEND COFFEE." Packaging is marked "JEWEL TEA CO. INC., LOS ANGELES, CAL." *Hamilton Collection.*

Two different views of "WEST COAST BLEND COFFEE," each bag contained 3 lb. *Hamilton Collection.*

Key-Wind

A 2 lb. key-wind "JEWEL BLEND COFFEE," "ROASTED AND PACKED BY JEWEL TEA CO. INC., BARRINGTON, ILLINOIS." *Byerly Collection.*

A "Valuable Coupon" was enclosed in this package of "JEWEL BLEND COFFEE." Marked "ROASTED AND PACKED BY JEWEL TEA CO., INC., BARRINGTON, ILLINOIS." *Randall Collection.*

The reverse side of the 2 lb. "JEWEL BLEND COFFEE." The coffee was VACUUM PACKED and directions for Drip Method and Glass Vacuum Method were provided. *Byerly Collection.*

The reverse side of "JEWEL BLEND COFFEE" providing directions for "DRIP METHOD, GLASS VACUUM METHOD, COFFEE POT METHOD and PERCOLATOR METHOD." A list of IMPORTANT directions was printed. *Randall Collection.*

Two different key-wind 1 lb. tins. Top tin is "JEWEL PRIVATE BLEND COFFEE" and the bottom is "JEWEL PRIVATE BLEND COFFEE." Both are marked "ROASTED AND PACKED BY JEWEL TEA CO., INC., BARRINGTON, ILLINOIS — LOS ANGELES, CALIFORNIA." *Byerly Collection.*

The reverse side of "JEWEL PRIVATE BLEND COFFEE" with directions for FINE GRIND. Note the green band around the top. *Byerly Collection.*

Note the orange band around the top, this "JEWEL PRIVATE BLEND COFFEE" was REGULAR GRIND. *Byerly Collection.*

Note the "Jewel Home Shopping Service" in the wreath on the side of the "JEWEL PRIVATE BLEND COFFEE." This tin can be dated to the 1950s. *Casey Collection.*

DRIP GRIND, "The coffee that makes the whole meal better," "Royal Jewel Coffee." *Orr Collection.*

Shown here are 6 ounces of "Royal Jewel Instant Coffee." *Orr Collection.*

Two key-wind "Royal Jewel Coffee." The top coffee is REGULAR GRIND and the bottom is DRIP GRIND. *Byerly Collection.*

A large REGULAR GRIND Key-Wind "Royal Jewel Coffee." *Sivils Collection.*

A key-wind 100% Colombian Coffee "Jewel Private Blend" FINE GRIND. *Sivils Collection.*

Jewel Key-Wind Coffee tins can be dated between the 1950s - 1960s. Also watch for "Troxa" Coffee in two different key-wind tins. One has the following printed across the front "A special blend of COFFEE, CEREAL, CHICORY." "Jewel Troxa" was used for mixing with coffee or as a coffee substitute. See "Mary Dunbar" Key Wind in this Chapter.

Jewel Jems

Two different 1953-1954 "Jewel Jems" Coffee 24 Bags containers can be found. Roasted and Packed by the Jewel Tea Co., Inc., at Barrington, Illinois, these coffee containers were not popular. The Key-Wind has never been opened. *Byerly Collection.*

The "Jewel Jems" has a snap on lid. Jewel Jems were a "quick and easy way to enjoy the full-bodied flavor and aroma of the world's finest coffee." *Lemons Collection.*

A closer view of the "Jewel Jems" lid. "ROASTED & PACKED BY JEWEL TEA CO., INC., BARRINGTON, ILLINOIS," 24 bags were enclosed. Patent No. 2,224,942 can be seen under the "Quick 'n Easy Directions." The patent date is 1940 - 1941. It is wise to remember patient dates and dates of manufacture may vary by several years. *Lemons Collection.*

Instant Coffee

A 6 oz. "Jewel Blend Instant Coffee." In 1978 this 6 oz. coffee sold for $6.99. *Lemons Collection.*

"Jewel Special Blend Instant Coffee." *Lemons Collection.*

The front and back views of "Jewel Blend Instant Coffee." This "New Vacuum Packed" coffee was "Approved by Mary Dunbar." *Lemons Collection.*

During 1975 - 1976, a 6 oz. "Jewel CF Brand Instant Coffee" was promoted in a Jewel Grocery Stock Card. This Instant Coffee was 97% caffeine-free and was regularly priced at $3.59. A photograph was not available.

Coffee Pot Cleaner

Shown here is the "Jewel Coffee Pot Cleaner." This carton contained 5 envelopes. This cleaner was safe for coffee or tea pots and plastic dishes. *Hamilton Collection.*

On the reverse side, directions and other uses for the "Jewel Coffee Pot Cleaner" were listed. This cleaner was "Approved by Mary Dunbar." *Hamilton Collection.*

Miscellaneous

This cardboard carton held twelve 2 lb. cans of "Jewel Blend Coffee." *Vogel Collection.*

This beautiful receptacle is believed to be a tea hopper. *Hedges Collection.*

This hopper is approximately 10" high and 5-1/2" in diameter. The logo shown on the top dates this receptacle to the early twentieth century, from 1903-1915. *Hedges Collection.*

This receptacle lacks the beautiful pattern design that appears on the one shown previously. I believe this receptacle is the same coffee tin that appears earlier in this Chapter, but without the paper label. *Barnes Collection.*

The logo on the lid to the receptacle dates to 1903-1915. *Barnes Collection.*

These beautiful tins consist of the tea hopper, a "JEWEL TEA CO. BREAKFAST COCOA," and a unknown tin with the Jewel logo. The cocoa tin had a paper label with the a picture of the Washington Boulevard and Ada Street building. It is not uncommon for tins to survive with missing paper labels. *Hedges Collection.*

Jewel Prefect Blend Coffee Pouches

In 1978, Jewel offered a FREE 12 ounce, non-dairy coffee creamer with the purchase of Jewel Prefect Blend Coffee Pouches. Seven packages, one pouch made a full pot. Priced at $7.29 plus FREE creamer.

"So many of my customers tell me the reason they buy Jewel Coffee is because their husbands like good coffee." This statement and the above promotional advertisement appeared in numerous Jewel publications during the mid-1930s.

TEA

In 1923, the new triple-seal packages, in which Jewel teas and coffees were being distributed, were considered the last word in modern, efficient, and safe packaging.

After performing various experiments with a wide variety of tea before 1928, and after serious study, Jewel adopted a variety of better brands for its line. Jewel's assortments of teas included: Orange Pekoe and Pekoe (Black) from Ceylon, India Black (Black) from India, Pan Fired (Green) from Japan, Basket Fired (Green) Japan, Imperial Gunpowder (Green) from China, Oolong and Gunpowder (Mixed Brown and Green) from Formosa and China.

Jewel found that the best grade of leaves from two different sources would not always produce exactly the same flavor. In order to provide customers with a tea that would not vary in flavor, they adopted a specific standard of cup quality for each brand of tea Jewel handled. Jewel blended leaves of the same quality from several source to produce that standard taste. Following this procedure in every brand of tea, all teas obtained by Jewel were rigidly tested in the cup by Jewel experts. Jewel claimed that, "These experts maintained a sense of smell and taste so keen they were able to detect the slightest variation in aroma and flavor."

Jewel teas were double tested, first by experienced representatives in the producing countries, then by Jewel experts. All representatives and experts had to keep in mind the Jewel standard of quality and flavor. Tea buyers were reminded not to buy from late summer or fall crops of India, China, Japan, or Formosa. Jewel used only the first crops from these countries.

In 1928, in the Jewel plant in Hoboken, New Jersey, all teas were delivered directly to the company in the chests in which they had been packed in their originating countries. From this shipment, samples from each lot were tested, all teas that passed the test where then ready for blending and cleaning.

Tea, like roasted coffee, would deteriorate with age (although not rapidly) and when exposed to the oxygen and moisture in the air. Poorly packaged teas and bulk tea were at a big disadvantage. Jewel avoided this problem with their triple-sealed package, designed to be air-tight and moisture proof. Jewel suggested that as soon as a package of tea was opened, it should be placed in an air-tight glass container, a container available from Jewel.

Jewel stated that their method of distribution was "... superior because they had the advantage of getting its teas to there customers in a wholesome condition. The Jewel Tea Co., Inc., not only imported and packaged its teas, but had its own salesmen who delivered the teas directly to the customer within four to five weeks from the packaging date." To the most distant points, Jewel guaranteed it was not longer than six to eight weeks.

Jewel salesmen were to demonstrate to the customer that they were real authorities on tea by explaining the merits of Jewel teas. Jewel conducted a survey during the mid-1920s and found out that Black, Green, and mixed teas were popular in all sections of the country; however, like all things, there were those territories in which one kind was more popular. In Illinois, Indiana, Iowa, Minnesota, North and South Dakota, Wisconsin, Michigan (except Detroit), Ohio, select parts of New York and Pennsylvania, Kansas, the northern part of Mississippi, and from there west to Denver, Jewel's Green teas were the greatest in demand.

In the territory south and southwest of the Ohio River, in mid-Atlantic states, the New England states, along the Pacific coast, and in the largest cities located in the "green tea area" (Detroit and Denver), Black tea was popular.

Prior to 1928, Baltimore, located in the "Black tea area," consumed more Oolong and Gunpowder than straight Black or straight Green tea. Jewel estimated that the average consumption of tea in the United States prior to 1928 was approximately 5-1/4 pounds per year per family.

Jewel equipped there salesmen with a guide to provide customers with information showing which particular Jewel brand could be substituted for the brand of tea the customer was using. "Either Jewel 'Orange Pekoe and Pekoe' or 'India Black' should be sold to users of any type of fully fermented black tea or any combination of two or more kinds of black tea. The consumer with a preference for a mild, mellow and sweet flavor should be sold 'Orange Pekoe and Pekoe'. On the other hand, the consumer who prefers a strong, sharp taste, not quite as sweet or delicate as the 'Orange Pekoe and Pekoe', should be sold the 'India Black'." *What You Should Know About Tea,* 1928.

"Jewel 'Pan Fired' should be sold to consumers who are now using any one of the several grades of Pan Fired, or who are using any of the Japan green teas known as 'Sun Dried', 'Uncolored Japan', 'Natural Leaf Japan', or 'Green Japan'." *What You Should Know About Tea,* 1928.

Jewel pointed out that there were several different grades of "Basket Fired" tea, all which was marketed under the name "Basket Fired." According to Jewel, their "Basket Fired" should be sold to customers using any type of Basket Fired tea.

Jewel "Imperial Gunpowder" would satisfied the taste of customers using either "Gunpowder," "Imperial," "Young Hyson," or any mixture of two or more kinds of China green teas.

Jewel's "Oolong and Gunpowder" teas were a mixture of green and brown teas. Jewel suggested that customers who were using any mixture of either brown and green or black and green teas would be satisfied with Jewel "Oolong and Gunpowder."

The Difference Between Black and Green Tea

From the Camellia Sinensis, an evergreen shrub, both Black and Green Tea were derived. The differences in the individual characteristics are found in the growing conditions and the processing. Black teas are fermented, heated, and dried, producing leaves that provide a strong, dark brew. Green tea leaves are not fermented.

Green Tea

In 1946, New York Jewel buyers purchased a large shipment of green teas for the first time since the outbreak of World War II. Processed and packaged in the Barrington, Illinois plant, Jewel salesmen carried it in their baskets. It was a blend of unfermented green tea, that had been treated to retain its "rare, delicate tang and pleasing aroma."

It had been some time since customers had been served this tea. World War II had curtailed its production and it would be years before the supply would reach pre-war levels. Jewel customers were among the first to serve Green Tea, because Jewel was among the first to acquire it.

There was a difference between Green and Black Tea. Green Tea was treated immediately after the leaves were picked, sealing the pores, and the green tea was preserved in natural green state. With Black Tea, the leaves were exposed to the air for a length of time, changing the nature of the leaves. These different leaf treatments accounted for the differences in taste.

In 1946 there were three times as many people who drank tea as those who drank coffee, and there were five hundred million coffee drinkers.

Jewel Brand Pan Fired Japan Tea was "Imported and Packed with special care by JEWEL TEA CO., CHICAGO, U.S.A." This container is metal with a paper label. As no "Inc." appears on this label, it dates before 1916. *Hamilton Collection.*

The Bar 'n Circle logo appears on this "Jewel Brand Pan Fired Japan Tea" container. The lid is hinged. *Hamilton Collection.*

Jewel promoted the above selection of tea in the customers choice of 1 or 1/2 pound packages during the mid-1920s. The selection was "Orange Pekoe and Pekoe a fine, black tea, Imperial Gunpowder - unfermented and Pan Fired - Green tea." A 15¢ credit was given on a premium with a pound package and a 5¢ credit on a premium with each half pound package.

In 1926, Jewel promoted this Jewel Orange Pekoe Tea. Priced at $1.00 per pound or 50¢ per half pound. (P.S.C. 10¢ and 5¢ respectively).

An original late 1970s advertisement promoting Earl Grey Tea and Strawberry Tea. FREE Jewel Money was offered with these Jewel Special Teas. In a Jewel Grocery Stock Card dated 1978, these teas were advertised as "INTRODUCING 2 NEW JEWEL TEAS," "priced Your Choice $2.99."

In the 1970s Jewel offered JEWEL Black Tea, Orange Pekoe, and Pekoe at the price of two for $2.49. It was regularly priced at $1.29 each.

This canister held 24 bags of "Orange Spice Tea" Net Wt. 15 oz. The paper label could be removed and the canister could be re-used. Also available was "Naturally Flavored Orange Spice Tea." This tea may have been introduced later, as my collection of Jewel Grocery Stock Cards is limited. See page 31 in "The Jewel Tea Company. Its History and Products." *Hamilton Collection.*

Postwar Packaging

In Barrington, Illinois in 1946, on a new post-war packaging machine, an extra large tea bag was packaged. Made from a fine texture, tasteless, odorless heat sealing paper, those tea bags were billed as "giving Jewel customer's a clear cup of tea." Proud of the new machine, Jewel wanted their customers to know what it meant to them in the way of better tea bags.

A feature writer for the Jewel News, in 1946, decided to investigate the operation of the new tea bag line. Viewing the operation of this new machine he saw a long strip of heat sealing paper being feed into the machine from one side. From the floor above, a blend of tea came down a pipe and the two, tea and paper, came together in the center. This operation formed the tea bags that were pushed forward out through a metal chute.

The writer closely watched the intricate mechanism and could see how the paper was heat-sealed, the edges crimped, and each bag cut apart from the next one. He noticed that the most "miraculous" feature about the whole operation was that the same amount of tea went into each bag. This feature was controlled by an adjustment in the angle of the pipe through which the tea flowed. Thus, he concluded, "Jewel Black Tea was the highest quality that anyone could get."

A picturesque Dragon appears on this carton. The carton contained 48 bags of Jewel Tea. (See the "American's Groceryman" 1952 in this publication. This carton can be seen in the promotional advertisement along with two other Dragon tea packages.) *Hedges Collection.*

From a 1970s Jewel Grocery Stock Card, the JEWEL FREE-FLO TEA BAGS were promoted. The carton of 48 Orange Pekoe and Pekoe Blend tea bags sold for 2 for $2.49 in a limited offer.

During the 1970s, Jewel paid 50¢ in "Jewel money" to try their Jewel Jumbo Iced Tea Bags. One bag made a whole pitcher of iced tea. Two for $4.98 + 50¢ free Jewel Money with two.

In 1978 Jewel sold the above 6 oz., "Jewel Jumbo Iced Tea Bags" for $2.29, listed as No. 15-040. *Byerly Collection.*

"Jewel Instant Iced Tea Mix" with lemon flavor and sugar. Net weight 8.33 oz. The carton contained 5 packages. Priced at $1.49, a customer in 1978 could purchase 2 for $2.88. No. 15-057. *Ferriera Collection.*

In 1978, "Jewel 100 Tea Bags" in Orange Pekoe and Pekoe Cut Black Tea was priced at $2.99, a savings of 50¢ off of the regular price.

This original carton has an illustration of the Autumn Leaf Newport teapot, breakfast cup, and saucer. Net weight 3-3/4 oz. This tea appeared in a 1978 Jewel Grocery Stock Card. *Hedges Collection.*

The side panel of the "Jewel 48 Tea Bags." Directions were provide on the bottom of this carton for making tea in your automatic coffee maker. *Hedges Collection.*

In the late 1970s, Jewel promoted the "Jewel 48 Tea Bags" in Orange Pekoe and Pekoe Cut Black Tea, 3 for $4.49.

Dated to the 1970s, Jewel offered the above "Jewel Black Tea" in 1/2 lb. cartons.

A Dragon appears on the above 1/2 lb. "Jewel Black Tea" Orange Pekoe and Pekoe. *Vogel Collection.*

A side panel and back of "Jewel Black Tea." The back panel provided direction for "The Art of Making Good Tea." *Vogel Collection.*

This carton of "Black Currant" tea held 20 tea bags. Note the logo and horse and wagon appearing near bottom right side. *Lemons Collection.*

These 48 tea bags were in the above "Jewel Tea Bags" carton. Packed by Jewel Tea Co. Inc., Jewel Park, Barrington, Illinois. *Hedges Collection.*

A glass covered display case is used to display this collection of Jewel Tea Bags. Also shown in the case is a "Victory" label used on a tea container. Covered display cases are available at most antique shows or flea markets. *Vogel Collection.*

Displaying loose tea bags has been accomplished by placing loose bags in a small container. This container is discussed in a later chapter. *Hamilton Collection.*

Three tea cartons, "Iced Tea Blend," "Imperial Gunpowder Green Tea" and "Pan Fired Green Tea." Packed by the Jewel Tea Company Inc., Jewel Park Barrington, Ill. Each carton held 8 oz. *Hamilton Collection.*

"The Art of Making Good Iced Tea" and directions appear on the back panel (center). On the reverse side panel the Long-Spout Teapot appears (right) and the Mary Dunbar Seal of Approval (left). *Hamilton Collection.*

An 8 oz. carton of "Oolong and Gunpowder Mixed Tea," Packed by Jewel Tea Company Inc., Jewel Park Barrington, Illinois. The Mary Dunbar's Seal, directions, and the Long-Spout appear on the side panels and back of this carton. *Hedges Collection.*

End panels on this selection of tea cartons are printed with, "Your Purchases of Jewel Groceries Bring You Beautiful and Useful Premiums." An illustration of the Long-Spout Teapot appears with the following, "For Flavorful Tea — The Jewel HALL CHINA TEAPOT." *Hamilton Collection.*

A full 3 oz. jar of "Jewel "T" Instant Tea," 100% Tea, Serve Hot or Cold. *Sivils Collection.*

In 1978 this 3 oz. jar of Jewel Instant Tea was priced at $2.99. It was "100% tea with no additives."

The reverse side of the "Jewel "T" Instant Tea" provided directions for Iced and Hot Tea. Distributed by Jewel Companies Inc. Barrington, Illinois 60010. *Sivils Collection.*

The label would have been on the raised, hinged lid, shown here. This missing label is not an uncommon occurrence. Jewel instructed customers to peel the label off and use the canister to start "YOUR" collection. The label indicated the "Jewel Tea Co." *Eisnaugle Collection.*

This decorated tea canister should have a paper label on the lid. The collector of this tea canister acquired the canister at a local flea market.

This highly decorated tea tin displays an Oriental scene on each side panel. A paper label appears on the hinged lid. *Lemons Collection.*

The tin tea chest held Jewel Tea bags and is scripted inside the lid: "This Imported Treasure Chest Contains 150 Jewel Tea Bags 'Famous for Delightful Flavor'." Jewel offered this Imported Tea Chest in 1947. Richly embossed and lavishly decorated in gold, red, blue, and green, this Chest is 9" long, 6" wide, and 4" deep. *Hedges Collection.*

This decorated tin has been laid on its side. It held "30 English Break Tea Bags." The paper label is marked "Distr Jewel Companies Inc. Barrington, Il. 60010." *Hamilton Collection.*

Two "Jewel Extra Fancy Darjeeling Blend Tea" canisters. Once the lid was removed, an insert liner provided instructions for the enjoyment of this tea. Each canister held 4 oz. *Hamilton Collection.*

The famous "Jewel" name does not appear on the colorful canister shown here. In 1978 this canister was promoted in a Jewel Grocery Stock Card with two other canisters, "Boston's Mint-in-Tea, Boston's Ginseng Tea." Jewel advertised them as "Get 1 FREE When You Buy 2." Priced at 3 for $5.98. Instructions were provided to "Peel OFF Label Start Your Collection Reusable Decorator Canisters." *Eisnaugle Collection.*

COCOA

In 1929, Jewel Tea stated that "Jewel agents purchased only the perfect fermented and cured cocoa beans. These beans were distinguished by the richness and even color, for those beans provided a richer flavor and aroma during manufacturing process and commanded a higher price." *Other Quality Groceries,* 1929.

When cocoa beans arrived at the Jewel factory, they were inspected and cleaned prior to roasting. Three varieties of beans were used to produce Jewel cocoa. Each bean selected was blended, "allowing only the highest quality of its type, which resulted in a mild, delicious chocolate flavor and aroma of maximum strength and nourishment."

Ensuring its "perfect texture," Jewel cocoa was run through the finest sieve twice, involving a process cooling machine, which brought out the rich, red brown color. No chemicals were used by Jewel in the manufacture of its cocoa. Jewel stated that "Their cocoa was richer than most on the market because it contained more than 24% cocoa butter, while others contained only 12 to 14%."

Jewel cocoa was packed in one-pound tin containers. Each package of Jewel cocoa made 125 cups of cocoa.

Cocoa solved the problem during the First World War when the need was acute for a concentrated food that could be eaten quickly and provide strength immediately. In 1929 government statistics showed that over 400,000,000 pounds of cocoa was used in the United States alone. Before World War I, an average of about 140,000,000 pounds of cocoa was used.

If Jewel salesmen sold each customer her total requirements in 1929, Jewel would have sold 2,850,000 pounds of cocoa per year. In 1928 Jewel sales were only 572,542 pounds, and the average per service salesman was 10 pounds. Jewel pointed out this disparity to its sales force, believing there was room for larger cocoa sales.

It is not impossible to acquired a collection of Jewel Cocoa tins like those shown here. Time, patience, money, and desire — are all that you need. *Lombard Collection.*

This 1 lb. "Pure Cocoa" tin is marked "Jewel Tea Co. Inc., Jewel Park Barrington, Ill." On the back Jewel gave directions for "HOT COCOA." At the very top on the back appears "©1933 J.T. INC." This Cocoa was "Richer in Cocoa Butter than required for Breakfast Cocoa." *Byerly Collection.*

The 1 lb. Jewel "RICH IN FLAVOR" Cocoa container is missing its lid. Marked "JEWEL TEA CO., INC., NEW YORK CHICAGO." Lids are almost impossible to locate. *Randall Collection.*

On a side panel of "Pure Cocoa" Jewel promoted "Jewel Coffees, Teas, Baking Powder, Coconut, Jell, and Butternut Cookies." *Byerly Collection.*

A 1 lb. container of Jewel "ABSOLUTELY PURE COCOA." Marked "JEWEL TEA CO., INC., NEW YORK CHICAGO." Directions were provided on the side. *Byerly Collection.*

Three exceptional Jewel "COCOA" tins. These 1 lb. tins are in mint condition. Packed by "JEWEL TEA CO. INC., JEWEL PARK BARRINGTON, ILL." *Byerly Collection.*

Jewel provided various recipes on each side of the Jewel "COCOA" tins. This Cocoa was Approved by Mary Dunbar. *Byerly Collection.*

This "DUTCH PROCESS COCOA" appeared in a 1952 Jewel catalog. Packed by Jewel Tea Co. Inc., Jewel Park Barrington, Illinois. *Vogel Collection.*

The back panel of "DUTCH PROCESS COCOA" provided recipes. "YOUR MONEY BACK WITH A SMILE IF YOU ARE NOT SATISFIED." Jewel stood behind their products. *Vogel Collection.*

The Jewel Scale logo introduced in the late teens appears on each side of the Jewel "COCOA" tin. *Byerly Collection.*

A 1 lb. Jewel Home Shopping Service "Jewel Instant Cocoa Mix." Approved by Mary Dunbar. *Byerly Collection.*

Front and side panels of "Jewel Instant Cocoa Mix" from the Jewel Home Shopping Service. *Byerly Collection.*

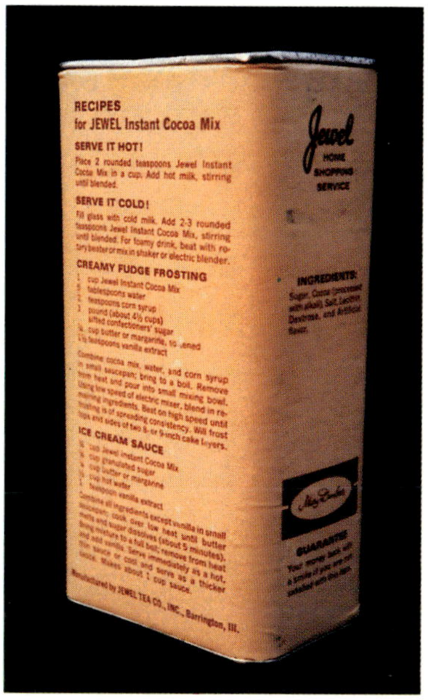

The back and opposite side panel provides recipes for JEWEL Instant Cocoa Mix. *Byerly Collection.*

A different packaging for the 1 lb. Jewel Home Shopping Service "Jewel Instant Cocoa" mix. *Byerly Collection.*

Recipes for "Jewel Instant Cocoa" mix were provided on the back and side panel, along with the Mary Dunbar Seal of Approval. *Byerly Collection.*

This cardboard carton held "JEWEL "T" INSTANT HOT COCOA MIX." *Sivils Collection.*

CHAPTER 3
SPICES, EXTRACTS, DRESSINGS, CORNSTARCH, BAKING POWDER AND SODA

Spices

On the subject of spices Jewel proclaimed that, "Reaching the American housewife, all Jewel spices were fresh, full strength, and rich in the natural oil that gave each spice its distinctive flavor. Jewel spices were carefully granulated, not pulverized, by what was referred to as the 'cold grind' method." *Other Quality Groceries,* 1929.

The benefits of granulation were described as follows, "Jewel spices were left with all the natural flavoring strength and aroma which provided the qualities in pepper, mustard and ginger. Small particles were torn apart when spices were pulverized which effected the oil and flavor. Oil cells in Jewel spices were not broken." *Other Quality Groceries,* 1929.

Jewel claimed their spices provided greater strength and flavoring while being cheaper to use than other spices. When customers used Jewel Spices, a smaller quantity was deemed necessary to give the required "zest" to any dish.

A revolving "twin turntable" was offered in 1966. With just a spin of the finger, neatly stored spices were right at the fingertip. This plastic turntable revolved on steel bearings and was easy to assemble. The "twin turntable" was 10-1/2" in diameter x 5-1/2" high and sold for $2.98. A "single turntable" sold for $1.98. On close examination, a variety of Jewel spices can be seen on this turntable.

Cinnamon

From the inner bark of a small tropical evergreen (cassia tree), Cinnamon is taken. Jewel Cinnamon was a blend of two cinnamon barks. Jewel Cinnamon was all cinnamon, with no filler. Jewel Cinnamon would go further than a lot of stale, dry, or artificial cinnamon.

Jewel instructed salesmen to inform the customers that an artificial preparation made from coal tar was sometimes used as a cinnamon flavor. A small amount of real cinnamon was also sometimes added to a powder made of cheap barks similar in appearance. Jewel Cinnamon was never prepared, nor were ingredients added under the above procedure.

The Jewel "Black Pepper" and "Ground Cinnamon" appeared in the Jewel Home Shopping Service Spring and Summer 1952 Catalog. These products were "PACKED BY JEWEL TEA CO., INC. JEWEL PARK BARRINGTON, IL." *Hamilton Collection.*

The original Jewel Cinnamon appeared in a 1927 Jewel News. The 5-oz. can sold for 30¢. (Profit Sharing Credit 5¢.) "Jewel Cinnamon was of high quality, convenient, and handy to use."

An original 1940s advertisement promoting a 2-lb. package of Jewel Prepared Biscuit Flour, Jewel Cinnamon 5-oz. can, and a Jewel Nutmeg 5-oz. can. These items were used to create the spicy doughnuts shown in this advertisement.

Three identical 5 ounce Jewel "Cinnamon" tins. "Packed By JEWEL TEA CO., INC. JEWEL PARK BARRINGTON, ILL." *Byerly Collection.*

Jewel "Cinnamon" Net Weight 5 ounces. "Packed By JEWEL TEA CO., INC. JEWEL PARK BARRINGTON, ILL." *Randall Collection.*

The three identical 5 ounce Jewel "Cinnamon" tins include various side views providing recipes, directions, and the "Mary Dunbar Seal of Approval." *Byerly Collection.*

A 5 ounce Jewel "Cinnamon" container, marked "JEWEL TEA CO., INC. NEW YORK — CHICAGO." *Byerly Collection.*

A 5 ounce container of Jewel "Cinnamon," this product was "TESTED AND APPROVED BY MARY DUNBAR JEWEL HOMEMAKERS INSTITUTE." Marked "JEWEL TEA CO., INC. JEWEL PARK BARRINGTON, ILL." *Byerly Collection.*

A side and back view of the above 5 ounce Jewel "Cinnamon." Jewel used this as a form of advertising for other products. *Byerly Collection.*

A cardboard carton of Jewel Brand "Ground Cinnamon." This carton is marked "PACKED BY JEWEL TEA CO. INC. HEADQUARTERS NEW YORK - CHICAGO - NEW ORLEANS - SAN FRANCISCO." *Hamilton Collection.*

The "Diamond Jewel Trade Mark" appears on this carton. The carton has been sealed for protection. This logo was in use between 1916 and 1919. *Hamilton Collection.*

During the 1970s, Jewel developed a line of products they referred to as "Quick Chef." This name would appear on various Jewel products: Quick Chef potatoes, Lasagna Dinner, Bakery mix's and a variety of spices. Shown here is a 3 ounce "Quick Chef Ground Cinnamon" container. *Lemons Collection.*

Partridge or Dove Tins

These "Ginger" and "Nutmeg" tins were "DISTRIBUTED BY JEWEL TEA CO., INC. BARRINGTON, ILL." Note the side panel on the spice tin in the center; each container held 2 ounces of spice. *Hedges Collection.*

Note the unusual design pattern around the word "JEWEL" and then repeated around each of the spice names on this container. *Byerly Collection.*

Referred to as the "Partridge" or "Dove" tin's, these items are highly sought by Jewel collectors and have recently escalated in the secondary market.

These are metal tins with paper labels. Note the coloring of the "GINGER" tin. *Byerly Collection.*

Dates can not be ascertain for these highly illustrated "Partridge" or "Dove" spice tins. Prepare yourself, they take time to find and can be somewhat expensive. *Byerly Collection.*

Allspice

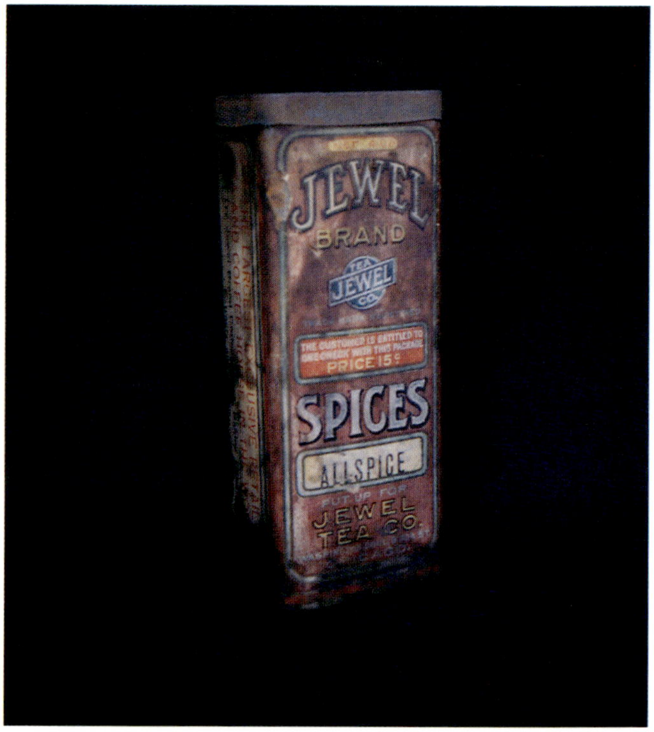

A metal "Allspice" tin with a paper label. Note the slant Jewel Bar 'n Circle logo on the front section. This logo was popular between 1903 and 1910. Marked "PUT UP FOR JEWEL TEA CO." *Hamilton Collection.*

The Jewel Tea Company building, located at Washington Boulevard and Ada Street, appear on the back of this "Allspice" tin. It is not uncommon to see the above street address also listed as "Washington Boul." *Hamilton Collection.*

Pepper

Black pepper berries, from a climbing tropical shrub, were picked while still green and allowed to dry. Then the entire berry was ground. White pepper was obtained by allowing the pepper berries to ripen and was less pungent than black pepper. Jewel Black Pepper contained no "adulterants" or fillers.

Jewel Pepper was obtained from the blending of the body of the pepper berry with the black outer hull. Jewel customers could, they claimed, hold their pepper under their noses without sneezing. Jewel Pepper had not dried out or been adulterated, the cause of peoples' sneezes.

The original Jewel "Black Pepper" appeared in a 1927 Jewel News. The 5 ounce can sold for 35¢. (Profit Sharing Credit 5¢). Jewel Pepper was ground to retain the flavor and conserve the oils.

This metal "Pepper" tin has a paper label and the slanted Jewel logo. Marked "PUT UP FOR JEWEL TEA CO. WASHINGTON BOUL. & ADA ST. CHICAGO." "THE LARGEST EXCLUSIVE RETAIL TEA AND COFFEE HOUSE IN THE WORLD." *Hamilton Collection.*

A tin with the slanted Jewel logo, marked "PACKED FOR JEWEL TEA CO. CHICAGO." No "INC" appears on this tin. A side panel reads: "Guaranteed under the Food and Drug Act June 30, 1906. Serial No. 28. (Original price 15¢)." On the other side: "Spices, Baking Powder & Cocoa are of superior quality, Full Weight and Strength and Dealers are Authorized to Refund the price paid in case purchasers are dissatisfied." *Lombard Collection.*

Distributed by "JEWEL COMPANIES INC. BARRINGTON, ILL. 60010," this Jewel "Black Pepper" was available during the mid-1970s. Net Weight 4 oz. Sold for 99¢. *Eisnaugle Collection.*

"DISTRIBUTED BY J.T'S GENERAL STORE IHSS INC. BARRINGTON, ILLINOIS 60010," this 4 ounce "Ground Black Pepper" is similar to the previous pepper container. J.T.'s General Store grocery products are becoming very collectible. *Hedges Collection.*

The original advertising photograph for the Jewel "Black Pepper" available during the mid-1970s. *Eisnaugle Collection.*

A 4 ounce container of Jewel "Black Ground Pepper." Packed by "Jewel Tea Co., Inc. Barrington, Ill." *Lemons Collection.*

Note the variation in color on the "BLACK PEPPER" tins. It is not uncommon to find tins from the same period with different coloring. Each tin is marked "PACKED BY JEWEL TEA CO. INC. JEWEL PARK BARRINGTON, ILL;" these containers held 5 ounces of black pepper each. On the side panel a recipe for "Brown Gravy" was provided and the opposite side the seal of Mary Dunbar appeared. *Byerly Collection.*

Note the Jewel logo on this exceptional "Black Pepper" tin. Marked "JEWEL TEA CO. INC. JEWEL PARK BARRINGTON, ILL." *Byerly Collection.*

The reverse side and a back panel of the Jewel "BLACK PEPPER." Instructions were provided for "Use as a seasoning for GRAVIES - SAUCES, VEGETABLES, SALADS, FISH, DRESSINGS, MEATS." This pepper was approved by Mary Dunbar. *Byerly Collection.*

A collection of Jewel spices bearing the same logo. Shown for variation of color and size, each is marked "PACKED BY JEWEL TEA CO. INC. JEWEL PARK BARRINGTON ILL." *Byerly Collection.*

Ground Mustard

Jewel Ground Mustard was obtained from carefully selected mustard seeds grown in England. Seeds were properly aged and cleaned before grinding and packaging. No artificial coloring, turmeric, or other ingredients were added to this mustard.

Jewel claimed their Ground Mustard was a real necessity as a medicine as well. Jewel salesmen told their customers that they could not only use Jewel Prepared Mustard for food flavoring but they could save lives with it by applying mustard plasters in cases of lung congestion and pneumonia. Jewel salesmen told their customers that if a stronger table dressing than "Jewel Prepared Mustard" was desired, it could be obtained by mixing the needed quantity of Jewel Ground Mustard with water.

The original photograph for Jewel "Ground Mustard" appeared in 1929. Marked "If You Like Mustard - Try Jewel Ground Mustard for varying the flavor of your favorite dishes. It has that rich, genuine mustard flavor - snappy and pungent; is made from a selected stock and is absolutely pure." A 5-oz. can sold for 35¢. (Profit Sharing Credit 5¢).

The 5 ounce metal container of "Ground Mustard" is marked "PACKED BY JEWEL TEA CO. INC. JEWEL PARK BARRINGTON, ILL." *Byerly Collection.*

The opposite side of the "Ground Mustard" container provided instruction for "Deviled Eggs" and was "Approved by Mary Dunbar." *Byerly Collection.*

Prepared Mustard

Jewel Prepared Mustard was produced from California yellow and brown mustard seeds. Turmeric was added for coloring to meet the public demand for a highly colored dressing. Jewel added no foreign ingredients.

Jewel Prepared Mustard was packed in 12 ounce glass jars with metal screw lids. This preserved the flavor and moisture and would not turn the product black.

The original photograph for Jewel "Prepared Mustard" appeared in a 1927 Jewel News. The 12 ounce jar sold for 25¢. (Profit Sharing Credit 5¢). Jewel Prepared Mustard came ready to use and could be used to enhance the flavor of roasts, cold meats, and tasty scalloped dishes.

Assortment of Spices

Jewel Spices "Cinnamon," "Allspice," and "Ginger," each tin is marked "JEWEL TEA CO., INC. NEW YORK — CHICAGO" and holds 5 ounces. Note the scale logo and the word "INC." Jewel was incorporated in 1916. *Hedges Collection.*

The reverse side provided instructions for using the product and information that "Spices vary in bulk. All our spice cans are uniform in size. This can is filled full weight as specified." *Hamilton Collection.*

These examples of Jewel "Nutmeg," "Cinnamon," and "Black Pepper" were offered in 5 ounce containers. Marked "TESTED AND APPROVED BY MARY DUNBAR JEWEL HOMEMAKERS INSTITUTE JEWEL TEA CO., INC. JEWEL PARK, BARRINGTON, ILL." Some tin's can be found marked with a date as well as the above logo. *Byerly Collection.*

Note the variation in coloring on these tins. These 5 ounce tins are highly sought by collectors. Each is marked "JEWEL TEA CO., INC. NEW YORK - CHICAGO." The two tins on the bottom would demand more than the worn tin on top. *Byerly Collection.*

Condition, coloring, and type of material has an effect on the price of a container. Many collectors search for coloring variation of tin's, others collect only those from an era of history or a particular logo, and many collect Jewel in general. It is wise to remember that prices vary from region to region and that the condition is very important.

A form of Jewel advertising was to promote other products on the reverse side of any product. *Byerly Collection.*

Nutmeg

Jewel Nutmeg was made from small Penang mace nuts, "famous for their richness in oil and flavor." Sometimes the oil could be seen when loose lumps formed in the can. This oil was considered to be proof of the quality of Jewel Nutmeg. Jewel customers received their Nutmeg in shakers.

This 5 ounce "Nutmeg" container is marked "PACKED BY JEWEL TEA CO., INC. JEWEL PARK BARRINGTON, ILL." *Byerly Collection.*

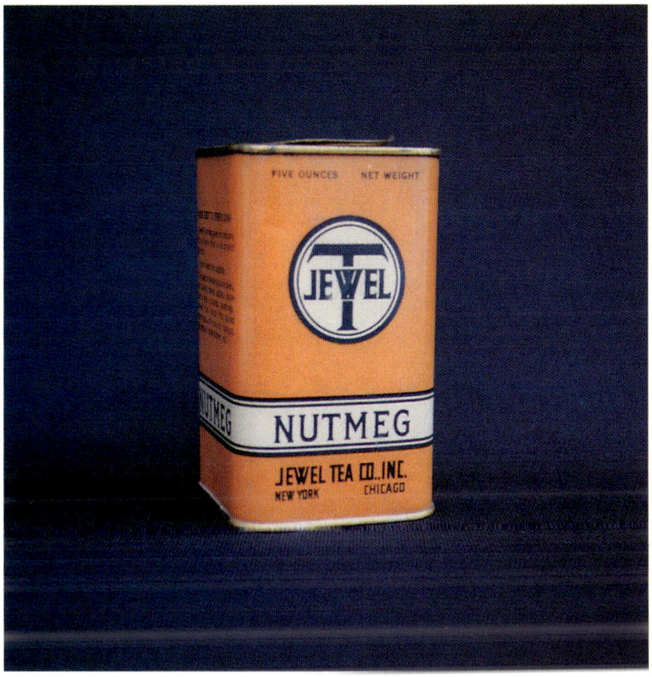

A 5 ounce container of Jewel "NUTMEG." Marked "JEWEL TEA CO., INC. NEW YORK — CHICAGO." Note the Jewel logo. *Byerly Collection.*

These "Nutmeg" tins are marked "©1933 J.T. CO., INC." This marking can be found on the back near the bottom. *Byerly Collection.*

The side panel of Jewel "Nutmeg" that "ADDS ZEST TO EVERY DISH." *Byerly Collection.*

Ginger

Jewel "Ginger" was an African ginger, "of special strength and purity, which is known for its hot, spicy flavor." Jewel "Ginger" was a favorite for Mrs. Brown's cooking and was used also as a medicine.

In 1929, Jewel promoted Jewel "Ginger" as "...a dash of ginger that gave unusual flavor that made an ordinary dish distinctive." It could be added to the syrup poured over canned fruits or to boiling water when preparing fowl. A 5-oz. can sold for 35¢. (Profit Sharing Credit 5¢).

The only difference with the 2 ounce "Ginger" container is the net weight of 5 ounces. *Randall Collection.*

A 2 ounce "Ginger" container. "PACKED BY JEWEL TEA CO., INC. JEWEL PARK BARRINGTON, ILL." The marking appearing on the front is "REG. U.S. PAT. OFF." *Randall Collection.*

A 5 ounce container of "Ginger." Marked "JEWEL TEA CO., INC. NEW YORK — CHICAGO," with "Bulls eye" logo. *Byerly Collection.*

The front and side view of the Jewel "Ginger." *Byerly Collection.*

Extracts

In this historical photograph, employees of the Jewel Tea Company fill extract bottles. Jewel staff expert, Frank Farwell, oversees the operation. *Andrews Collection.*

Jewel's extract bottling equipment was designed by Frank Farwell, production foreman, along with Henry Dreckman and Waldo Shuett. The bottling machines they designed were described as "almost human after installation."

This equipment was developed in the office of Plant Superintendent E.J. Courrier, with actual construction being pieced together between regular jobs and after closing time. This new equipment cost less than $400 and increased Jewel's production by 50 percent. Construction allowed for lower maintenance cost, with all pipes made from stainless steel and non-corrosive metal, which was not true of the standard equipment available during 1938.

The reserve tanks were glass-lined allowing for easy cleaning and sterilizing. It is very important to note here that the extract bottling equipment was not the first machinery built by Jewel experts. Throughout the Barrington facilities, machines could be found that had been modified in one way or the other. There were also machines designed and built directly by Jewel experts.

Refining companies, breakfast food companies, and other firms in 1938 - 1939 asked permission to send their draftsmen and engineers to the Barrington facilities to watch these machines in operation.

Vanilla Extract

The Jewel Tea Company, Inc. purchased vanilla beans from orchards on the Bourbon Islands. This extract was described as possessing the "... rare, delicate flavor of genuine Bourbon vanilla beans." The Bourbon Islands bean was dark brown in color, waxy to the touch, and covered with "fine sparkling crystals of vanillin" (the active flavoring principle of vanilla). Proof of high vanillin contents could be found in only the best cured beans having these fine crystals.

Jewel Vanilla Extract was manufactured in a giant percolator, to which chopped vanilla beans, sugar and pure grain alcohol were added. The alcohol dissolved the sugar and extracted the vanillin and resins as it passed over the chopped beans. This percolation continued until all the flavor was taken from the beans and the extract was a rich, dark brown color.

Jewel Vanilla was aged in special glass lined storage tanks which allowed "... a smooth and mellow extract with a perfect blend of flavoring and alcohol." This process was the last before the vanilla was automatically bottled for shipment.

Jewel claimed that the economy to be found in this product was in "... its full, rich flavor, each drop was uniform and delicious."

During the mid-1970s Jewel promoted an Imitation Vanilla Flavoring. Regularly priced at 79¢ each, Jewel offered customers a savings of 19¢ when 2 bottles were purchased at $1.39. *Lemons Collection.*

A 6 ounce Jewel Imitation Vanilla Flavoring. *Lemons Collection.*

Jewel "Imitation Vanilla Extract" with the original carton. "Manufactured By Jewel Tea Co., Inc. Jewel Park Barrington, Ill." Original packaging increases the value of a product. *Lemons Collection.*

Jewel "Maid Vanilla" Extract shown here with the original carton. Marked "Jewel Companies Inc. Melrose Park, Illinois." *Hedges Collection.*

Melrose Park

In 1953, Jewel Tea Company directors approved plans for the development of a new two-story office and warehouse facility in Melrose Park, Illinois at a cost in excess of $4 million dollars. This new warehouse served as a distribution center, supplementing existing facilities serving Jewel's Chicago food store.

Jewel President George L. Clements announced that a third of the personnel from both the Barrington and the Jewel food store department headquarters would be transferred and consolidated into the new location. Numerous grocery product's can be found marked "Jewel Companies Inc. Melrose Park, Illinois."

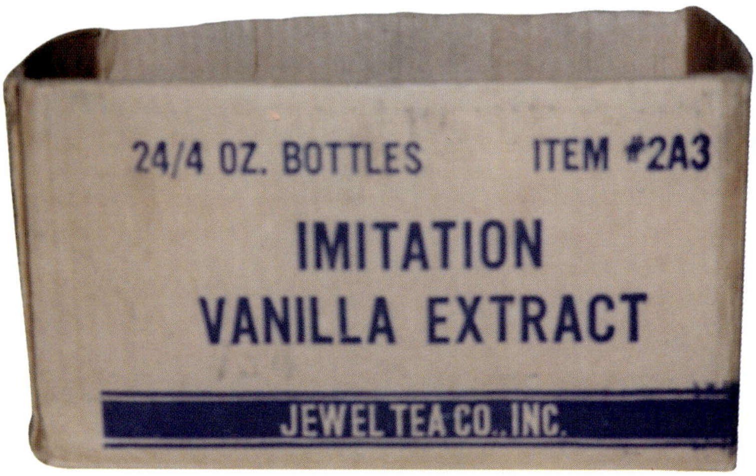

An original "Imitation Vanilla Extract" packing carton. Marked "Jewel Tea Co., Inc.," this carton held 24 - 4 oz. bottles. Item #2A3. *Lombard Collection.*

Jewel "High Quality Imitation Vanilla Extract" in 4 fluid ounces. This product appeared in the Spring and Summer 1952 Jewel Home Shopping Service Catalog. *Hedges Collection.*

Lemon Extracts

Jewel Lemon Extract was "... a combination of fragrant natural lemon oil, finely ground lemon peel (only of the highest quality) and government tested pure grain alcohol." Jewel Lemon Extract was of the same high standard as their Vanilla Extract.

Jewel Lemon Extract was guaranteed to be "pure and wholesome." The taste of real lemons could be given to pies, cakes, sherbets, ice cream with a little Jewel Lemon Extract.

The Home Service kitchen found that lemon flavoring brought out and improved the flavor of other recipe ingredients.

A 2 ounce bottle of "Pure True Lemon Flavor Lemon Extract." Marked "JEWEL TEA CO., INC. NEW YORK — CHICAGO." *Hamilton Collection.*

"Jewel Brand Non-Alcoholic Concentrated Tube Flavors Lemon Flavor," Price 30¢. The Diamond logo appears on the top flap and the bottom and on the back with "THE WORLDS LARGEST RETAIL TEA AND COFFEE HOUSE." One side of the carton says "BUY THE JEWEL WAY FROM PRODUCER TO CONSUMER" while the opposite side provides a list of Jewel products. *Lemons Collection.*

This Jewel "Pure Orange Extract" glass bottle, with a paper label, contains 2 fluid ounces. *Vogel Collection.*

Dating prior to 1916, this Jewel "Brand Food Coloring" was priced at 30¢. This is a Yellow Color bottle with a paper label and a cork stopper. "Manufactured By Jewel Tea Co. Chicago." *Byerly Collection.*

Jewel Brand "Flavoring Extracts Imitation Raspberry," a 2-1/2 ounce bottle with a paper label. Note the diamond logo. This product was "Manufactured By Jewel Tea Co., Inc. Headquarters New York — Chicago — San Francisco — New Orleans. Price 30¢." *Vogel Collection.*

The collection of extract bottles shown here include "Lemon," "Almond," and "Maple." They are stamped with the "Diamond" and the "Bar 'n Circle" logos. These bottles were sealed with cork stoppers. *Hamilton Collection.*

Dressings

This "Homogenized Jewel Italian Dressing" was promoted in the 1970s Grocery Stock Cards. Each bottle contained 12 fluid ounces.

Twelve fluid ounces of Jewel "French Dressing." *Hamilton Collection.*

This 3 ounces carton of Jewel "Whole Mixed Pickling Spice" was "Distributed by JEWEL TEA CO., INC. JEWEL PARK BARRINGTON, ILL." *Ferriera Collection.*

Mayonnaise

In 1929, Jewel informed the American housewife that Jewel Mayonnaise was the perfect salad dressing. Jewel "... knew that absolute uniformity in materials, careful measurements, equality of temperatures during the mixing process and the tendency of the oil was the major factor in producing Jewel Mayonnaise, only the highest quality of oil was used." Their mayonnaise was billed as mild, palatable, and spicy in flavor. To cut the oiliness of Mayonnaise, a "scientific" blend of spices, "pure and specially aged vinegar," a dash of mustard, a little sugar, and "only the freshest eggs" were used in making Jewel Mayonnaise smooth and creamy.

If a Jewel customer preferred a thinner mayonnaise, cream or lemon juice could be added. Jewel Mayonnaise could be used for the base in making Thousand Island dressing or sandwich spreads, or it could be used directly on bread.

Jewel promoted the 16 ounce jar of spicy "Mayonnaise" as a way to add tempting flavor to salads, sandwiches, cold meats, and hot vegetables. (Credit on Premium 5¢).

"Eat salads — they are healthful!" The Jewel "Mayonnaise," shown here, is marked "©1934 J.T. Co., Inc. 16 ounces. Distributed by Jewel Tea Co., Inc. Jewel Park Barrington, Ill." *Vogel Collection.*

Cornstarch

A Jewel customer was not afraid her custard would have lumps, her gravy would refuse to thicken, or that her white sauce would fail, if she used Jewel Cornstarch. The company reassured her that their cornstarch "... was pure, glistening white, highly refined and pulverized, with a uniform thickening power resulting in the best results." The Jewel cornstarch manufacturing process was identical with that of Jewel Gloss Starch. This process used the same selection of corn and extraction of starch and was all that was needed for a laundry starch; but, edible starch required a through process of refinement. This involved pulverizing the cornstarch to a fine powder and thoroughly sifted it. Tests were made in the Jewel Home Service Kitchen under the direction of an expert. Jewel pointed out that cooked cornstarch was almost 100% digestible.

Jewel Cornstarch was sold in one-pound packages and was fine for starching delicate linens and laces. It was not recommended for ordinary cold starch or laundry because Jewel Gloss Starch was good for those purposes and less expensive.

Mary Dunbar and Jewel customers discovered various uses for cornstarch and these were made available to Jewel customers through the Idea Exchange in THE JEWEL NEWS. If a Jewel customer experienced tired feet, simply apply Jewel Cornstarch.

Photographs of Jewel Cornstarch were not available.

Baking Powder

Jewel Baking Powder was a double acting baking powder that was assured under all conditions. There were four main classes of baking powder on the market during the 1920s. These classes were: 1) Tartrate, 2) Phosphate, 3) Alum, and 4) A Composite — which Jewel Baking Powder belonged to.

Jewel Baking Powder was composed of bicarbonate of soda (baking soda), calcium acid phosphate, sodium aluminate, and cornstarch, all skillfully blended. During the mid-1920s government standards required that a baking powder yield at least 12% of leavening gas, or carbon dioxide. Jewel Baking Powder exceeded government standards, releasing 14%.

In Jewel Baking Powder, cornstarch was used as the base to hold the other ingredients and to keep them from breaking down. The other elements used in making Jewel Baking Powder were selected, mixed, and blended under the direction of Jewel chemists. These chemists tested each lot so that they were certain of the proper proportions and of the uniformity of the powder. The soda, phosphate, sodium aluminate, and cornstarch used were of "the highest quality obtainable."

There were approximately 189 teaspoons of baking powder in the Jewel one-pound can, or 63 bakings. In 1929, Jewel Baking Powder sold for 50¢.

The colorful 1 lb. Jewel "Baking Powder" tin, shown here, is marked "Jewel Tea Co., Inc. New York — Chicago." This is the same container as shown in the 1927 advertisement. *Steelman Collection.*

An original Jewel "Baking Powder" container that appeared in a 1927 Jewel News. "Melt-in-Your Mouth Biscuits are easy to make with Jewel Baking Powder, for it has double leavening power. That means it 'works' both in the dough, before it is placed in the oven, and continues 'working' after it is in the oven. It is inexpensive because, on the average, only one teaspoon to a cup of flour is needed. It makes uniform baking. Made of absolutely pure ingredients. 1-pound can."

Jewel Baking Powder is promoted in a 1938 photograph. Jewel Baking Powder acted twice. Once when in contact with liquids and a second time with the application of heat. The china seen here is "Floral Dresden." *Andrews Collection.*

During the late 1930s, this group of Jewel employees gathered in the Jewel test kitchen and sampled a new cake recipe using Jewel Baking Powder. The group included, from left to right: Doris Olson, ediphone operator; Frances Neumann, typist; Gertrude Grom, expense section payroll clerk; Sally Banks, switchboard operator; and F.C. Fleming, chief of the stock control division. *Housel Collection.*

Four of the most common Jewel containers found for "Jewel Baking Powder." Each container is marked "Manufactured By Jewel Tea Co., Inc. Jewel Park Barrington, Ill." *Hedges Collection.*

The two Jewel Baking Powder jars shown here are slightly different in height and labeling. *Hedges Collection.*

Full containers will command higher prices than those found empty. Never use old products! *Lemons Collection.*

This one pound metal container of Jewel "Continuous Action Baking Powder" was "Manufactured By Jewel Tea Co., Inc., Jewel Park Barrington, Ill." This product appeared in the 1952 Spring and Summer Jewel Home Shopping Service Catalog. *Randall Collection.*

Directions for Baking Powder Biscuits were provided on the label. Jewel Baking Powder was "Approved by Mary Dunbar." Missing parts are impossible to find. *Byerly Collection.*

"Jewel Continuous Action Baking Powder," in one pound metal containers. "Jewel Home Shopping Service." 1950s - 1960s. *Byerly Collection.*

Sixteen ounces of "Jewel Home Shopping Service Baking Powder." *Randall Collection.*

Jewel provided a recipe for "Baking Powder Biscuits." This product was "Approved by Mary Dunbar." Sold from 1960 - 1966. *Randall Collection.*

Shown here is a metal "Jewel Baking Powder" container with a screw on lid. Note the printing on the lid, "A COMPLETELY MODERN BAKING POWDER more efficient USE 1/4 TO 1/2 LESS IT GOES FARTHER." *Byerly Collection.*

"Manufactured By Jewel Tea Co., Inc. Jewel Park Barrington, Ill.," this Baking Powder is a different packaging than the two shown previously . . . note the variation in the wording. *Byerly Collection.*

Baking Soda

Promoted in 1978, this Jewel Baking Soda sold for 2 for $1.98. Net weight was 32 oz. The old style logo makes this product most collectible and it can be somewhat hard to find.

The perfect Baking Soda Keeper, promoted during the mid-1970s for 99¢.

This historical photograph was used in an advertisement to promote Jewel "Baking Powder" and Jewel "Vanilla" during the mid-1930s. The china is the "Floral Dresden" pattern. *Housel Collection.*

In 1932, the Vol. 10, No. 6 issue of "The Jewel News" used a historical photograph promoting a selection of Jewel premiums and a container of Jewel "Black Pepper." The promotional photograph was titled "EASY TRAVELING TO THE PICNIC." Mary Dunbar, the Director of the Jewel Homemakers Institute, made comments concerning "interesting things that your serviceman will have within the next month."

Expanding on this comment, Mary Dunbar continued, "In the photograph above is the home refrigerator bottle which we have developed, and it is mighty convenient for keeping water cold in the ice box, storing milk, iced tea, coffee, and other summer beverages. It is a two-quart size so that the quantity it holds is sufficient for the family serving of iced tea and is shaped so that it is quite easy to grasp in one hand for pouring or other handling. It takes up a minimum amount of room for carrying the iced drinks to the picnic. We have made graduations on the panels in the back so that the pint, quart, three pints and two quart marks are easily notes."

Furthermore, "The cake safe, plate, bowl, and cooker shown above are not new items . . ." Mary Dunbar then continued to pointed out the convenient method for using these items on a picnic.

Does any collector have the above "Refrigerator Bottle" which was developed in the Jewel Homemakers Institute kitchen? The Jewel "Black Pepper" is shown elsewhere in this Chapter.

CHAPTER 4
BREAKFAST PRODUCTS

Rice

Jewel Tea sold Blue Rose rice, which they stated was the best variety grown in the United States. It was an extra fancy head rice that was cleaned, polished, and which did not contained indigestible coating mixtures such as glucose and talc. Blue Rose was deemed to contain the nutritive qualities of milled rice. Jewel Tea assured its customers that every lot purchased was inspected and tested by Jewel Company experts. These experts examined the rice's appearance, cooking qualities, and flavor. Jewel rejected all rice that did not pass these tests.

At the Company's plant in Hoboken, New Jersey, the rice was received directly from the mills. Jewel experts inspected and tested the rice and then cleaned it again. A special cleaning machine removed all dirt and dust that had worked through the burlap bags during shipment. The rice was cleaned then automatically weighed and packaged in air-tight and dust-proof triple-seal cartons.

Jewel salesmen indicated to every customer that Jewel rice did not cook down into a sticky mass, but was tender and flaky as each grain separated and became light and fluffy. The salesman continued, stating that Jewel rice was pure, had no indigestible coatings, and was the most nutritious of all cereals.

Jewel experts suggested that customers refer to the "Mary Dunbar Cook Book" and "Jewel News" for the use of Jewel rice.

A 1 pound, 10 ounce cardboard carton of "Extra Fancy Jewel Rice" from the Jewel Home Shopping Service. "Packed by Jewel Tea Co., Inc., Jewel Park Barrington, Ill." This carton appeared on the back page of the 1952 Jewel Home Shopping Service Spring and Summer Catalog. *Hamilton Collection.*

On the reverse side, recipes were provided using Jewel Rice. This Rice was "Approved by Mary Dunbar." *Hamilton Collection.*

Tastiflakes

From the mid-western corn belt, white dent corn grown in the area was selected to become Jewel's Tastiflakes. After a thorough cleaning to remove dirt, dust, and foreign particles, the heart of the corn, which contained a large percentage of fat, would become rancid in a short time. Therefore, after another cleaning, this heart was removed together with the skin. Broken into pieces the corn became known as hominy or grits.

In large rotating steam cookers, the grits were combined with malt flavoring, pure cane sugar, salt, and distilled water and cooked for two hours. This process made Jewel corn flakes "tasty" flakes. The grits were then on a constant rotation and were fanned for two hours during a cooling and drying cycle; this removed surplus moisture and heat. The dried and cooled grits were then placed in curing bins where they were properly tempered and seasoned. From the curing bins, they were removed to the flaking rolls, from which they emerge ready for toasting.

In carefully regulated and controlled gas ovens, the flakes were placed on a wire belt and moved back and forth. In the oven, all flakes reached a delicate, golden brown color which insured a pleasing taste. Before going to the packaging machinery, the flakes passed over a screen to remove all broken particles. According to Jewel, "This process resulted in comments often heard from Jewel customers about Tastiflakes, 'They have less fine material at the bottom of the package than any other flakes we can buy.'"

Jewel's packaging had a wax inner lining, used both as additional protection for the flakes and to keep the flakes crisp. Jewel Tastiflakes were packaged by automatic machinery, no hands touched the contents during the packing, weighing, and sealing process.

Mary Dunbar had many new uses for Jewel Tastiflakes that she published from time to time in "The Jewel," "Jewel News," and recipe folders.

Shown here are Jewel "Whole Wheat Flakes With All The Bran." Net weight 8 ounces in the cardboard carton. "Distributed By Jewel Tea Co., Inc., New York — Chicago." *Lombard Collection.*

Oats

From Minnesota and northern Illinois farms, Jewel Quick Oats were made from best grade white oats. When the grain arrived at the mill, after being carefully selected and inspected, it was again subjected to inspection and placed into machines that removed all foreign matter, leaving only the full-berried grains for milling.

The 2 lb. 10 ounce carton of "Quick Oats" appeared in a mid-1920s Jewel publication. Jewel Quick Oats had been cooked by steam under pressure during the manufacturing process. (Priced at 26¢ P.S.C. 5¢). "Distributed By Jewel Tea Co., Inc., New York Chicago."

These "Quick Oats" have been sealed for protection. "Tested and Approved by Mary Dunbar Jewel Homemakers Institute." "Distributed By Jewel Tea Co., Inc., Jewel Park Barrington, Ill." *Lombard Collection.*

This is a colorful "Quick Oats" carton. "Distributed By Jewel Tea Co., Inc., Jewel Park Barrington, Ill." The lid to this carton is missing. *Lombard Collection.*

Jewel Quick Oats were touted as a valuable food for growing children because of the "high tissue and bone building content." Jewel also advertised that Jewel Quick Oats had a creamy, nut like flavor and tasted better than other oats because of a special toasting system which used a direct coke fire heat. Finally, Jewel added that "Quick Oats were flaked, steamed and packed in air-tight containers all in the same day and never touched by human hands."

Jewel "Quick Oats. Rich In Vitamin B." *Vogel Collection.*

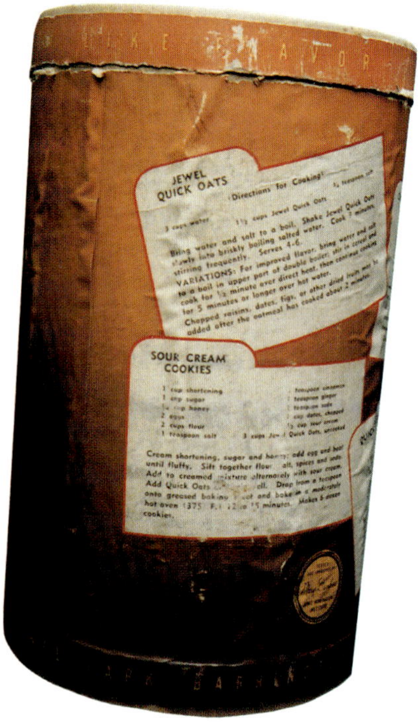

The "back" side of the "Quick Oats" packaging provided recipes. This product appeared in the 1952 Spring and Summer Jewel Home Shopping Service Catalog and was "Tested and Approved by Mary Dunbar." *Vogel Collection.*

These Jewel "Quick Oats" appeared in a different packaging. Cooks in 3 minutes, this product was "Distributed by Jewel Tea Co., Inc., Jewel Park Barrington, Ill." *Vogel Collection.*

The "Quick Oats" reverse side provided recipes and promoted additional Jewel grocery products. *Vogel Collection.*

This original advertisement appeared in a 1940s "Jewel News," promoting Jewel Quick Oats, Vanilla, Shredded Coconut, and Jewel Mince Meat. This advertisement also included a "Mincemeat Fruit Cookies" recipe using all of the above Jewel products.

"Quick Oats" were rich in Vitamin B1. "Distributed by Jewel Tea Co., Inc., Barrington, Ill." *Eisnaugle Collection.*

Three different "Jewel Quick Oats," each carton marked "Distributed by Jewel Tea Co., Inc., Barrington, Ill." *Hedges Collection.*

Corn

In the original advertisement, Jewel promoted their "Corn Flakes" in 1927. Marked "JEWEL TEA CO., INC., NEW YORK — CHICAGO."

An original 1938 promotional advertisement for Jewel "Prepared Biscuit Flour."

A 2 lb. Jewel "Prepared Biscuit Flour" manufactured by the "JEWEL TEA CO., INC., JEWEL PARK BARRINGTON, ILL." This product has been sealed for protection. *Hamilton Collection.*

Biscuit Flour

Jewel considered its Biscuit Flour to be the best made. Unlike other biscuit flours, Jewel Biscuit Flour did not deteriorate or turn rancid. It also contained a Jewel-developed baking powder that left no bitter after-taste. It was simple and quick to use in making rolls and biscuits of every variety, as well as griddle cakes, coffee cakes, waffles, doughnuts, and dumplings. There were no lumps of fat in Jewel Biscuit Flour.

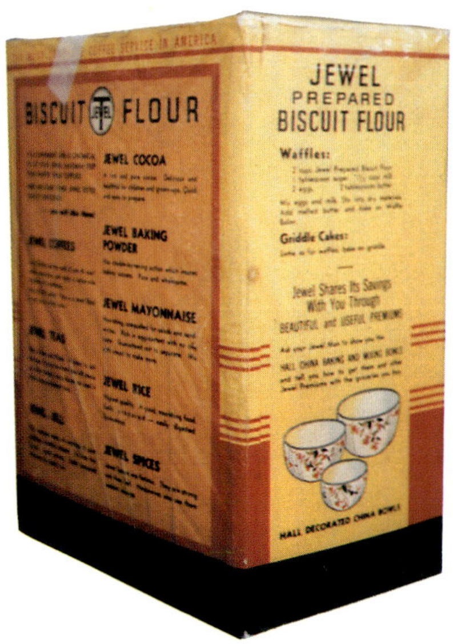

The back panel of the "Prepared Biscuit Flour" promoted a variety of Jewel products. The side panel provided recipes and promoted the "Hall Decorated China Bowls." *Hamilton Collection.*

"Manufactured by Jewel Tea Co., Inc., Barrington, Illinois," this carton contained 2 lbs. of Jewel "Biscuit Mix." *Eisnaugle Collection.*

The promise "Your money back with a smile if you are not satisfied with this item" appears on a side panel of the Jewel "Biscuit Mix," along with the "Tested and Approved by Mary Dunbar" seal. *Eisnaugle Collection.*

Syrup

Shown here, a 22 ounce bottle of Jewel "Pancake Syrup." This glass bottle is marked "JEWEL TEA CO., INC., NEW YORK — CHICAGO," and has the "Bulls eye" logo that was introduced in approximately 1921 - 1922. See accompanying historical photograph. *Orr Collection.*

This photograph appeared in "The Jewel News Vol. 10 No. 6 1932." Various Jewel products can be seen in this photograph: Jewel Coffee, Jewel Syrup (Note this is the same 22 ounce Pancake Syrup bottle), Jewel Tea, Jewel Malted Milk, various Jewel premiums, a 9-cup capacity Drip Coffee Maker, a little one cup drip coffee maker that was efficient and practical (Item No. 66, sold for 50¢), Hall China lined Olive Green 7-cup capacity teapot (Item No. 330, sold for $1.55), malt shaker, glass baking pan, and a glass beverage pitcher and matching glass. Note, also, the Refrigerator Bottle (on the left). In the 1932 Vol. 10 No. 7 issue of The Jewel News, Mary Dunbar makes reference to this bottle. "The refrigerator bottles which we have developed in the kitchen are now ready for order taking. The flat shape requires a small amount of space in the refrigerator, and also makes for much easier handling. The bottles are graduated by pints to two quarts so that you can measure the liquid as you pour it in. Iced coffee, iced tea, fruit drinks or milk can be kept chilly cold in the refrigerator in this generous sized bottle." See Chapter 3.

Distributed by "JEWEL TEA CO., INC., JEWEL PARK BARRINGTON, ILL.," this 1930s carton contained seven 1 ounce packets that made 3 quarts and 1 pint of Syrup. When using this Jewel "Syrup-Mix," only Sugar and Water were added. The mix was then boiled for one minute. *Ferriera Collection.*

Eggs

The carton of Fresh Eggs shown here were "Distributed By Jewel Tea Co., Inc., Chicago, Ill." *Hedges Collection.*

A one dozen "Jewel Selected Grade A Egg" carton. *Hedges Collection.*

Breakfast Drinks

See "Chapter 2 Coffee, Tea and Cocoa Products" and "Breakfast Refreshment" in this Chapter for additional Breakfast Drinks.

In 1975 "JEWEL ADE MIXES" were available in three flavors, imitation CHERRY, STRAWBERRY and GRAPEADE MIX. In a special promotion, JEWEL ADE MIXES were offered at 2 cartons for $2.49 with a savings of 29¢. Each carton contained five 3 oz. envelopes that made 1 quart each by adding water. JEWEL ADE MIXES came complete with sugar.

The consumer saved $1.00 when 2 jars of "JOYA" Orange Breakfast drink were purchased in 1976. JOYA was described as a natural tasting instant drink fortified with Vitamins C and A.

Jewel "Concentrated Pure Apple Juice." *Ferriera Collection.*

"New Instant . . . the Jewel 'Pineapple-Grapefruit Flavor Breakfast Drink' provided thirty-six 4 ounce servings." Marked "Manufactured by Jewel Tea Co., Inc., Barrington, Ill." *Byerly Collection.*

Jelly and Preserves

Remember the smell of jams, jellies, and preserves in grandmother's kitchen? The fruit cooked and the smells filled the house. Mason jars, paraffin sealing the jars, lids tightly shut... Jewel knew these were fond memories, and they wanted to provide customers with these fine, delicate flavors of grandmother's jams, jellies, and preserves.

Jewel used modern stainless steel manufacturing equipment, combined with a special low temperature process to insure customers the finest jams, jellies, and preserves. Jewel bought fruits from throughout the continent. From upper New York and Michigan, currants were acquired; Concord grapes from Michigan; raspberries from Washington and Michigan; blackberries from the West Coast; and from the Pacific Northwest, the finest strawberries. Jewel acquired apple juice from Nova Scotia.

Immediately after picking, the fruits for preserves were frozen to maintain their fresh "just picked" flavor. The juices for jams and jellies were immediately refrigerated.

Arriving in Barrington, Jewel chemists selected samples and actually made jams, jellies, and preserves in their laboratory. This process was done on a scaled-down version to assure that the fruit actually resulted in quality products.

Modern equipment was also used in the Jewel preserve line. The fruit was cooked at low temperatures and jars were vacuum sealed. After this process was being done, samples were taken every half hour to insure product quality.

Jewel "Grape Jelly" was promoted during the 1970s.

A 1960s original advertisement promoting Jewel preserves.

Jewel "Old Fashion Grape Jam" featuring the "Script" logo on this jar, appeared during the 1950s and was used for approximately 10 years (1960). The glass container is missing its lid. *Hedges Collection.*

Shown here is an example of Jewel "Crabapple Jelly." In 1976, Mrs. Brown saved 19¢ on Jewel Jellies when she purchased two for $2.19. Jewel offered both "Crabapple" and "Apple." *Randall Collection.*

"Seedless Blackberry Preserves" in an 18 ounce container. *Randall Collection.*

During the 1970s, Jewel offered an 18 ounce container of Jewel "Peach Preserves." *Randall Collection.*

This crate held two containers of Honey. Embossed on the front of the jars is a bee hive and the phrase "Jewel Pure Honey." In 1976 Jewel listed this as Item No. 45-203 2 - 1# Jars. It sold for $5.95. "Jewel Pure Honey" also appeared in a Jewel Christmas catalog. *Lemons Collection.*

The "Jewel Pure Honey" marking on the top of the crate, note the original tag on this jar. *Private Collection.*

A crate holding three containers of "Jewel Pure Honey, Clover, Wild Flower and Basswood." Each container held 4 ounces. *Private Collection.*

Graham Crackers

Note the Jewel logo on this package of "Honey Flavored Graham Crackers." The "Bulls eye" logo was introduced in approximately 1921 - 1922. Distributed by "JEWEL TEA CO., INC., NEW YORK — CHICAGO." *Hamilton Collection.*

A 1 pound, 6 ounce cardboard carton of "Honey Flavored Graham Crackers." This carton has been sealed for protection. *Hamilton Collection.*

This original 1930s advertisement promoted the Jewel Graham Crackers, a 17-1/2 oz. package of Butternut Cookies, and a 1 lb. can of Jewel Cocoa. Note that "Jewel Park" does not appear on the "Graham Crackers" or the "Jewel Cocoa" carton but does appear on the Butternut Cookies. Jewel moved into their Barrington headquarters in 1930. Old packaging was depleted before the new was issued.

This 1 pound, 6 ounce "Graham Crackers" box was "Distributed by JEWEL TEA CO., INC., JEWEL PARK BARRINGTON, ILL." The Jewel logo is basically the same logo that appears on the "Honey Flavored" grahams. *Hedges Collection.*

The front and side panels of the 1 pound, 6 ounce "Graham Crackers" box. *Hedges Collection.*

Breakfast Refreshments

See "Chapter 2. Coffee, Tea and Cocoa Products" and "Breakfast Drinks" for additional Breakfast Refreshments.

Shown here, a Jewel one pound metal tin of "Sweetened Chocolate Flavored Malted Milk." *Vogel Collection.*

The back panel of the "Sweetened Chocolate Flavored Malted Milk" provided "Directions for Cold Drinks and For Hot Drinks." Manufactured by "Jewel Tea Co., Inc., Jewel Park Barrington, Ill." This product was "Tested and Approved by Mary Dunbar." *Vogel Collection.*

This one pound "Chocolate Flavored Malted Milk" metal container was "Manufactured by JEWEL TEA CO., INC., JEWEL PARK BARRINGTON, ILLINOIS" and appeared on the back cover of the Spring and Summer 1952 Jewel Catalog. *Byerly Collection.*

The back panel of the "Chocolate Flavored Malted Milk" metal container carries the "Tested and Approved by Mary Dunbar" seal. *Byerly Collection.*

"Manufactured by JEWEL TEA CO., INC., JEWEL PARK BARRINGTON, ILLINOIS," this metal tin held one pound of "Sweetened Chocolate Flavored Malted Milk." *Hedges Collection.*

The highly decorated snap on "IT'S GOOD" lid from the tin of "Sweetened Chocolate Flavored Malted Milk." *Hedges Collection.*

Shown here are two 14 ounce containers of "Jewel Chocolate Flavored Milk Shake Mix," manufactured by "JEWEL TEA CO., INC., BARRINGTON, ILL." On the side panel the "Guarantee and Ingredients" were provided along with the Mary Dunbar seal. This is a metal and cardboard container. *Byerly Collection.*

On the back panel, direction for a Milk Shake and an Extra Rich Milk Shake were provided. This "Jewel Chocolate Flavored Milk Shake Mix" container is of metal and cardboard manufacture. *Byerly Collection.*

This 12 ounce container of "Jewel Instant Cocoa Mix" was manufactured by "JEWEL TEA CO., INC., BARRINGTON, ILLINOIS." *Byerly Collection.*

Instructions and Recipes were provided on the back and side panel of the "Jewel Instant Cocoa Mix." Note the 1950s Jewel Home Shopping Service "Laurel Wreath" logo. *Byerly Collection.*

During the 1930s Jewel offered this 2-quart capacity aluminum double boiler, promoting it as an excellent boiler to prepare cereal or milk for the baby. This item was No. 65 and sold for $1.75. "Perfect for any morning breakfast!"

CHAPTER 5
HOME MAINTENANCE

The historical photograph shown here appeared in a 1932 Jewel News. Note the various products and premiums shown in this photograph. It is believed the lady with her back to the camera at the far right is Ruth Leone Rutledge Carroll. Note the hand painted cookie jar on the counter.

To give you a general idea of what the lid to this Cookie Jar looks like, it has been removed and placed to one side. As lids were damaged first, check the lid carefully, making sure it is the right lid and not a replacement. This cookie jar also has been seen with a black background. *Hamilton Collection.*

This cookie jar was popular among Jewel customers. First appearing in 1931, the hand painted cookie jar was promoted as follows:
"The extremely smart appearance of this Cookie Jar is due not alone to the brilliant poppy design but quite as much to the gracefulness of line. The well proportioned jug shaped jar is made with smooth, neutral pottery material which makes a splendid background for the splashy poppy design of red petals and green stem and leaves. The inside border of the neck has a strip of the same brilliant red as has the top of the knob which makes the cover easy to lift. The Cookie Jar is particularly fine for storing cookies, crackers, small cakes, doughnuts and the like. It may be used as a canister for quick oats, rice, sugar, noodles, and many other staple supplies. A kitchen of any proportion would be more attractive with such a row of canisters. An excellent gift or bridge prize." *Hamilton Collection.*

"The crockery jug [cookie jar] stands nine inches high with seven inches diameter at base and measures five inches diameter at the neck. Plenty large enough to reach into with perfect ease or to dip in a cup for measuring. The flat, deep set cover is equipped with an easy grip knob and the painted flower decoration which is on one side only is baked into the pottery ware. The Cookie Jar is sufficiently attractive to serve as a vase for extra large garden bouquets. Unusually reasonable in price. Item No. C-6141 Priced $1.00." *Jewel News,* 1931.

In the Jewel test kitchen all recipes and Jewel products were tested and all of the Jewel premiums were used. Products offered by Jewel Tea all underwent extensive testing and use in this kitchen and laboratory before being approved for distribution to customers. Any products not meeting Jewel specifications were rejected.

Soap

Jewel toilet soaps filled the needs of the whole family, each Jewel toilet soaps were designed to suit an individual purpose.

"Tender Skins Require a Gentle Soap," Jewel Castile Soap was a mild soap used as a protection against constant sun exposure. Six cakes were sold in a carton, 10¢ credit were given on a premium.

"For the Guest," four different perfumes and four colors were available in Jewel French Process Soap. Six cakes came in a carton and a 10¢ credit was given on a premium. These were billed as ideal for guest soap.

Jewel Palm Soap, shown here in an original advertisement, "lathered freely" and left the skin "refreshed and clean." This Palm Soap was popular.

The original 1930s advertisement, shown here, promoted a selection of Jewel soaps. "An Every Day Soap," Jewel Palm Soap was "delightfully fragrant and refreshing." It contained pure vegetable oils that were blended to give the best results. Six cakes were packaged in a carton and a 5¢ credit was given on a premium.

Jewel's Toilet Soaps.

In 1938 a survey was taken in large American cities revealing that over 99% of all families used toilet soaps, consuming an average of five and one-half bars per month. Jewel promoted their own line of Jewel Toilet Soaps. Jewel salesmen were advised in 1938 to insert two bars of "French Process Soap," of different colors, in the ends of a French Process package; in the center of the package were placed one bar each of Pine, Castile, and Health Soap.

The sample package was then shown to each Jewel customer. As a customer examined the soap products, the salesman removed one of the bars of French Process Soap. The customer was then allowed to smell the product. As each bar was removed and smelled by the customer, Jewel salesmen quickly sold the product. As he observed Mrs. Brown's reactions, he was finding out what soap the family used. By listening to her comments and questions he was able to promote the Jewel Toilet Soap product.

Five colored bars of Jewel "French Process Soap" in the original cardboard carton. *Hedges Collection.*

The Jewel "French Process Soap" was "Distributed by JEWEL TEA CO., INC., JEWEL PARK, BARRINGTON, ILLINOIS." *Vogel Collection.*

Jewel "Pine Toilet Soap." Distributed by "JEWEL TEA CO., INC., JEWEL PARK, BARRINGTON, ILLINOIS." *Byerly Collection.*

Four bars of Jewel "French Process Soap." Each bar is embossed with "Jewel French Process" and the Jewel logo. This is a cardboard container. *Byerly Collection.*

Four embossed bars of Jewel "Pine Toilet Soap." This soap appeared in the December 2, 1946 edition of "The Jewel News" and sold for 39¢. *Vogel Collection.*

A single bar of "Jewel Castile Soap." An original 1930s advertisement for this soap appears elsewhere in this book. *Hamilton Collection.*

This cardboard carton held 5 cakes of Jewel "French Process Soap." Each soap bar is embossed "Jewel of Barrington." This soap appeared on the back of the Spring and Summer 1952 Jewel Home Shopping Service catalog. *Vogel Collection.*

A cardboard container of 4 large cakes of Jewel "Velvetouch Bath Soap." The brand name "Velvetouch" first appeared during the 1920s and continued to be used into the 1970s. *Orr Collection.*

A cardboard carton of Jewel "Floral Bouquet" Toilet Soap. Distributed by "JEWEL TEA CO., INC., JEWEL PARK BARRINGTON, ILL." *Lemons Collection.*

Distributed by "JEWEL TEA CO., BARRINGTON, ILL.," these 5 cakes of "Velvetouch Beauty Soap" appeared on the back of the Spring and Summer 1952 Jewel Home Shopping Service catalog. *Lombard Collection.*

A window carton of Jewel "Soap Zoo." Distributed by "JEWEL TEA CO., INC., JEWEL PARK BARRINGTON, ILL.," these animal figures were a delight to youngsters. *Ferriera Collection.*

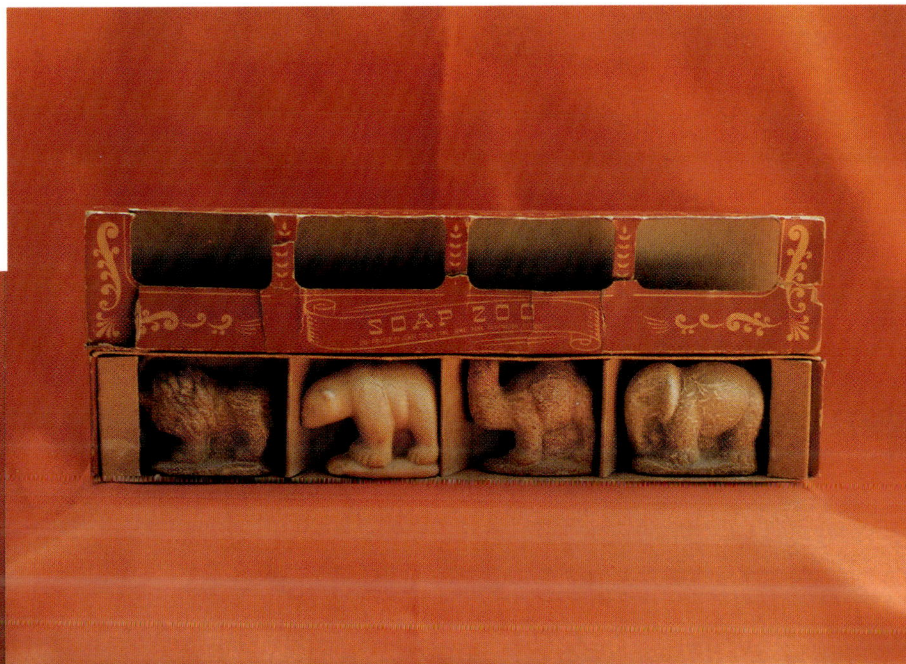

A lion, bear, camel, and elephant represented the four animal soaps that were enclosed in the above Jewel "Soap Zoo" carton. This soap appeared in the 1942 Christmas Jewel News edition. *Ferriera Collection.*

Four cakes of Jewel "Castile Soap" were packaged in this carton, which was distributed by "JEWEL TEA CO., INC., JEWEL PARK, BARRINGTON, ILLINOIS." It is wise to remember that the packaging design for Jewel changed regularly ... but the product remained the same. *Ferriera Collection.*

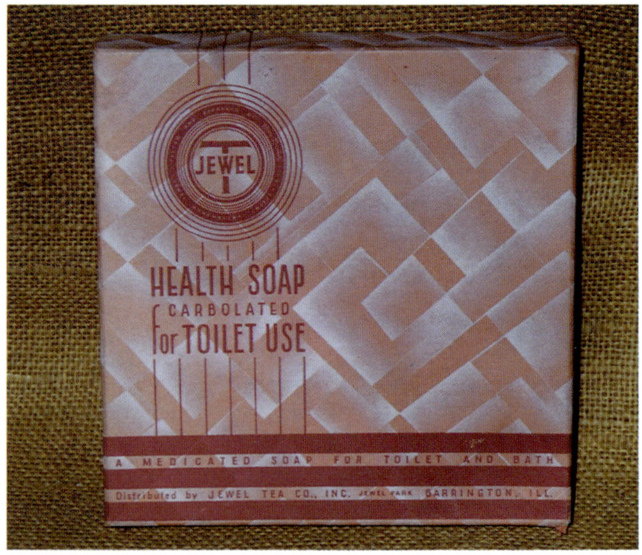

"A Medicated Soap For Toilet and Bath," distributed by "JEWEL TEA CO., INC., JEWEL PARK BARRINGTON, ILL." Six cakes of "Health Soap Carbolated for Toilet Use" were offered in this cardboard container. *Lombard Collection.*

Marked "JEWEL TEA CO., INC." the cardboard carton held "Lilac Supreme Bath Soap." *Orr Collection.*

Jewel "Pine Toilet Soap." *Byerly Collection.*

This 7" square x 1-1/4" deep cardboard carton held Jewel "French Process Soap." Six pastel colored soap bars were enclosed, each bar embossed with "Jewel French Process" on one side and the Jewel "T" logo on the reverse. Circa 1931. *Lemons Collection.*

The single bar of JEWEL "White Laundry" soap dissolved when added to the weekly laundry water. *Hamilton Collection.*

The "Velve-Touch" carton is marked "A PRODUCT OF JEWEL OF BARRINGTON." This cardboard carton held five cakes of Beauty Soap. *Hamilton Collection.*

This cardboard carton held five cakes of embossed Cold Cream Soap. *Hamilton Collection.*

Cold Cream Soap by Jewel, its virtues were extolled as follows: "A Dainty, Delightful Soap - Delicately Perfumed." Distributed by "JEWEL TEA CO., INC., JEWEL PARK BARRINGTON, ILL." *Hamilton Collection.*

Beauty and Health Products

This cardboard carton held one 3 ounce bottle of Sara Lotion and two embossed cakes of Lilac Supreme Bath Soap. Distributed by Jewel Tea Co., Inc. *Hedges Collection.*

A cardboard window carton which held an assortment of Jewel "Velve-touch" Bubble Bath. *Vogel Collection.*

Enclosed were 20 envelopes containing four individual scents described as: "Lily of the Valley, Forest Pine, Carnation, and Apple Blossom." This bubble bath carton was redesigned during the 1970s and can be seen in a Jewel Grocery Stock Card. Jewel sold this redesigned packaging of Velve-touch Bubble Bath, 20 envelopes, in "woodsy and floral" scents, two for \$2.49. "Velve-touch" also appeared as "Velvetouch" on many products and in numerous publications. *Vogel Collection.*

Distributed by Jewel Home Shopping, this 1970s glass container could be used as a vase when empty. This container held 4 ounce of Jewel Classic Bubble Bath and had a paper label. *Randall Collection.*

This container of "Velvetouch" Dusting Powder has never been used. Net weight 5 ounces. Distributed by "JEWEL TEA CO., INC., BARRINGTON, ILLINOIS." In 1975 this Dusting Powder sold for $2.00. Jewel reduced the price for a limited time to $1.75, a savings of 25¢. *Byerly Collection.*

This "Jewel Home Shopping Service" container, held "Velvetouch Perfumed Bath Crystals." *Ferriera Collection.*

"Baby Powder" from the Jewel In-Home Shopping Service, 14 ounces worth. *Lemons Collection.*

A container of "Velvetouch Bath Powder." *Lemons Collection.*

The "Scripted Jewel" logo, on the JEWEL "Skipper" bubble bath was popular during the 1950s - 1960s era. "Gets your children clean while they have tubs of fun in tubs of bubbles!." Net weight 12 ounces. This packaging was redesigned and appeared in the Jewel Grocery Stock Cards during the 1970s as JEWEL "SKIPPER Instant Bubble Bath." Jewel offered this colorful character on "Ani-Shapes Vitamins" and "Skipper Children's Shampoo." *Ferriera Collection.*

Getting children to bathe was almost impossible without offering them a rubber duckie or colorful toy character. The "Jewel Skipper" is a rubber toy used for this purpose. *Hamilton Collection.*

One "Jewel Skipper" has been turned ... using a magnifying glass the words "Jewel Skipper" can be seen just above the edge of his jacket. This item may have been popular during the 1970s. Also see the "Jewel Skipper Whale" in this Chapter. *Hamilton Collection.*

The original cardboard carton and 6 ounce bottle of Jewel "Liquid Shampoo," billed as "THE SECRET OF BEAUTIFUL HAIR." Marked "JEWEL TEA CO., INC., JEWEL PARK BARRINGTON, ILL." *Lombard Collection.*

Shown here is the reverse side and back panel of Jewel "Liquid Shampoo." This Shampoo was "Tested and Approved by Mary Dunbar." *Hamilton Collection.*

This carton of Jewel "Liquid Shampoo" has been sealed for protection. Manufactured by "JEWEL TEA CO., INC., JEWEL PARK BARRINGTON, ILL." *Hamilton Collection.*

The original cardboard carton and bottle of Jewel "Antiseptic Mouth Wash and Gargle." *Vogel Collection.*

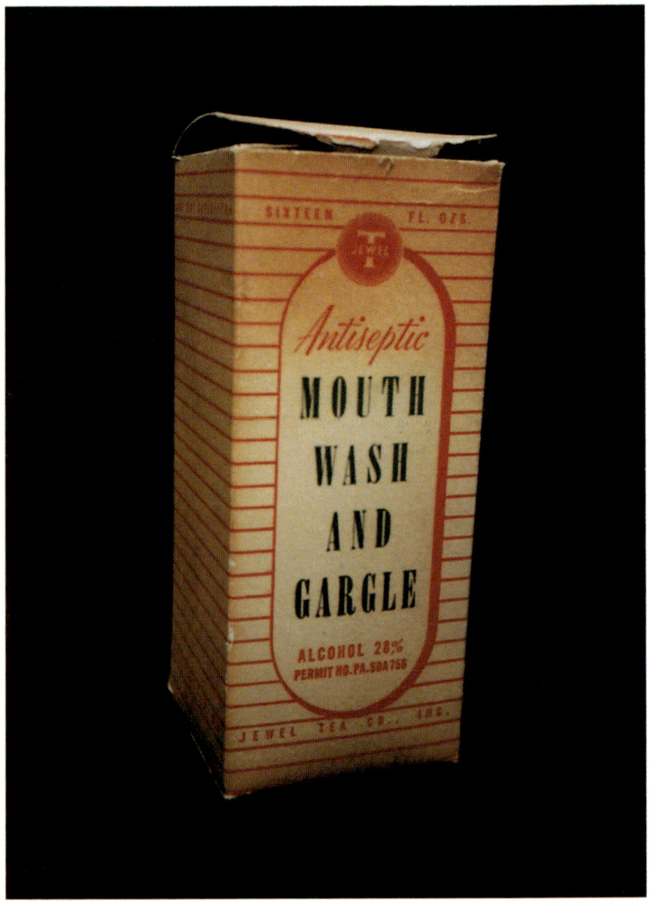

Jewel "Antiseptic Mouth Wash and Gargle" was distributed by "JEWEL TEA CO., INC., JEWEL PARK BARRINGTON, ILL." Original packaging increases the value of an item. *Vogel Collection.*

The bottle, shown here, held 16 ounces of Jewel "Antiseptic Mouth Wash and Gargle." *Vogel Collection.*

Jewel "Mouth Wash and Gargle." *Vogel Collection.*

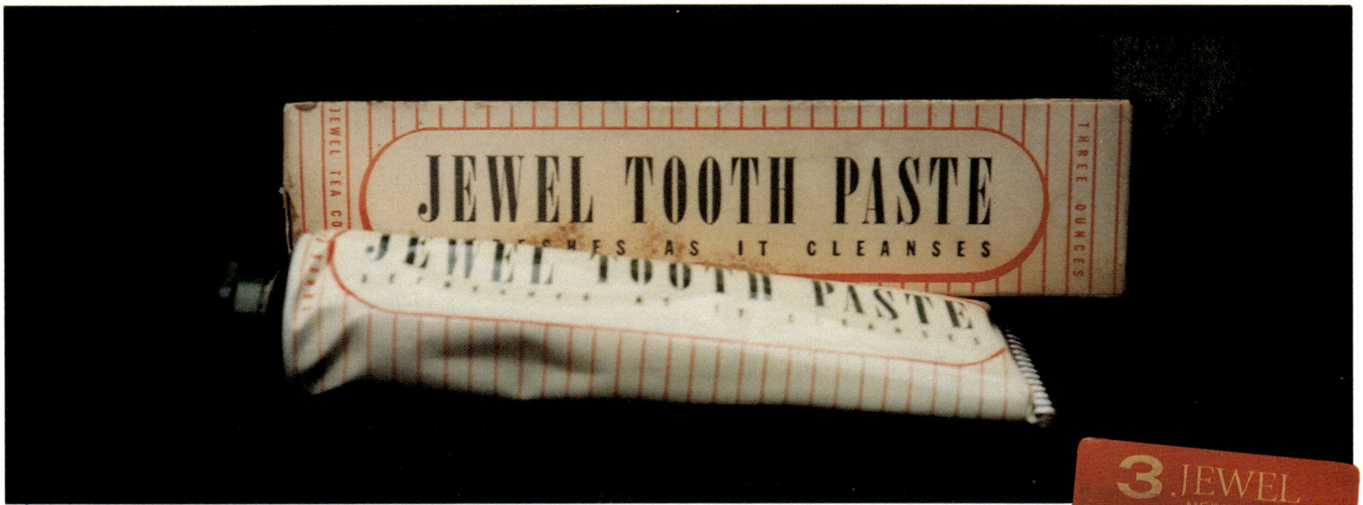

The original carton with a 3 ounce tube of "Jewel Tooth Paste." *Vogel Collection.*

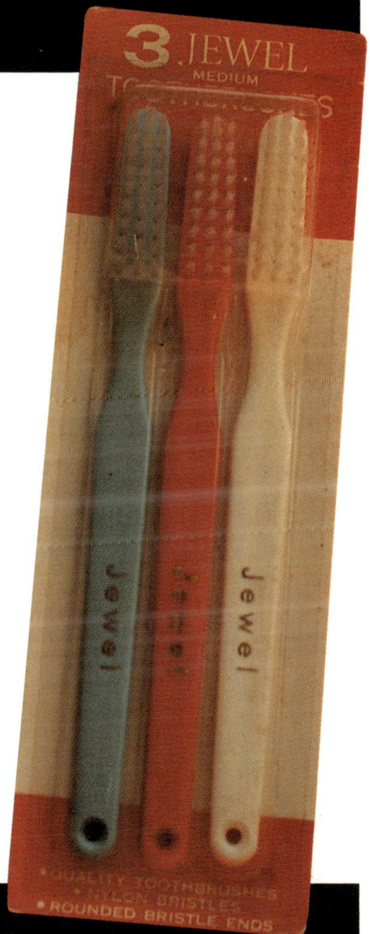

A package of 3 "Jewel Medium Toothbrushes." These toothbrushes were available from Jewel in 1976, priced 2 packages for $1.88. A package of 2 Jewel Junior Toothbrushes were priced at 2 for $1.29. These items were promoted along side a tube of Jewel Imitation Strawberry Toothpaste which sold for 2 for $1.29 or regularly priced at 69¢. *Ferriera Collection.*

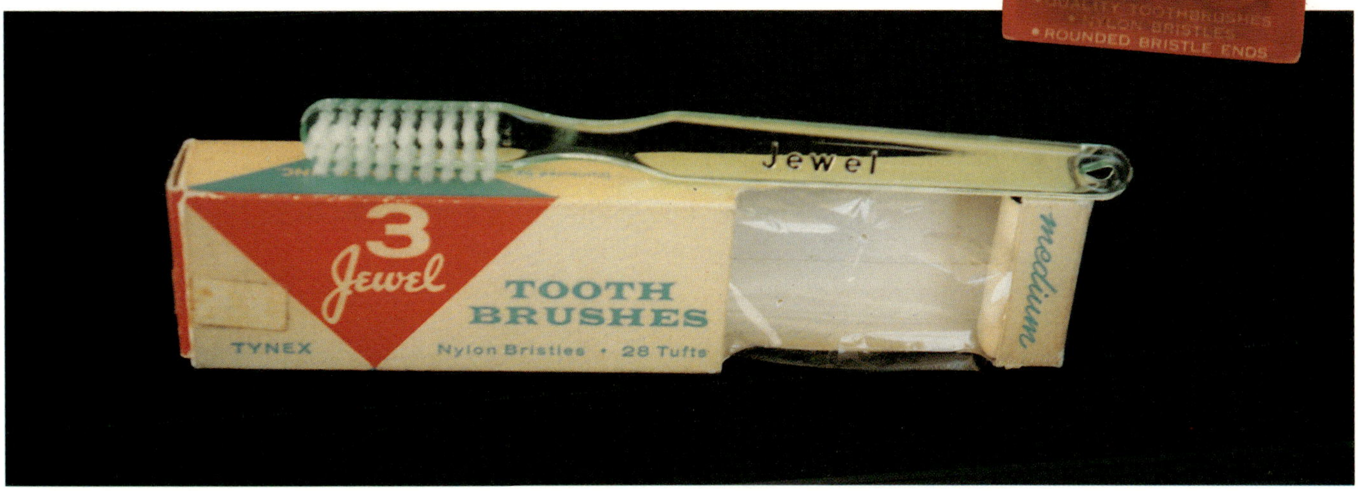

This original carton is missing two of the original tooth brushes. Each brush was embossed with the word "JEWEL." *Vogel Collection.*

A full 16 ounce plastic bottle of Jewel "baby oil" with Lanolin. In 1976, Jewel sold this "baby oil" for $1.49. *Vogel Collection.*

"Velvetouch Bubbling Bath Liquid." *Vogel Collection.*

"Velvetouch Bath Oil." *Vogel Collection.*

This glass container with its cork stopper held 5 ounce of "Velvetouch Milk Bath Salts," and was distributed by Jewel from the Barrington (60010) plant. *Hedges Collection.*

Three containers of "Velve-touch." The top container is marked "PRODUCT OF JEWEL OF BARRINGTON." *Hamilton Collection.*

"Velvetouch" Finest Quality All Nylon Hosiery With Seams. Priced to sell at 89¢. *Hamilton Collection.*

A 9 ounce jar of Jewel "Medicated Skin Cream." *Ferriera Collection.*

"Velvetouch" Finest Quality All Nylon Hosiery Seamless with Run Stop Bands at Top and Toe. Priced at 89¢. *Hamilton Collection.*

A 7-1/2 ounce "Sara" Cleansing Cream jar. Distributed by "JEWEL TEA CO., INC., JEWEL PARK BARRINGTON, ILL." *Lombard Collection.*

"Sara" Lilac Cologne was distributed by "JEWEL TEA CO., INC., JEWEL PARK BARRINGTON, ILL." *Hamilton Collection.*

A one ounce and a three ounce bottle of "Sara Lotion." Manufactured by "JEWEL TEA CO., INC." *Ferriera Collection.*

An original 1932 advertisement for a bottle of "Jewel Shampoo," one jar of "Jewel Velvetouch Skin Lotion," and a tube of "Jewel Toothpaste." A 10¢ credit on a premium was given when Jewel Shampoo was purchased. A 5¢ credit on premiums were given for Skin Lotion and Toothpaste.

The original 1916 carton and bottle of "Jewelette Perfume Jewelette Laboratories Perfumers New York — Chicago — New Orleans — San Francisco." Note the 1¢ Luxury Stamp. This was the last year the Government required this stamp. *Hamilton Collection.*

The original carton for "Chatnay Velvetouch" Skin Lotion. *Hedges Collection.*

The carton of Chatnay Velvetouch has been turned on its side (the box top is not substantial enough to hold the jar). The "Chatnay Velvetouch" jar is marked "JEWEL TEA CO., INC., NEW YORK — CHICAGO." *Hedges Collection.*

A single pint of "Sara Lilac Cologne," distributed by "JEWEL TEA CO., INC., JEWEL PARK BARRINGTON, ILL." *Sivils Collection.*

Note that this one pint bottle held "Sara Lilac Cologne" is decorated with blue accessories, whereas the other has pink accessories. *Ferriera Collection.*

The pint bottle of "Sara Lilac Cologne" with the original carton. *Sivils Collection.*

"Velvetouch Lilac Cologne," shown here in the original window carton. *Ferriera Collection.*

A full bottle of "Velvetouch" lotion. *Vogel Collection.*

Jewel "Kleen-Wipes" for household use. *Hamilton Collection.*

This plastic container is marked "JEWEL BUTTONS UP SAVINGS." This may have been a give-away. *Hamilton Collection.*

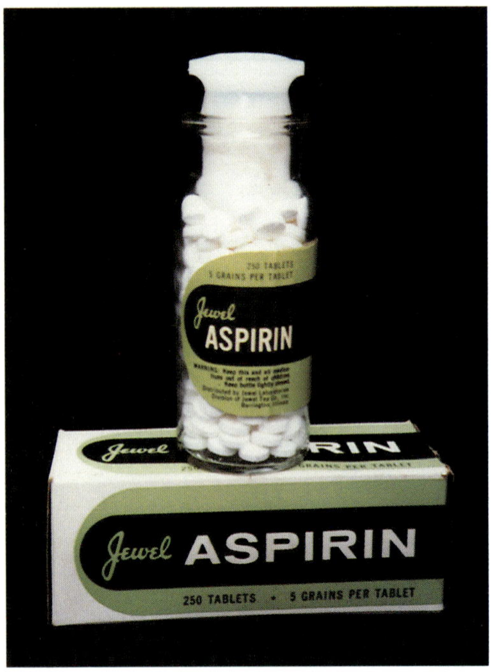

Jewel "100 Kleen-Wipes." Also see "Paper Products" in this Chapter. *Hamilton Collection.*

Jewel "Aspirin" with the original carton. This asprin was distributed by "Jewel Laboratories Division of Jewel Tea Co., Inc., Barrington, Illinois." *Vogel Collection.*

A 3-1/2 oz. spray can of Jewel "First-Aid and Bandage Spray." In 1975 Jewel promoted this product as follows: "Save 20¢ on First Aid Spray — Soothes without stinging — acts as a protective bandage." Priced at $1.49. *Byerly Collection.*

An original 1950s shipping carton, shown here, is marked "It's easier to shop with Jewel Home Shopping Service." *Sivils Collection.*

Enclosed in this shipping carton were yard goods in "Wash-N-Wear," "Drip-Dry," and "Wash-Rinse-Dry." *Sivils Collection.*

Welcome To Jewel

In 1974 Jewel "Welcomed" customers when they joined the ever growing list of homemakers who had discovered the "world of In-Home Shopping." Jewel wanted every customer to enjoy shopping with them and to make sure that every customer took "full advantage of the many products and service offered."

Jewel indicated that they wanted the customer to be satisfied. Should they need additional information about any item sold in their catalog or desired to comment on any aspect of the Jewel customer service, Jewel directed them to write to: Mrs. Joan Brinkman, Director of Customer Affairs — Jewel Home Shopping Service Jewel Park Barrington, Illinois 60010.

In a Jewel catalog from 1974, these beauty products were promoted: Jewel 40 3-inch Medicated Complexion Pads; Jewel Skipper Children's Shampoo, 9-1/2 fluid ounces; Jewel Skipper Liquid Bubble Bath, enough for 25-30 baths; Velvetouch Orange Blossom Bubble Bath, net contents 16 fluid ounces; Jewel Family Spray Deodorants – choose Regular Formula or Anti-Perspirant in 7 ounces; 16 ounces of Velvetouch Bath Oil Beads; and two forms of Velvetouch Personal Deodorant, in either cream or roll on.

A selection of beauty aids was promoted in a JEWEL GROCERY CARD STOCK in 1977. The following selections were offered at 99¢ each: Bubble Bath, Bath Oil Beads, Velvetouch Cleansing Bar and Baby Powder.

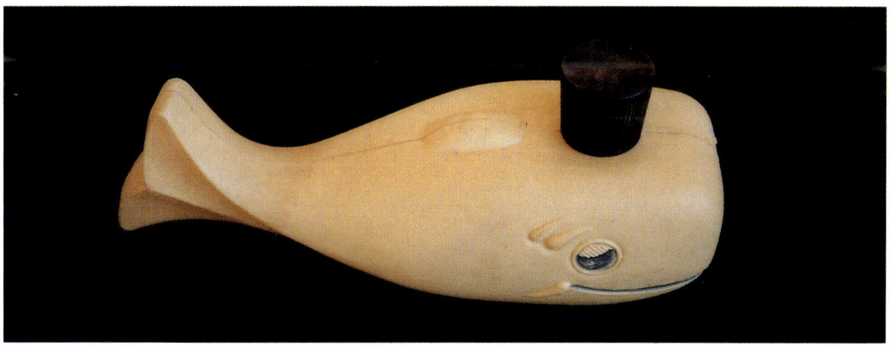

The "Whale" bath toy held 11 fluid ounces of "Jewel Liquid Skipper." *Hamilton Collection.*

The bottom of the "Whale" bath toy is marked "MANUFACTURED BY JEWEL TEA CO., INC., BARRINGTON, ILL." *Hamilton Collection.*

Vitamins

Jewel offered a selection of Vitamins during the 1970s.

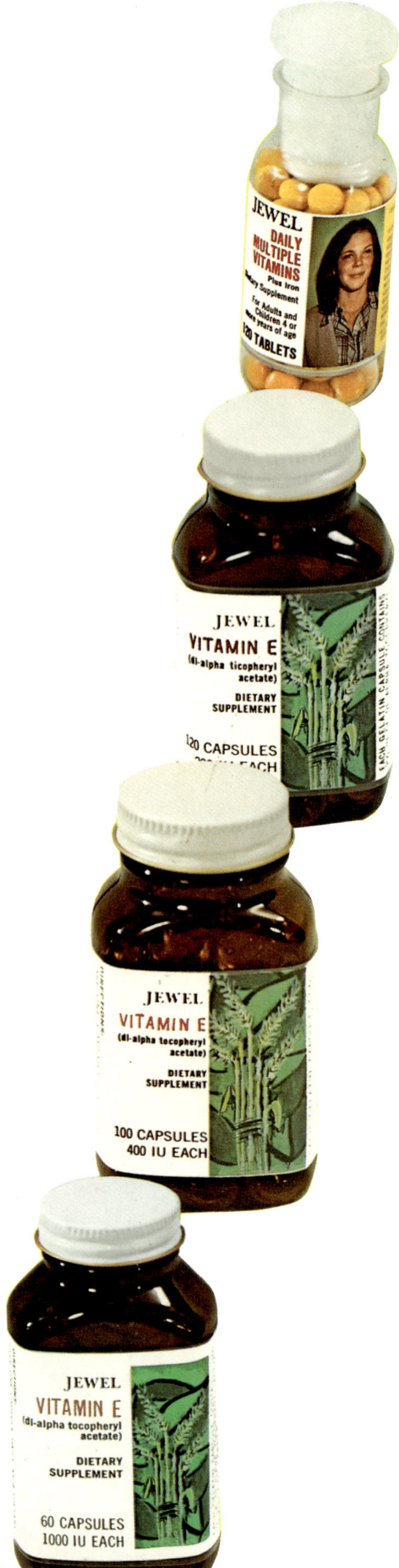

Also offered were the Vitamins shown here.

A bottle of 125 Ani-Shapes Chewable Vitamins, pictured "Skipper." This is from a 1970s Jewel Grocery Stock Card.

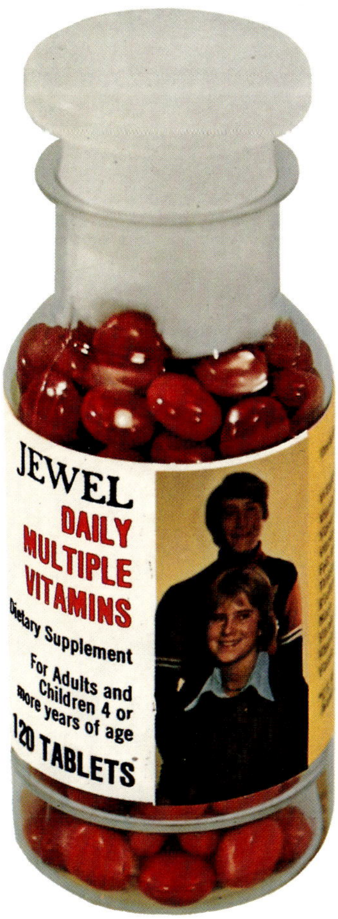

A 120 tablet bottle of Jewel "Daily Multiple Vitamins" for adults and children, ages 4 or older.

Laundry Soap

The original 1930 advertisement for JEWEL LAUNDRY TABLETS.

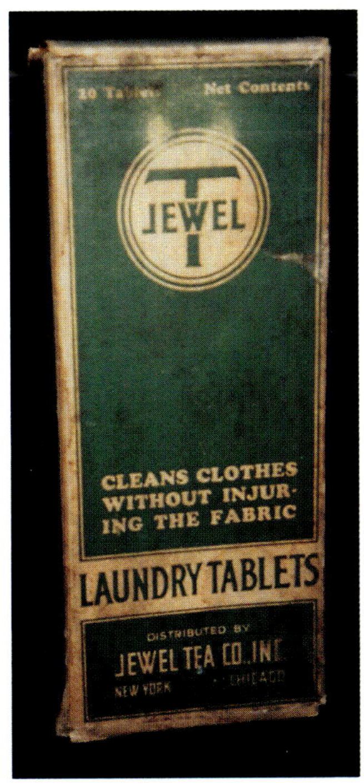

An original "Laundry Tablets" carton distributed by "JEWEL TEA CO., INC., NEW YORK — CHICAGO." When I photographed this product, tablets were still inside. According to the company, "JEWEL LAUNDRY TABLETS served well. They loosened dirt, help to remove stains, whiten clothes and soften water. Priced 25¢." *Vogel Collection.*

In these historical photographs the processing of Jewel "Grano" soap is shown and explained. In the top left photograph high grades of fats and oils in large kettles are converted to soap, top right: in a crutcher liquid soap is pumped, where other ingredients are added and mixed. Second from top: the soap product is dried, then granulated, which was considered by Jewel to be the most economical form for packaging at the time. Third from top: before Jewel "Grano" cartons were glued and sealed, two-stages automatically filled accurate amounts into each carton. Fourth from top: "Grano" filled packages were wrapped in their characteristic tight-sealed wrapping by machines. Fifth from top: cases of Jewel "Grano" were moved by conveyor belts to freight cars for distribution throughout the United States.

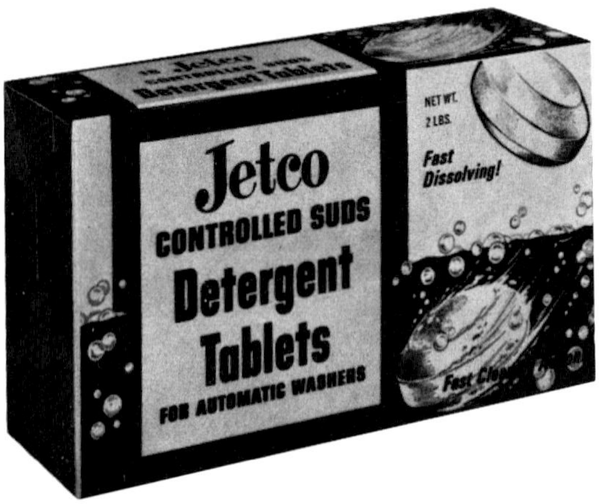

An original promotional advertisement for "Jetco Controlled Suds Detergent Tablets."

During the late-1930s all Jewel branches that stocked small packages of Jewel "Grano" had to completely sell their existing stock before new, larger "Grano" packages were introduced. During this period of time, all requisitions for "Grano" were being filled with the new packages.

Jewel "Grano" contained two and one-half pounds per package which made 24,360 cups of suds. Jewel indicated that good suds were necessary for cleansing.

"Grano" was a concentrated soap designed to remove dirt or grease while producing a large volume of suds from a relatively small amount of product. Jewel stated, "When Mrs. Brown used Jewel 'Grano' she found it unnecessary to add more soap to her laundry or to the dish pan. Mrs. Brown simply swished the water producing more suds."

Jewel "Grano" was made from a blend of tallow and vegetable oil, "... producing the best cleaning value." Jewel advertised their "Grano" contents as being of a higher qual-

ity than that of "other" granulated soaps. The absence of alkali made it easy on hands, clothes, and colors.

"Grano" was also described as containing an added cleaning ingredient, not found in other soaps, "... giving a good sudsy quality even in hard water." The fine granulation prevented lumping by permitting the product to dissolve quickly with normal agitation in hot water. Jewel customers sprinkled "Grano" over the surface and swished the product into their laundry water. Jewel pointed out that clothes never needed boiling or scrubbing.

Jewel "Grano" was recommended for washing clothes and for washing dishes without a greasy film left behind. It was also described as useful for cleaning woodwork and for general household jobs. "Grano" also worked well in hard or soft water.

What Users Say About Our Wonderful New Soap

In 1932 Jewel told their customers, "If You Haven't Used It — Try It Just Once — That's All We Ask."

The following article appeared under the 2-1/2 lb. box Jewel Grano, shown here.

"Here are just a few of the statements picked from customers' letters describing their experiences with Grano."

The economy of this wonderful soap is one of the outstanding features. So small a measure makes such abundant, lasting suds. Also, you do not need to have several soaps on hand when Grano is at your service, for it is truly an all-purpose soap. Just as fine for dish washing and household cleaning as it is in the laundry. The same quality which keeps it from injuring fabric or color is appreciated by the housewife whose hands it does not redden or roughen.

Martha E. Phillips, from Baltimore, Maryland wrote Jewel. "I use Grano for all purposes. Dishes just sparkle. Stains from sinks and bathtubs are removed without injuring enamel. Grease, grime and dirt, removed from woodwork like magic, without destroying pain, etc."

Mrs. Guy L. Cooley, Elmira, New York wrote, "After comparing the merits of different soaps and reviewing the facts, I find that Grano is the most economical soap I have ever used, saving both time and money."

Mrs. Geo. M. Johnson from East Toledo, Ohio said, "Not one of the best, but the best soap on the market. I think the outstanding quality is the clean, fresh-like odor it leaves everything with.

From Wichita Falls, Texas Jewel customer Mrs. George H. Osborne wrote, "Having three small children, laundry is one of my biggest problems. I find Grano a long sought answer. Baby's little shirts, dresses, blankets, sister's little dresses and big brother's heavy playsuits can all use the same nice suds. Grano is safe and thorough, too. Gets clothes clean by soaking. So little rubbing is necessary because there is so much more suds than other soaps. It dissolves quickly — even in this hard Texas water. The suds last all thorough a big wash and the clothes are soft and white."

"It lasts twice as long as other soaps, therefore, it's economical."

"The nice hot suds get even the greasiest of dishes clean, keeps silver bright and glasses sparkling."

"We have never found anything superior to it for keeping linoleum like new. It is wonderful for tile floors, woodwork, and white shoes. It prevents roughness of my hands." *Jewel News,* 1932.

It was not uncommon for Jewel reader's to share family photographs with Mary Dunbar. Described as one of the most precious photographs submitted to Jewel, along with her letter, was the picture from Mrs. L.G. Soule, 3644 Askew Avenue., Kansas City, Mo.

Mrs. Soule, in 1932, enclosed this photograph of her 10 month old daughter Marilyn Mae Soule and wrote, "Where are my clothes? Why, my mamma is washing them in Jewel Granulated soap. I smile and am so happy because things feel so good on my body and smell so clean and sweet."

One Jewel customer compared herself to the old woman who lived in the shoe when she wrote Jewel about using Grano. "I am like the old woman who lived in the shoe without Grano I wonder just what I would do. It takes such a little to make suds foamy white. Cleaning all over the house becomes a delight." *Jewel News,* 1932.

"Now, all Jewel products are tested, tried and true, so order some Grano, and I am certain that you, after using it once, will be a satisfied customer, too." Mrs. R.M. Lindsay, Knoxville, Tennessee. *Jewel News,* 1932.

Mrs. H.C. Roesch, 1463 Chestnut St., Terre Haute, Indiana wrote and sent this photograph, along with the following statement: "The above is my reason for using Grano."

During the 1930s this promotional advertisement appeared in "The Jewel News." "For quick, better, and easier cleaning. Jewel Powdered Ammonia 12 oz. can, Daintiflakes 12 oz. box, 2-1/2 lb. box, Jewel Gloss Starch, 2-1/2 lb. box Jewel Grano, and 1 lb. can Jewel Cleaner."

A 2 lb. cardboard carton of Jewel "Grano," distributed by the "JEWEL TEA CO., INC., JEWEL PARK BARRINGTON, ILL." *Hamilton Collection.*

The back and side panel of Jewel "Grano." A six quart kettle was promoted on the side and various Jewel products on the back. *Hamilton Collection.*

This 2 lb. 8 oz., "Grano" box has been sealed for protection. It was distributed by the "JEWEL TEA CO., INC., JEWEL PARK BARRINGTON, ILL." Note the side panel promotion for an iron. This was a common form of Jewel advertising. *Lombard Collection.*

This "Grano" was distributed by the "JEWEL TEA CO., INC., LOS ANGELES, CALIFORNIA." *Lemons Collection.*

Note the side panel on this box of "Grano." Jewel is promoting the Silex Coffeemaker. Note: see page 69, *Jewel Tea. Sales and Houseware Collectibles. Vogel Collection.*

The back and side panel of "Grano." Instructions were provided, along with the seal of Mary Dunbar. Note the photograph as well. *Byerly Collection.*

On a side panel of the "Grano" box, Jewel promoted "Jewel Gloss Starch" and Jewel Daintiflakes. *Vogel Collection.*

Won

From the mid-1950s to the 1960s the majority of wash day powders sold were detergents. Pure, granulated soap powders were no longer the volume soap powder sellers used. Jewel believed there were several reasons for the growth of synthetic detergents — performance, power, and cost. Soap was the best cleaner, but left a film on clothing that Jewel called "tattle-tale gray." There was no effective way to remove this film as long as pure soap was used. Pure soap would not perform well in hard water. Scientists developed synthetic cleaning agents or detergents that equaled the cleaning power of soap, left no film, and worked in hard water. Because of the brightening agents in detergents, clothing looked cleaner and brighter than when washed with soap.

A 1 lb., 14 ounce box of "Won," distributed by the Jewel Tea Co., Inc., Jewel Park Barrington, Illinois. *Lombard Collection.*

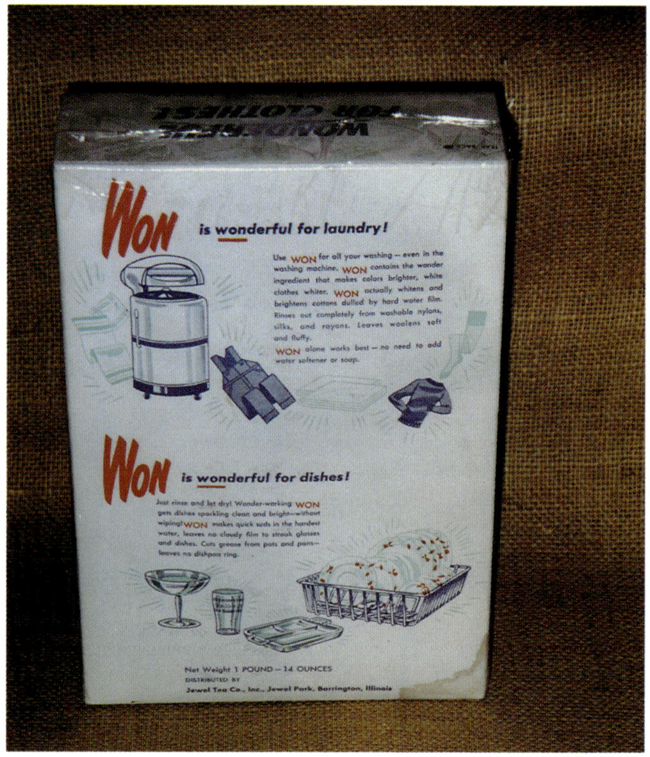

The back panel for "Won" extolled its virtues: "Won was wonderful for Laundry! Won was wonderful for dishes!" *Lombard Collection.*

A different packaging for "Won." The product was always the same. *Lemons Collection.*

This promotional photograph appeared in an early 1960s advertisement. New Blue Won was a "low sudsy" detergent similar to Dash and had the blue "action" of Blue Cheer.

Regular Won, seen here in a promotional advertisement from the early 1960s, was a "high sudsy" detergent. Manufactured by Procter and Gamble, it had fantastic cleaning power and could be used in non-automatics. It could even be used to wash cars.

U-No-Me

Jewel conducted a contest in 1934, asking Jewel customers to submit a name for a new soap product. The contest ended May 30, 1934, and Jewel announced the grand prize winner as D.S. Downing of Michigan. The winning name was announced in Issue No. 10 in 1934 as "U-NO-ME."

Packed by "JEWEL TEA CO., INC., BARRINGTON, ILLINOIS," U-NO-ME Heavy-Duty Cleaner "Makes Soap Go Farther." This product has been sealed for protection. *Byerly Collection.*

The back and side panels of "U-NO-ME" suggested that it could be used on painted walls, woodwork, and floors — either linoleum, marble, and tile. U-NO-ME was used to remove grease and for removing paint as well. See U-NO-ME Soap Stretcher in this Chapter. *Byerly Collection.*

Daintiflakes

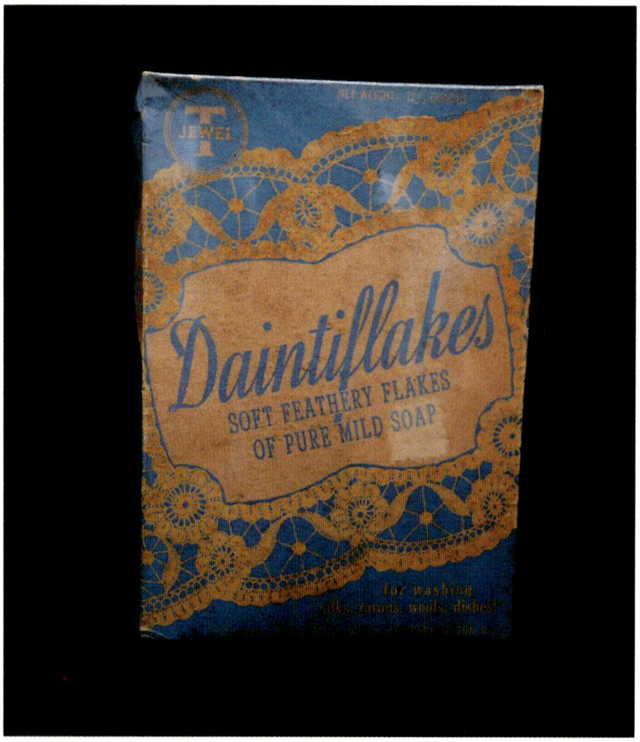

For washing silks, rayons, wools, and dishes, use Jewel 12-1/2 ounce carton of "Daintiflakes." Marked "JEWEL TEA CO., INC., JEWEL PARK BARRINGTON, ILL." *Hamilton Collection.*

The back panel of "Daintiflakes" listed instructions and recommendations for use. *Hamilton Collection.*

Two different packaging for Jewel "Daintiflakes." Both packages held the same product and are marked "Distributed by JEWEL TEA CO., INC., JEWEL PARK BARRINGTON, ILL." *Hamilton Collection.*

The side panels of "Daintiflakes." On one panel Jewel promoted their Oven Proof Hall Autumn Leaf China Mixing Bowls. *Hamilton Collection.*

Soap Stretcher

A 2 lb., 1 ounce carton of "U-NO-ME" Soap Stretcher makes soap go farther. "PACKED BY JEWEL TEA CO., INC., JEWEL PARK BARRINGTON, ILL." *Vogel Collection.*

The back and side panel of "U-NO-Me." Jewel recommendations were provide and the Seal of Mary Dunbar. See "U-NO-Me" in this chapter for more information. *Vogel Collection.*

Jetco

A 1 lb., 8 ounce carton of 1970s "JETCO" Condensed Detergent. Distributed by "JEWEL TEA CO., INC. JEWEL PARK BARRINGTON, ILL." *Vogel Collection.*

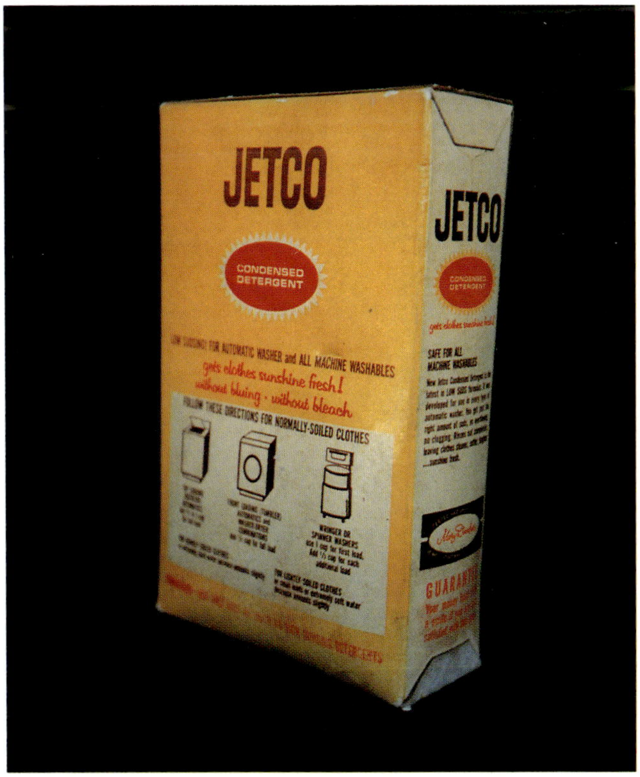

The side and back panel of "JETCO." Directions and the Seal of Mary Dunbar appeared on these panels. Numerous "JETCO" products appeared in "Jewel Grocery Stock Cards" during this period. *Vogel Collection.*

Meteor

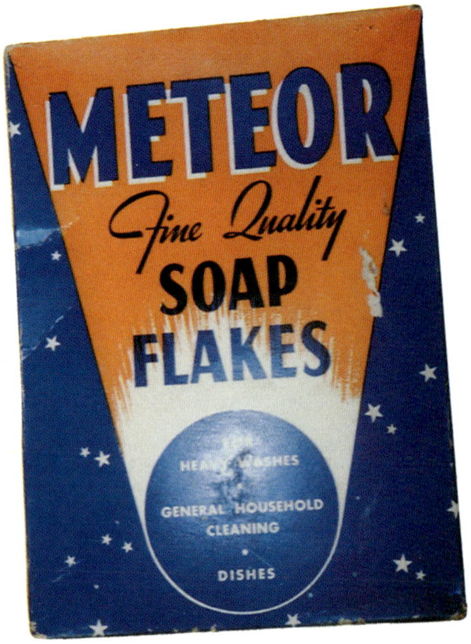

A 2 lb. carton of "Meteor" Fine Quality Soap Flakes. *Lemons Collection.*

HD

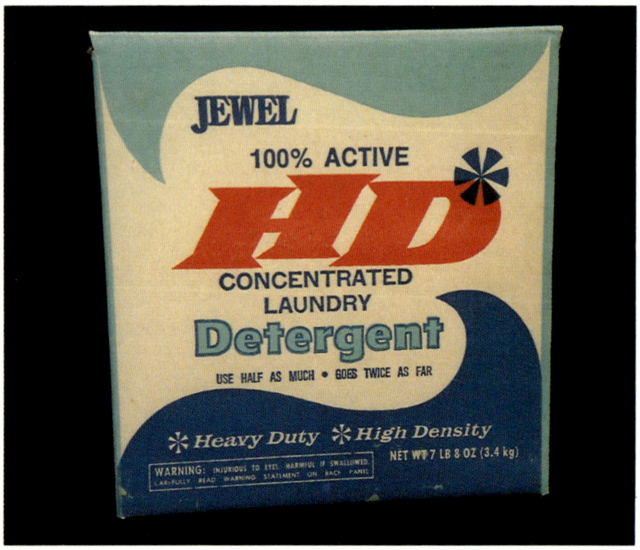

Jewel 100% Active "HD" Concentrated Laundry Detergent appeared in various "Jewel Grocery Stock Cards" during the 1970s and was offered in various weights. In 1974, "HD" (Heavy Duty) was available in a 10 lb. carton and sold for $4.99. The 7.5 lb. carton sold for $4.49 in 1978. Jewel suggested that customers compare it to Cheer™. *Lemons Collection.*

In 1967, H.D. (Heavy Duty) was introduced and Jewel stated that "... immediately housewives were impressed with this economical and effective detergent. It was 100% active, meaning 'concentrated' and more cleaning power to the cupful." *1967 Jewel Grocery Stock Card.*

In 1970, "Sell it where we ain't!" was the new slogan when Jewel Blue was produced. Jewel Blue catered to perma-press fabrics. Jewel Blue was introduced as a compliment to H.D.

In 1971, Jewel praised three of their laundry detergents — H.D. (Heavy Duty), Jewel Blue, and P.F.D. (Phosphate Free Detergent) which was the newest and most popular in their laundry detergent line. According to Jewel, "P.F.D. excelled in cleaning power, economy, and in phosphate-free, non-polluting detergent."

Phosphate water pollution was a prime concern of communities attempting to protect and conserve their water supplies. Phosphate Free Detergent fulfilled the needs of conscientious housewives determined to do their part for the environment.

This original advertisement appeared in a "Jewel Grocery Stock Card" during the 1970s. The "Laundry Corner" promoted various Jewel products including "JETCO, HD, and Tender Touch Fabric Softener." Bonus Credits were also given.

During the 1970s Jewel introduced this "NEW BLUE DETERGENT." The carton contained 7-1/2 pounds and was packed in a space-saving non-tip carton. NEW BLUE DETERGENT contained BORAX for extra cleaning boost, BLUING for sparkling laundry, and BRIGHTENERS which "was a special system for radiant results." It was a "Super Concentrated detergent" — only 1/4 cup for top-loading washers, 55 loads per box, which was easy rinsing and had a low phosphate content.

During the introductory offer, NEW BLUE DETERGENT and a 1/2 gallon of JETCO FLUFF could be purchased together, "both for $4.98." JETCO FLUFF is covered in HOUSEHOLD PRODUCTS.

During the 1970s, Jewel introduced a 7 lb. carton of DAYBREAK Laundry Detergent. DAYBREAK sold for $4.99 plus $1.00 in FREE JEWEL Money. In this advertisement Jewel reminded customers of a big Blanket sale approaching.

JEWEL NEW BLUE DETERGENT appeared on the cover of a Jewel Stock Card; it is believed a child may have marked on the cover which resulted in the pencil marks appearing on this photograph.

Starch, Softener and Bluing

Shown in the photograph is a 3 lb. cardboard carton of Jewel "Pure Gloss Starch" which was distributed by "JEWEL TEA CO., INC., JEWEL PARK BARRINGTON, ILLINOIS." *Edelman Collection.*

The back and opposite panels of "Pure Gloss Starch." Jewel provided instructions for making "HOT" or "QUICK" Starch. This carton contained enough starch for 50 average washings and was guaranteed by Jewel. *Edelman Collection.*

The front and side panel of the above "Pure Gloss Starch." Mary Dunbar's own signature appears. *Edelman Collection.*

An example of 1970s "Jetco" New Water Softener and Perfumed Starch. *Vogel Collection.*

The 30 ounce cardboard carton of "Jetco" perfumed Starch was "PACKED BY JEWEL TEA CO., INC., BARRINGTON, ILL." *Vogel Collection.*

This carton of "Jetco" water softener, with built in detergent action, held 40 ounces. *Vogel Collection.*

Side panels promoted various "Jetco" products. *Vogel Collection.*

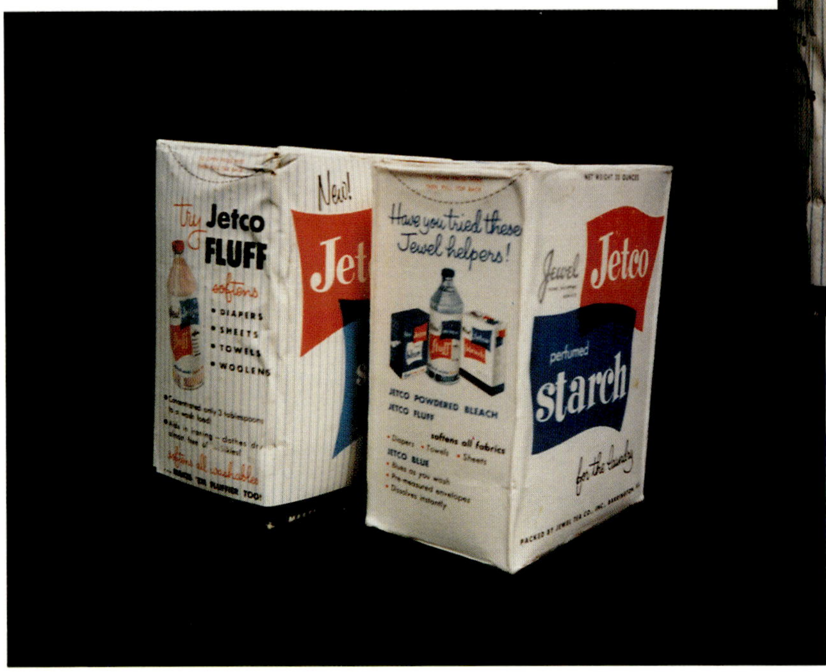

"Jetco" New Economy Size Bead bluing. *Vogel Collection.*

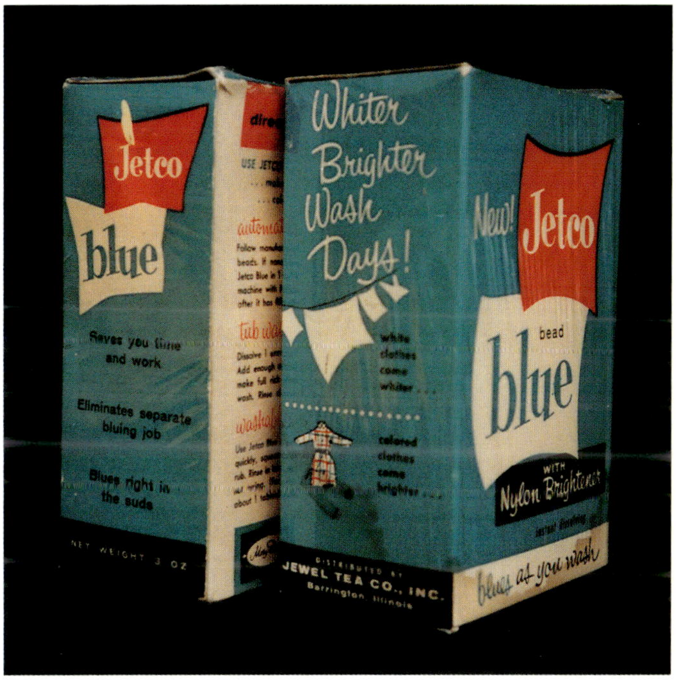

Different packaging for New "Jetco" bead blue. Distributed by "JEWEL TEA CO., INC., BARRINGTON, ILLINOIS." These cartons have been sealed for protection. *Hamilton Collection.*

The back and side panel of the "Jetco" bead blue. Directions for use and the Seal of Mary Dunbar appeared. *Hamilton Collection.*

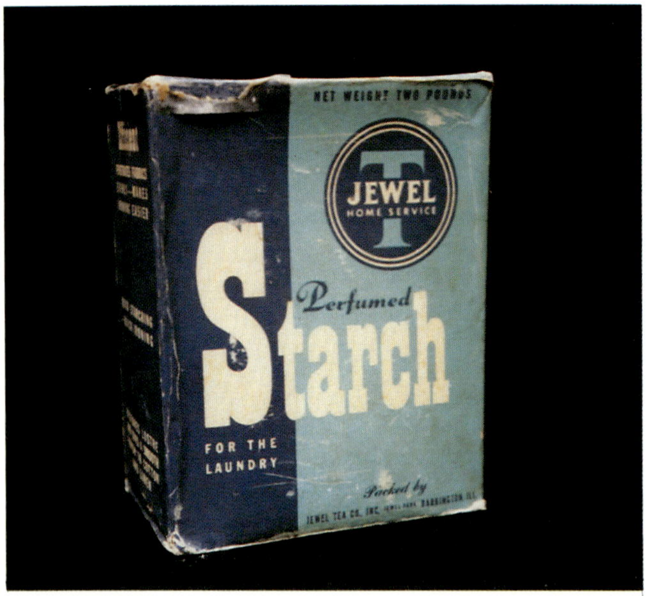

A 2 lb. cardboard carton of Jewel "Perfumed Starch." Packed by "JEWEL TEA CO., INC., JEWEL PARK BARRINGTON, ILL." *Hamilton Collection.*

A side panel of the "Perfumed Starch" carton. This product was "Guaranteed" by Jewel. *Hamilton Collection.*

The multicolored carton held 3 lbs. of "JEWEL GLOSS LUMP STARCH," marked JEWEL TEA CO. WASHINGTON BOUL. & ADA ST. CHICAGO, ILL." The Bar 'n Circle logo appears on this carton and can be dated between 1903 - 1910. On a side panel, a multicolored illustration of the Washington and Ada Street headquarters appears along with "The driver will be pleased to take your orders today for LAUNDRY and TOILET SOAPS" and "JEWEL WASHING POWDER is one of the JEWEL products that pleases everybody." This product offered "25 CENTS WITH 1 CHECK." *Sipes Collection.*

A sealed carton of Jewel Blue, distributed by "JEWEL TEA CO., INC., JEWEL PARK, BARRINGTON, ILL." *Lombard Collection.*

An envelope of Jewel Blue. Note the different packaging of these items. *Lombard Collection.*

Household Products

The original carton and package of Jewel Blue. The envelope is marked "© BY THE STEVENS WILEY MFG. CO. INC., 1938." The carton is marked "Distributed by JEWEL TEA CO., INC., JEWEL PARK BARRINGTON, ILL." *Hamilton Collection.*

The back and side panel of the "Jewel Blue" carton. Directions were provided for the Machine or Tub Method and for preparing Jewel Blue. *Hamilton Collection.*

A 1 lb., 4 oz. box of Jetco Dishwasher Detergent. *Edelman Collection.*

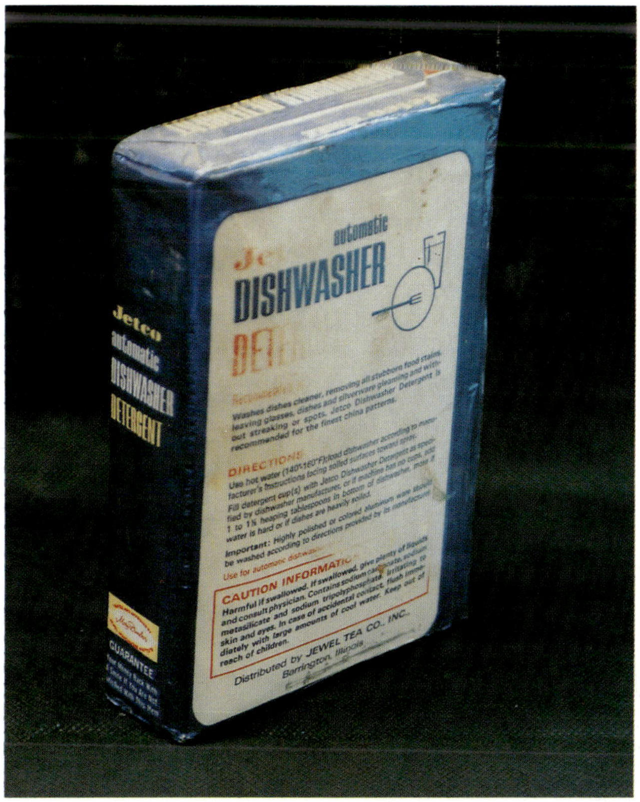

The back and side panel of Jetco Dishwasher Detergent provided directions and the Seal of Mary Dunbar. This product was "Distributed by JEWEL TEA CO., INC., BARRINGTON, ILLINOIS." *Edelman Collection.*

The selection of Jewel products appeared in a Jewel publication in the early 1970s. Note the different packaging for Jetco Dishwasher Detergent. In 1976 this detergent sold for two for $3.88. It was regularly priced at $1.99. Products often underwent a change in packaging but the product remained the same.

A "Jewel Home Shopping Service" glass bottle of "New Jetco laundry no rub." *Housel Collection.*

"Jetco" Laundry Brightener, shown here in a 32 ounce plastic bottle, sold in 1976 at two bottles for $2.98. *Housel Collection.*

In 1976, two 1/2 gallon plastic bottles of "Jetco" fluff sold for $3.88. A one gallon plastic container was also available during this period. On this container "Jetco" does not appear, it was replaced by the word "JEWEL." This one gallon container sold for $3.49. *Housel Collection.*

In 1978, "Jetco" spray fabric finish appeared in a Jewel Grocery Stock Card. Three cans of this products sold for $3.57, plus a free key chain with rain bonnet was given away with the purchase. *Edelman Collection.*

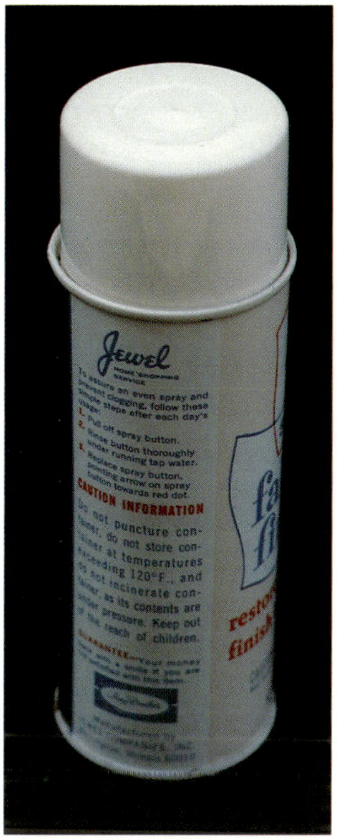

The back panel of "Jetco" fabric finish. Marked "Jewel Home Shopping Service" and "Manufactured by JEWEL COMPANIES, INC., BARRINGTON, ILLINOIS 60010." *Edelman Collection.*

"Jewel Hand Cleaner" cleaned with or without water. This plastic bottle, with a paper label, was "Distributed by JEWEL HOME SHOPPING SERVICE BARRINGTON, ILL. 60010." *Housel Collection.*

Two 32 oz. plastic bottles of "HD" Concentrated Fabric Softener "with the light touch." Marked "JEWEL COMPANIES INC., BARRINGTON, ILLINOIS 60010." *Housel Collection.*

"Jewel Mr. Rust" in a 1 pint plastic pump bottle. This product was a 10 minute rust and stain remover. *Vogel Collection.*

The original carton and Jewel Automatic bowl clean container. This 6 ounce container appeared in various Jewel Grocery Stock Cards of the 1970s. In 1976, this bowl cleaner sold for 5 containers for $4.96. With this offer, a customer received a free handmade wicker and hemp planter (plant not included). *Vogel Collection.*

Perfect for cleaning around the cooking area! "Jewel Kitchen Degreaser" appeared in a 1976 Jewel Grocery Stock Card. This 16 ounce plastic pump bottle sold for $1.29. *Lemons Collection.*

Two 1970s cleaners containers. Distributed by "JEWEL TEA CO., INC., JEWEL PARK BARRINGTON, ILL." *Byerly Collection.*

Jewel "glo" cleaner. *Hamilton Collection.*

The back panel of the "glo" cleaner. Distributed by the Jewel In-Home Shopping Service Jewel Companies Inc. *Hamilton Collection.*

Jewel "Spot Remover." *Hamilton Collection.*

In 1976, the 1 qt. "Jetco" Pine Oil Cleaner was sold at two cans for $3.49. Jetco was an all purpose cleaner which cleaned, disinfected, deodorized, and cleaned paint brushes. *Lemons Collection.*

The 1 qt. Jewel "Pine Oil Cleaner," was "Manufactured and Distributed by JEWEL COMPANIES, INC., BARRINGTON, ILLINOIS 60010." *Hamilton Collection.*

The back panel of the Jewel Pine Oil Cleaner provided directions of this All-Purpose Cleaner for all Household Cleaning. Manufactured by "JEWEL TEA CO., INC., JEWEL PARK BARRINGTON, ILLINOIS." *Hamilton Collection.*

This Pine Oil Cleaner appears under a new designed container. Jewel Jetco Home Service. *Hamilton Collection.*

The back panel of the Jewel Pine Oil Cleaner features directions and "Danger Information." *Hamilton Collection.*

The original advertisement appeared in a Jewel Grocery Stock Card from the 1970s.

An original advertisement for JEWEL lemon Dish Detergent. This advertisement appeared in a 1970s Jewel Grocery Stock Card.

The one quart Jewel "No Rubbing Floor Wax" was "MANUFACTURED BY JEWEL TEA CO., INC., JEWEL PARK BARRINGTON, ILLINOIS." *Vogel Collection.*

The back panel of Jewel "No Rubbing Floor Wax" provided directions and the Seal of Approval. *Vogel Collection.*

"New Economy Size Jewel Hi-Gloss Floor Wax." *Steelman Collection.*

"Jewel Home Shopping Service" Rug Shampoo, a liquid rug cleaner. *Randall Collection.*

Self-polishing "Jewel Wood Floor Wax." *Lemons Collection.*

Jewel Home Shopping Service "Fine Furniture Polish." *Lemons Collection.*

An 8 ounce Jewel Home Shopping Service "Moisturizing Furniture Lotion." *Lemons Collection.*

"Jewel Polish The Polish That Varnishes." Marked "Distributed by JEWEL TEA CO., INC., NEW YORK — CHICAGO." *Hamilton Collection.*

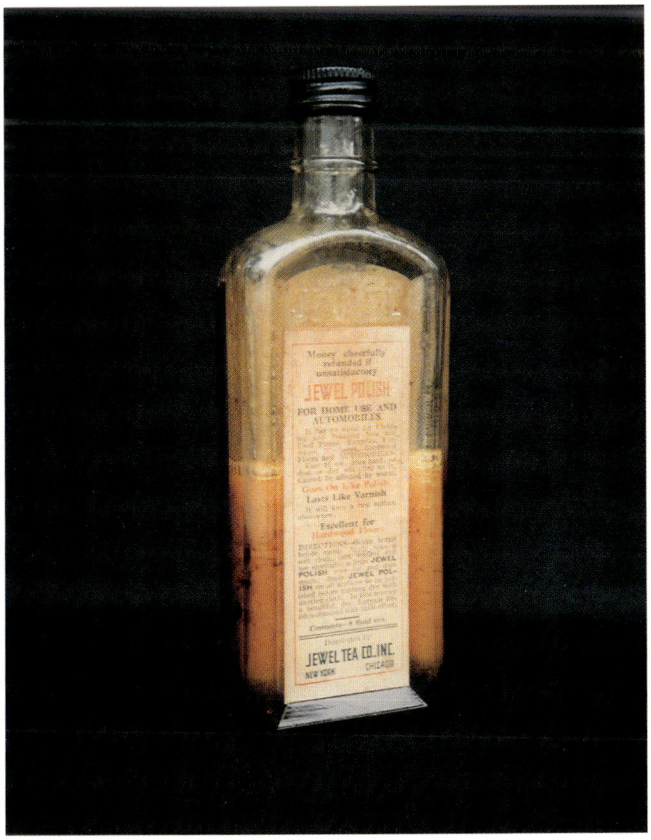

The back of this glass bottle of Jewel Polish includes instructions for use in the home and in automobiles. *Hamilton Collection.*

In 1974, Jewel promoted Jewel "Cedar Fresh Moth Block" as having a handy hanger for use in closets and a net weight of 12 ounces. Jewel also promoted Jewel Bath Room Deodorizer, in an easy-to-use aerosol spray, net weight 12 ounces and Jewel "Perfumed Toilet Bowl Deodorants" in a box of 3 deodorants, with a net weight of 9-3/4 ounces.

A 3 ounce Jewel "Moth Cake" and Jewel "Cedar Fresh Moth Cake." *Vogel Collection.*

Jewel "Cedar Fresh Moth Crystals." *Byerly Collection.*

Jewel Home Shopping Service "Moth Crystals."
Hamilton Collection.

A 22 ounce canister of Jewel "Moth Crystals."
Lemons Collection.

An advertisement promoting Jewel "Air Fresheners" appeared in a 1970s Jewel Grocery Stock Card.

In 1976, the advertisement for Jewel "Drain Cleaner" was stapled inside a Jewel Grocery Stock Card.

Aerosol Cans

In 1976, the "Jewel Overnight Oven Cleaner" was offered for sale at two for $2.70.

An original advertisement promoting "Jewel Power Spray Oven Cleaner" and "Jewel Foaming Bowl Cleaner." This advertisement appeared in a Jewel Grocery Stock Card from the 1970s.

From the 1970s, an advertisement for "Jewel Odor Kil" appeared in a Jewel Grocery Stock Card.

"Jewel Lemon Furniture Polish" with lemon oil. *Byerly Collection.*

In 1978, two cans of "Jetco Glass Cleaner with Ammonia" was sold for $2.58. *Lemons Collection.*

A 15 ounce can of "Jewel No Streak Glass Cleaner." *Lemons Collection.*

In 1975, two 12 oz. spray cans of "Jewel no-dust" sold for $2.88. Jewel no-dust was made from peppermint and coconut oils. *Housel Collection.*

A 16.6 ounce can of "Jewel Odor Kil" disinfectant deodorant. *Lemons Collection.*

A 6 ounce can of "Jewel spot remover." *Byerly Collection.*

Jewel Home Shopping Service's can of "NO-DUST." See "NO DUST" below. *Vogel Collection.*

"GMO," a multipurpose cleaner, disinfectant, and deodorizer. *Lemons Collection.*

"Jewel Bath Room" deodorizer. *Lemons Collection.*

Jewel "NO DUST." *Lemons Collection.*

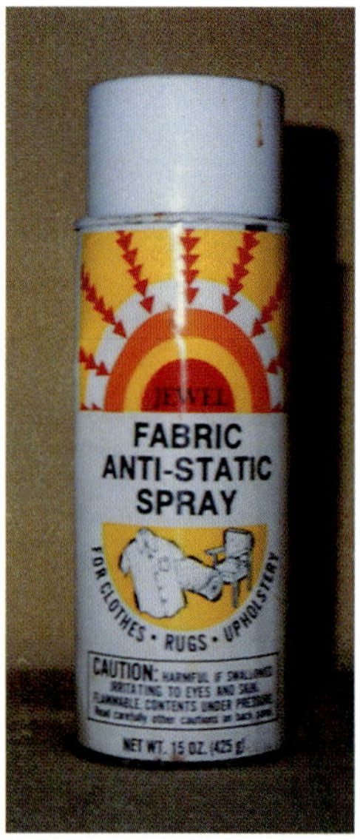

A 15 ounce can of "Jewel Fabric Anti-Static Spray." *Lemons Collection.*

This advertisement appeared in a 1970s Jewel Grocery Stock Card.

Scouring Pads

An advertisement appearing in a 1970s Jewel Grocery Stock Card.

This carton of "Jewel 20 Scouring Pads" has been sealed for protection. The side panel promoted "Jetco Suds" for speedy dish washing. *Vogel Collection.*

Enclosed in this cardboard carton were 18 fast shining "Jewel Scouring Pads," distributed by "JEWEL COMPANIES INC., BARRINGTON, ILLINOIS." *Hamilton Collection.*

"Jewel Twin Pack Scotch-Brite Nylon Web Scouring Pads." Two pads, measuring 4 x 6-1/4 x 5/16 inches, were enclosed. See original advertisement in this chapter. *Vogel Collection.*

An original 1970s advertisement for Jewel Scouring Pads.

On the carton of "12 Soap Filled Steel Wool Scouring Pads," someone has penciled in Nov. 1947. Distributed by "JEWEL TEA CO., INC., JEWEL PARK BARRINGTON, ILL." *Hamilton Collection.*

This cardboard carton has the original three "Jewel Stainless Metal Scrub Puffs" inside. See the original advertisement in this chapter. *Eisnaugle Collection.*

This cardboard carton still has the original "Jewel Stainless Steel Sponges" inside. Distributed by "JEWEL COMPANIES INC., BARRINGTON, ILLINOIS 60010." *Eisnaugle Collection.*

The back panel of these "Scouring Pads" included Directions and the Seal of Mary Dunbar. *Hamilton Collection.*

The back panel of "Jewel Stainless Steel Sponges" and the Seal of Mary Dunbar. *Eisnaugle Collection.*

Paper Products

"Jewel Home Shopping Service" 200 paper luncheon embossed napkins. *Housel Collection.*

This package held 160 Jewel Table Napkins. *Vogel Collection.*

Eighty Jewel embossed paper napkins. These luncheon size napkins are 13" x 13-1/2." *Vogel Collection.*

Jewel Garbage Bags. *Hamilton Collection.*

The Mary Dunbar seal appears on the back panel of the Jewel Garbage Bags. *Hamilton Collection.*

This "Dusting Paper" dates to 1942. This paper measures 11-3/4" long x 2-1/4" across and was 50 feet in length. Distributed by "JEWEL TEA CO., INC., JEWEL PARK BARRINGTON, ILL." *Lemons Collection.*

Jewel Home Shopping Service "Waxed Paper." *Sivils Collection.*

The reverse side of Jewel Home Shopping Service "Waxed Paper." It had 250 feet at finger tip convenience. *Sivils Collection.*

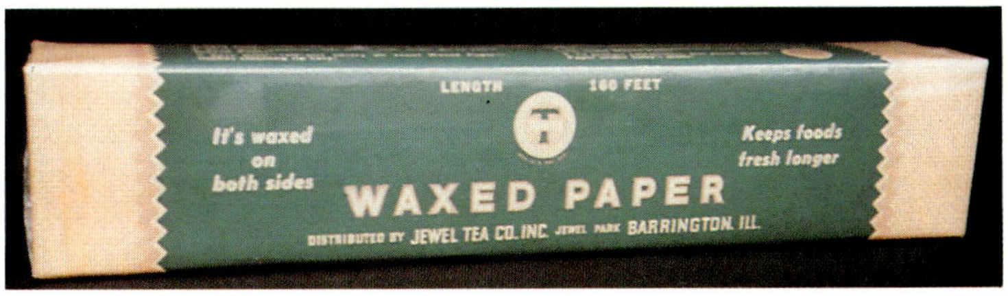

This 160 feet roll of Waxed Paper was "Distributed by JEWEL TEA CO., INC., JEWEL PARK BARRINGTON, ILL." *Hamilton Collection.*

A 200 square foot roll of Jewel "Plastic Wrap." *Sivils Collection.*

"Jewel Economy Garment Bags," 6 bags measuring 24" x 54" were included. *Lemons Collection.*

A series of Jewel products appeared in a 1970s Jewel Grocery Stock Card.

A roll of "Jewel Home Shopping Service" tape. *Randall Collection.*

A section from the "Jewel Home Shopping Service" roll of tape. *Randall Collection.*

"Jewel Quick Tape," this carton has been sealed for protection. Distributed by "JEWEL TEA CO., INC., JEWEL PARK BARRINGTON, ILL." *Hamilton Collection.*

The back section of the "Jewel Quick Tape" provided "Directions." *Hamilton Collection.*

Paint and Wallpaper

Jewel described the qualities of their paints as follows: "When Jewel customers choose Jewel 'Magic Touch' paints, they got proven quality. In laboratory testing, Jewel Paints ranked equal to or better than any of the best grades at popular prices. Colors were pre-mixed in most wanted colors." *1966 Jewel Catalog.*

These paint colors, with original captions from 1966, were reproduced as faithfully as it was possible with modern high-speed equipment. Colors varied slightly, in shade, from the actual colors. If a Jewel customer preferred to see actual swatch cards, they were instructed to ask their salesman or write directly to Mary Dunbar, Jewel Tea Co., Inc., Barrington, Ill. 60010 *Andrews Collection.*

INTERIOR LATEX OR ENAMEL...color-coordinated!

Dripless Satin Latex

Recommended for living rooms, bedrooms...durable, scrubbable! Needs no stirring, shaking or thinning... applies easily with roller or brush, no drip, no mess! Dries in 30 minutes to a smooth mat finish! Covers up to 450 sq. ft. per gallon. Hands & tools wash clean with soap, water.

Semi-Gloss Enamel

Recommended for kitchens, bathrooms and woodwork...wipes clean with a damp cloth, and repeated scrubbings won't dull its luster! Apply with brush or roller...dries overnight to a hard, semi-gloss finish. Non-toxic when dry. One gallon covers from 550 to 600 square feet.

Order 'Magic Touch' Interior Paints from chart below...10 matching colors!

Color	Dripless Satin Latex Cat. No.	Gallon Price	Semi-Gloss Enamel Cat. No.	Gallon Price	Semi-Gloss Enamel Cat. No.	Quart Price
White	X-11H 110	5.98	X-11H 120	5.98	X-11H 130	1.95
Off-White	X-11H 111	5.98	X-11H 121	5.98	X-11H 131	1.95
Golden Yellow	X-11H 112	5.98	X-11H 122	5.98	X-11H 132	1.95
Honey Beige	X-11H 113	5.98	X-11H 123	5.98	X-11H 133	1.95
Gay Lavender	X-11H 114	5.98	X-11H 124	5.98	X-11H 134	1.95
Wedgewood Blue	X-11H 115	5.98	X-11H 125	5.98	X-11H 135	1.95
Mint Green	X-11H 116	5.98	X-11H 126	5.98	X-11H 136	1.95
Turquoise Sky	X-11H 117	5.98	X-11H 127	5.98	X-11H 137	1.95
Doeskin (Tan)	X-11H 118	5.98	X-11H 128	5.98	X-11H 138	1.95
Crystal Pink	X-11H 119	5.98	X-11H 129	5.98	X-11H 139	1.95

WATER STOP MASONRY PAINT seals out moisture!

Heavy-duty coating...specially designed for application on stucco, concrete, cement blocks, cinder blocks, asbestos shingles and other surfaces...interior and exterior! Rubberized latex base paint gives you hard, durable, beautiful surface of elastic thermo-plastic film...fills and seals pores, resists moisture! Acid and alkali-proof, dries fast, retains its color longer. Economical, too... one coat provides a thickness of 3 to 4 times that of ordinary paint! Tough...surface can be cleaned with soap, water & a brush. Hands and equipment wash clean with soap and water. Gallon covers from 200 to 400 sq. feet.

Gal. Price	Turquoise	Bright Yellow	Honey Beige	Pearl Gray	Light Green	Coral Pink	White
5.98	X-11H 147	X-11H 148	X-11H 149	X-11H 150	X-11H 151	X-11H 152	X-11H 153

SPARKLE FINISH LATEX adds metallic highlights!

Add gleaming metallic highlights to walls and ceilings...give your home the decorator look! Finest quality latex paint has bright metallic flecks mixed right in with it... as paint is applied with brush or roller, the sparkle accents brighten your walls! Applies easily to clean surfaces...if used on new or porous surfaces, use a coat of Primer Sealer. Hands and equipment clean easily with soap and water. One gallon covers from 350 to 400 square feet.

Size	Price	Gold/White	Gold/Beige	Silver/Turquoise	Silver/White
1 gallon	5.98	X-11H 159	X-11H 160	X-11H 161	X-11H 162
1 quart	2.49	X-11H 163	X-11H 164	X-11H 165	X-11H 166

LATEX TEXTURE PAINT covers with just one coat!

Just one coat does it! Texture and paint in one operation, on old or new interior surfaces! Excellent for cracked or crazed plaster walls, hides small cracks and most surface defects. Finest quality latex paint covers from 100 to 150 square feet per gallon, depending on the texture desired and the condition of the surface. Dries to the touch in only 30 minutes and is hard in 4 to 5 hours. Apply with roller or brush...then use comb, sponge, brush or roller to produce the desired texture. Equipment washes clean with soap & water.

Gallon Price	Light Blue	Light Green	Sandalwood	Light Yellow	White
5.98	X-11H 154	X-11H 155	X-11H 156	X-11H 157	X-11H 158

VINYL LATEX HOUSE PAINT goes on quick 'n easy!

Gives a fast, professional job...with no brush or lap marks...even touch-ups won't show! Easy to apply with brush or spray in just about any kind of weather...on damp surfaces, even 30 minutes after rain! Dries in only 20 minutes to a low-luster sheen, you can apply two coats in one day! It dries so fast that dust or bugs won't stick! This flexible breather-type latex-emulsion paint is strongly resistant to moisture, blistering, cracking, peeling, mildew, fumes. Stays clean and retains its color longer. No paint odor! Hands and equipment wash clean quickly with soap & water. Note: On unsealed (new) wood surfaces, use any good oil-base primer. One gallon covers from 400 to 500 square feet.

Gallon Price	White	Mist Green	Warm Gray	Sandalwood
5.98	X-11H 106	X-11H 107	X-11H 108	X-11H 109

All Jewel Magic Touch paints were delivered by the customers' salesman and no postage was charged.

The original advertisement for "Jewel Vinyl Coated Wallpaper" appeared in 1972. *Andrews Collection.*

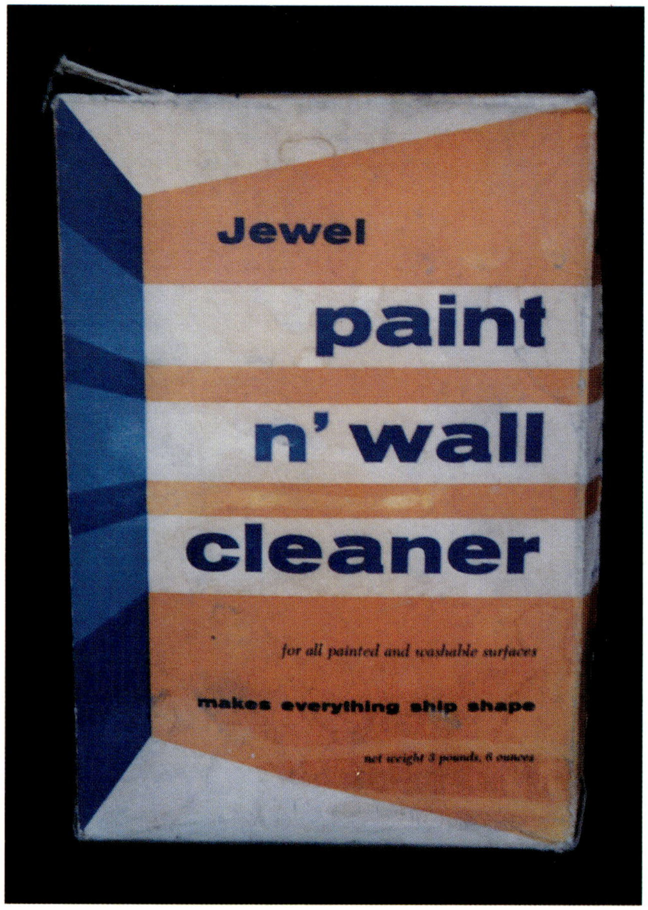

A 3 lb., 6 ounce carton of Jewel paint n' wall cleaner. *Hedges Collection.*

Dog Food

Jewel "Eukanuba Dog Food" was recommended for fussy eaters, older dogs, puppies, and small breeds. One carton was equivalent to approximately 7-12 cans or packets of moist dog food. Eukanuba was available in a half-gallon container, with a net weight of 2 pounds. Jewel Canned Dog Food came in a handy 6-pack carton, with a net weight of 5 pounds, 13 ounces. Jewel Variety Pack Ground Dog Food, each box of which contained 12 individually sealed packets, had a net weight of 4 pounds, 8 ounces.

Mother Hubbard would have danced for joy in 1974 when this promotional advertisement appeared in a Jewel publication. *Andrews Collection.*

"Jewel Dog Food" was distributed by "JEWEL TEA CO., INC., BARRINGTON, ILLINOIS." This cardboard carton contained 12 - 16-1/2 ounces ready-to-use cans. *Randall Collection.*

The side panel from "Jewel Dog Food." This product was good for cats, too! *Randall Collection.*

Cleaner

"Jewel Aluminum Cleaner." This carton contained seven pads and soap. Distributed by "JEWEL TEA CO., INC., JEWEL PARK BARRINGTON, ILL." *Hamilton Collection.*

A 64 ounce container of "Solventol" for laundry and dishes. "Mfg. By Solventol Chemical Products, Inc. Detroit, Michigan. Distributed by JEWEL TEA CO., INC., BARRINGTON, ILL." *Vogel Collection.*

The back panel of "Solventol." Note the logo along the top edge. *Vogel Collection.*

The cardboard cylinder carton held "Jewel Lustrex" The New Powdered Aluminum Cleaner. Distributed by "JEWEL TEA CO., INC., JEWEL PARK BARRINGTON, ILL." This product replaced steel wool. *Vogel Collection.*

A 21 ounce container of "Glorex Cleaner." *Eisnaugle Collection.*

This "New Cleanser" was "Tested and Approved by Mary Dunbar." Distributed by "JEWEL TEA CO., INC., JEWEL PARK BARRINGTON, ILL." *Byerly Collection.*

The side panel of "Glorex Cleaner," this product was "Distributed by JEWEL TEA CO., INC., JEWEL PARK BARRINGTON, ILL." *Eisnaugle Collection.*

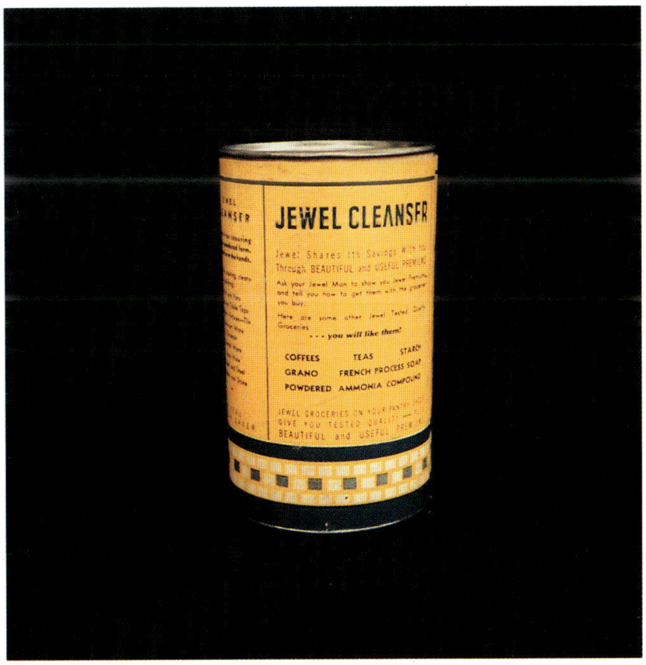

The back panel of "New Cleanser" promoted other Jewel products; Coffees, Teas, Starch, Grano, French Process Soap, and Powdered Ammonia Compound. *Byerly Collection.*

A 12 ounce container of "PowderedAmmonia Compound." Distributed by "JEWEL TEA CO., INC., JEWEL PARK BARRINGTON, ILL." *Hamilton Collection.*

The embossed lid of the "PowderedAmmonia Compound." *Hamilton Collection.*

The back panel of "PowderedAmmonia Compound" was where other Jewel products were promoted. *Hamilton Collection.*

A different packaging for "Jewel Cleaner." Distributed by "JEWEL TEA CO., INC., JEWEL PARK BARRINGTON, ILL." *Hamilton Collection.*

The back panel of "Jewel Cleaner," with the Seal of Mary Dunbar and directions. *Hamilton Collection.*

"Jewel Cleaner" was distributed by "JEWEL TEA CO., INC., JEWEL PARK BARRINGTON, ILL." The flat metal "Jewel Cleaner," shown on the back of the can, has not been formed into a usable can. *Byerly Collection.*

"Jewel Glorex Cleanser." *Lemons Collection.*

The bottle held 8 ounces of "2-Way" Insect Killer Paint was marked "Jewel Tea Co., Barrington Ill., by Nash & Kinsella Labs Inc. St. Louis, Mo." *Lemons Collection.*

"Jewel rust 'n stain" remover. *Lemons Collection.*

"Jewel Korex" Stove Cleaner. *Vogel Collection.*

The original packaging carton for "HD Detergent" from JEWEL COMPANIES, INC. See "HD" elsewhere in this chapter. *Sivils Collection.*

Jewel customers received a FREE 1976 "Bicentennial Edition" calendar. This calendar was filled with important dates and historical information of the country's history plus 12 pages of recipes and household hints. The calendar was FREE with the purchase of a 10 lb. carton of either "HD" Detergent, Fabric Softener, Jetco Laundry Ease, Jecto White Phosphate Free, or Jewel Liquid Laundry.

The original carton held 12 one quart cans of "Jewel Clean 'n Shine," Item No. 3F-23. *Vogel Collection.*

This original shipping carton printed "JEWEL COMPANIES, INC." is believed to have held "Bowl Cleaner." *Vogel Collection.*

The contents of the "JEWEL TEA CO., INC." shipping carton are unknown. *Vogel Collection.*

The reverse end of the "JEWEL COMPANIES, INC." carton. *Vogel Collection.*

CHAPTER 6
GROCERIES

Peanut Butter

Jewel Peanut Butter was made from the new crops of high grade Virginia peanuts which were large and oblong, combined with the small, round Spanish peanuts which had more oil than the Virginia nut. This oil produced rich and smooth Jewel Peanut Butter.

Jewel first shelled then roasted the fresh peanuts in ovens similar to those used for Jewel coffee and cocoa. Once properly roasted, they were removed from the ovens, blanched, and the skins and hearts were removed. If peanuts were over roasted they became bitter. The only ingredients that went into Jewel Peanut Butter were peanuts and salt.

Jars were sealed to retain the aroma and flavor. Jewel peanut butter was rich in protein, the food element, Jewel advised, that was most needed for children.

This original advertisement appeared in an early 1927 Jewel News. Because of its tasty flavor, Jewel Peanut Butter could be used as the base for many dishes: soups, cakes, cookies, candies, sandwiches, and salads. The 12 ounce jar was priced at 35¢.

This Jewel Peanut Butter jar is marked "JEWEL TEA CO., INC., NEW YORK — CHICAGO." *Hamilton Collection.*

The 14 ounce jar of Jewel Peanut Butter is marked "Distributed by Jewel Tea Co., Inc., Jewel Park Barrington, Ill." *Steelman Collection.*

Note the lid on this jar. It is the same lid that appears on the 14 ounce Jewel Peanut Butter jar. It is wise to purchase lose lids when available. The contents of this jar is unknown, since the paper label is missing. *Lombard Collection.*

The 1 lb. Jewel Peanut Butter jar is marked "JEWEL TEA CO., INC., JEWEL PARK BARRINGTON, ILL." This Peanut Butter appeared on the back page of the "Spring and Summer 1952 Jewel Home Shopping Service." *Randall Collection.*

Cake, Cookies, Mince Meat and Pudding

A 1 lb., 14 ounce cardboard carton of Jewel "Cake Flour." *Ferriera Collection.*

The back section of the "Devil's Food Cake Flour" where directions were provided. *Hamilton Collection.*

A 15 ounce cardboard carton of Jewel "Devil's Food" cake mix. "Manufactured by JEWEL TEA CO., INC., JEWEL PARK BARRINGTON, ILL." *Ferriera Collection.*

This cardboard carton held 18 ounces of "Quick Chef Carrot Cake Mix." The famous Autumn Leaf pattern china appears on this carton. *Byerly Collection.*

This cardboard carton held 15 ounces of "Quick Chef Chocolate Flavored Fudge n' Chips Cake Mix," which also made delicious cookies. Pieces of the famous Hall Jewel Autumn Leaf pattern china appear on this carton. "Quick Chef" was a brand name that appeared on numerous grocery products during the 1970s. *Byerly Collection.*

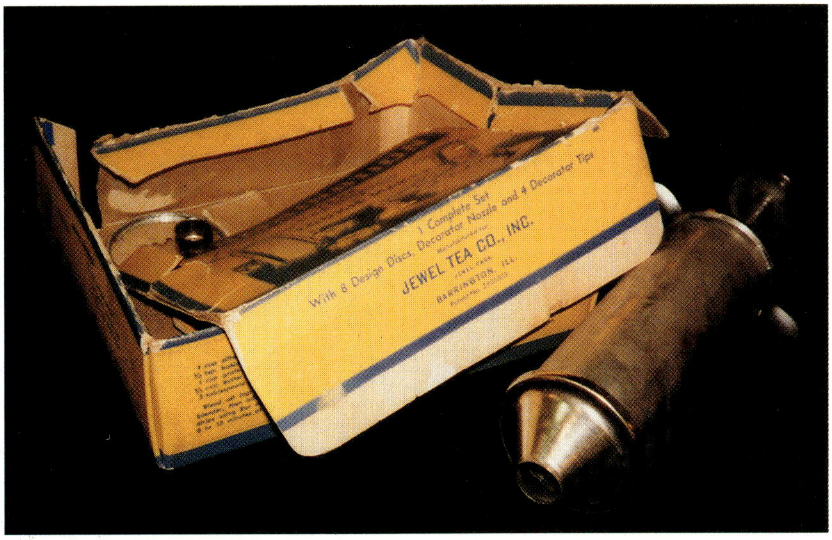

The original 6-1/2" x 5-3/8" x 2" carton for a "Combination Cake Decorator and Cookie Maker." Included was 1 complete set with 8 design discs, decorator nozzle, and 4 decorator tips. Manufactured for "JEWEL TEA CO., INC., JEWEL PARK BARRINGTON, ILL." The Patent No. 2,101,075 indicates a date of 1938, but does not necessarily indicate the year of manufacture. *Hamilton Collection.*

Three 1 lb. cardboard cartons of "Quick Chef" creative cookie mix sold for $2.77 in 1975. The mix was used as a base for a variety of cookies. *Ferriera Collection.*

Simple in packaging is the "Heritage German Chocolate Cake Mix." The autumn leaf motif appears on this 18.5 ounce cardboard carton. "Heritage" was a brand name popular during the 1970s. *Lemons Collection.*

This cardboard shipping carton held 12 sales item 2F57, Jewel "Double Chocolate Sandwich" cookies. *Lemons Collection.*

This cardboard shipping carton held six 1/2 lb. packages of Jewel "Country Kitchen Cookies." *Sivils Collection.*

The Jewel "chocolate chip" cookies shown here, appeared in a 1970s Jewel publication.

The Jewel "butternut" cookies appeared in a 1970s Jewel publication.

Shown here, JEWEL "Danish Style Cookie Assortment." The 1-1/4 lb. tin was "Dist. by Jewel In-Home Shopping Service, Barrington, Il. 60010." *Randall Collection.*

The "Banana Nut Loaf Mix" and Jewel "Nut Bread Mix" appeared in a 1970s Jewel Grocery Stock Card.

Mince Meat

This wooden shipping crate held 36 sales of Jewel Mince Meat. *Sivils Collection.*

This wooden shipping crate held 24 sales of Jewel Mince Meat. The crate is marked with the Jewel logo on both ends as well as "24 Sales Mince Meat Jewel Tea Co., Inc." On the front and back, the logo appears and is marked "JEWEL TEA CO., INC." *Spayde Collection.*

The wooden Mince Meat crate is 18-1/2" x 15-1/2" x 7-1/2." Even though the lid is missing, this crate is in exceptional condition. *Spayde Collection.*

Two variations of Jewel "Mince Meat" packaging. Each package held 1 lb., 2 ounces and has photographs of Jewel's oven-glass pie plate and casserole on the sides. *Orr Collection.*

A close-up view of the 1 lb., 2 ounce cardboard carton of Jewel "Mince Meat." Distributed by "JEWEL TEA CO., INC., JEWEL PARK BARRINGTON, ILL." *Lombard Collection.*

Pudding

In 1924 the Jewel Pudding Pan was listed as Item No. 3 (5 qt.) and sold for $1.00. Made of pure aluminum, the pan was also offered in a 2 qt. size and sold for 70¢. It was also listed as Item No. 4 (3 qt.), but no price was given. *Sivils Collection.*

The bottom of the Pudding Pan, marked with the Jewel logo. *Sivils Collection.*

A 10 ounce cylinder container of "Vanilla Pud'n Pie." This container appeared on the back of the "Spring and Summer 1952" Jewel Home Shopping Service catalog. Jewel also offered this product in "Chocolate" and "Butterscotch." *Hamilton Collection.*

This container of Jewel "Pud-N-Pie" Dessert Mixture held 8 ounces.

The reverse panel of the Jewel "Pud-N-Pie" Dessert Mixture, where directions were provided and the "Seal of Mary Dunbar" appeared. *Vogel Collection.*

Jewel "Cocoanut Dessert." Marked JEWEL TEA CO., INC., NEW YORK — CHICAGO. *Hamilton Collection.*

Jewel "Cocoanut Dessert." Marked JEWEL TEA CO., INC., NEW YORK — CHICAGO. Note the Jewel logo visible here. *Hamilton Collection.*

A 14 ounce container of Jewel "Chocolate Flavored Dessert" marked "JEWEL TEA CO., INC., JEWEL PARK BARRINGTON, ILL." This was a compound to be used for chocolate creme pie, pudding sauce, and cake filling. *Byerly Collection.*

Jewel "Lemon Flavored Dessert." *Ferriera Collection.*

Jewel "Lemon Flavor Pudding and Pie Filling" was manufactured by "JEWEL TEA CO., INC., JEWEL PARK BARRINGTON, ILLINOIS." *Vogel Collection.*

Jewel-Jell

In 1937 there were seven facts that helped the Jewel man sell Jewel-Jell. Jewel-Jell was considered by Jewel to be the finest gelatin dessert on the market, and just as economical as other brands.

FACT No. 1. The basic ingredient in Jewel-Jell was Grayslake gelatin, considered by Jewel to be the best available. The raw material used was the frozen, edible, fresh skin taken from animals slaughtered only for human consumption. The skins were thoroughly cleaned, United States government inspected, frozen, and shipped in refrigerator cars to the Grayslake factory. Distilled water was used throughout the cooking process in which the gelatin is drawn off. All manufacturing steps were automatically controlled and no human hands ever touched the product. All equipment coming into contact with the gelatin was aluminum, nickel, or stainless steel. Grayslake gelatin was made in "an immaculately clean" factory — live steam and boiling water was used on all equipment before every batch operation. The factory was located in the open country, away from city dust.

FACT No. 2. The "super-sanitary" conditions under which Grayslake gelatin was made gave Jewel customers safety — and a lot more. Jewel-Jell was described as "... crystal clean and brilliant — only pure gelatin could make such attractive desserts and salads."

In the photograph, packages of Jewel-Jell are shown through a sheet of pure Grayslake gelatin. The squares are mold-formations.

FACT No. 3. There was no trace of gelatin smell when boiling water was poured over Jewel-Jell, and there was no trace of any taste in Jewel-Jell except for the real fruit flavor.

FACT No. 4. Jewel-Jell was quick setting because the products included a quick-setting ingredient developed by Jewel chemists.

FACT No. 5. Jewel-Jell was a nourishing food. The Grayslake gelatin was accepted by the Council on Foods of the American Medical Association. Gelatin was a protein food similar to lean meat and the whites of eggs. It was to be touted as a valuable muscle-builder. The sugars in Jewel-Jell provided a rich source of carbohydrates, "body fuel for quick energy." The calorific value of a package of Jewel-Jell was 365 calories, which compared favorably with other desserts. Jewel claimed that a pound of prepared Jewel-Jell had the same food value as a pound of canned apricots or fresh sliced apples or pears and the same food value as a pound and a half of fresh pineapple or canned peaches. Jewel further asserted that Jewel-Jell was easily and quickly assimilated by the body — it was assimilated almost 100 per cent in the digestive process.

FACT No. 6. The company pointed out that Jewel-Jell was an economical food and was as economical as any other brands of gelatin selling for less money. One package of Jewel-Jell made almost a pound and a quarter of dessert. "Comparing the cost of Jewel-Jell with other desserts, and for the same quantity and food value it was invariably found cheaper." Experiments in the Jewel Homemaker's Institute kitchen showed that the amount of water added to Jewel-Jell could be greatly increased over the standard recipe on the package. Jewel-Jell compared favorably with nationally advertised brands, in flavor and consistency, when 3 cups of liquid per envelope of powder were used instead of 2 cups. Even more liquid per envelope could be used when fruits or vegetables were added in quantity and Jewel-Jell stood up well. The Jewel salesman would add, "The extra quality of Jewel-Jell made it go further, making it entirely unnecessary for housewives to sacrifice quality for price."

FACT No. 7. There were lots of "... appetizing and attractive ways to use Jewel-Jell. Jewel-Jell made a tasty dessert or salad all by itself, served plain or with lettuce, whipped cream, or adding other garnishments. It could be whipped to provide an entirely different taste and appearance. Jewel-Jell was popular for jellied meat loaf, vegetable salad, fruit salad, fruit dessert, and fruit pie. Jewel-Jell made Bavarian Cream, ice box cake, and coffee chiffon pie, and even made delicious, sparkling fruit drinks. However, when Jewel-Jell was used, it was uniformly smooth, brilliant, and had a pleasant flavor. Mrs. Brown couldn't go wrong with Jewel-Jell." *1937 Jewel Publication.*

The Jewel-Jell shown here appeared in a mid-1920s Jewel publication. The "Bulls eye" logo was introduced in the late teens and was eliminated during the early 1920s. This products is marked "JEWEL TEA CO., INC. NEW YORK — CHICAGO."

Three flavors of Jewel-Jell: Lemon, Lime and Orange. Marked "JEWEL TEA CO., INC., JEWEL PARK BARRINGTON, ILL." These three flavors appeared on the back of the "Spring and Summer 1952 Jewel Home Shopping Service" catalog. *Housel Collection.*

This carton of Jewel-Jell "Natural Raspberry Flavor" Gelatin Dessert is marked "Manufactured by JEWEL TEA CO., INC., JEWEL PARK BARRINGTON, ILL." *Byerly Collection.*

The back panel of Jewel-Jell. Additional Jewel products were promoted on this panel. *Byerly Collection.*

The four Jewel Jell glass jars, shown here, include two Strawberry, a Cherry, and a Pure Lemon flavor. Manufactured by "JEWEL TEA CO., INC., JEWEL PARK BARRINGTON, ILL." *Byerly Collection.*

This cardboard carton held 3-1/4 ounce of Jewel-Jell. Manufactured by "JEWEL TEA CO., INC., JEWEL PARK BARRINGTON, ILL.," this was a natural Lemon flavor gelatin dessert. Note the logo. *Sivils Collection.*

The back panel of this 3-1/4 ounce carton of Jewel-Jell was where Jewel promotod additional products. This product appeared in a 1930s Jewel publication. *Sivils Collection.*

Snacks

Three cardboard cartons of Jewel "Pop Corn" sold for $3.57 in 1978. With this purchase a customer received a FREE School Box, a 69¢ value. *Edelman Collection.*

An original $1.19 Value Jewel coupon. The Jewel popcorn was delivered FREE when a $5.00 grocery order was placed. *Edelman Collection.*

The Jewel Pop Corn side panel where the "Seal of Mary Dunbar" appeared. *Edelman Collection.*

The Pop Corn back panel where recipes were provided for preparing 10 cups of corn and how to make caramel corn. *Edelman Collection.*

Jewel "Salted Mixed Nuts" packed by "JEWEL TEA CO., INC., BARRINGTON, ILL." *Sivils Collection.*

The "Tested and Approved by Mary Dunbar Jewel Homemakers Institute" seal appears on the Salted Mixed Nuts can. *Sivils Collection.*

The 9" diameter "Frisbee," shown here, held 24 ounces (1 lb., 8 oz.) of popcorn. Marked "Dist. by Jewel Companies Inc. Barrington, Ill. 60010." The paper label reads "Jewel Popcorn" and provides a recipe for "tempting popcorn." This "Frisbee" was offered also in Blue, Yellow, and Red. This particular "Frisbee" is missing the original paper label and popcorn. *Eisnaugle Collection.*

This tin held Jewel "Deluxe Mixed Nuts." *Hedges Collection.*

This cardboard carton held Jewel "Jollie Spiced Drops." *Ferriera Collection.*

The contents of this colorfully illustrated Jewel cardboard carton is unknown. *Lemons Collection.*

The 1-1/4 lbs. of "Granny Dunbar Butter Crisp Peanut Brittle" was available during the 1970s. In 1977 Jewel offered customers a choice between Dunbar Peanut Brittle, Sugarless Candy, or Jewel Instant Chocolate Flavored Mix for $1.99. *Lemons Collection.*

The metal tin held Jewel "Sparkling Beauties." Manufactured by "Zion Institutions & Industries - Zion, Illinois" but distributed by "JEWEL TEA CO., INC., NEW YORK — CHICAGO." *Hamilton Collection.*

The reverse panels of the "Sparkling Beauties" tin. *Hamilton Collection.*

The metal cylinder container held Jewel "Mints." Distributed by "JEWEL TEA CO., INC., NEW YORK — CHICAGO." *Hedges Collection.*

Two variations of "Mary Dunbar" Holiday candy. The larger was offered in 1929. The paper label reads: "Mary Dunbar Candy - Soft Centers - 3 lbs. Net Weight. Distributed by Jewel Tea Co., Inc. New York — Chicago." The lid on the smaller jar indicates the Jewel Tea Co. *Hamilton Collection.*

A closer view of the paper label of Mary Dunbar Holiday candy. *Hamilton Collection.*

This glass jar held 32 ounces of Jewel "100% Filled Sunbrite Mix." *Vogel Collection.*

A 2 lb. round metal container for "Jewel Assortment." This container held either cookies or candy. *Hamilton Collection.*

The round metal container, shown here, held 14 ounces of Jewel "Fruity Snack Mix." If the sticker had been removed from this tin, no indication of this historical company would have been known. *Private Collection.*

This round metal container held 3 lbs. of Holiday candies. *Hamilton Collection.*

This metal tin held 14 ounces of Jewel "Fruity Snack Mix." Distributed by "Jewel Companies, Barrington, Illinois 60010." *Byerly Collection.*

This tin held an assortment of Jewel "After Dinner Mints" and was distributed by the Jewel Tea Company Inc. of Barrington, Illinois. *Ferriera Collection.*

Fruit Cake Tins

In 1940, Jewel believed Mrs. Brown would like to have several packages of these fruit cake mixes to make cakes for Christmas gifts. With this mixture, the fruit was cut into pieces "just the right size," so that there was no waste. The spices had already been added so there was nothing additional needed. A 10¢ premium credit was provided.

Angelic children appear on the lid to this fruit cake tin. *Casey Collection.*

The rim of the fruit cake tin lid is marked "Mfg. by JEWEL TEA CO., INC., BARRINGTON, ILLINOIS." *Casey Collection.*

Ice skaters grace the lid to this 2 lb. fruit cake tin. The rim of the lid is marked "Manufactured by JEWEL TEA CO., INC., BARRINGTON, ILLINOIS." *Vogel Collection.*

Owls appear on lid of the Jewel 1980 Fruit Cake tin. *Vogel Collection.*

A pair of cardinal's appear on this Fruit Cake tin. *Vogel Collection.*

The Jewel Fruit Cake tin is marked "Keepsake 1977." *Vogel Collection.*

Shown here are two lids to the most popular Jewel Fruit Cake tin. See "The Jewel Tea Company, Its History and Products" page 132 - 134. The lid, in poor condition, had washed ashore along an Ohio river and was retrieved by the collector's daughter. *Vogel Collection.*

This Jewel Fruit Cake tin is marked "Keepsake 1978." *Vogel Collection.*

Miscellaneous

Note the 1950s - 1960s Jewel logo appears on this Jewel Whip Dessert Topping Mix. Same packaging, but different time periods. *Lombard Collection.*

In 1976, this Jewel Whip sold for 85¢. A twin pack made 1 quart of whipped topping. *Housel Collection.*

A 12 ounce jar of JOYA "Egg Nog" Flavor Beads. *Ferriera Collection.*

These "Quick Chef Scalloped Potatoes" date to the 1970s. The carton held 5-1/2 ounce. *Lemons Collection.*

A 15-1/2 ounce carton of JT's General Store Heritage Creative Corn Muffin Mix. JT's General Store is still in business and their products are highly sought by Jewel collector's today. On October 3, 1994, J.T. General Store was sold and the new name is "JT Dealer Sales and Services Corp." In the late 1970s Jewel offered customers a Jewel Creative Corn Muffin Mix, similar to this example. Two cartons sold for $1.49. Recipes were on the box for corn waffles, corn bread, and cheese muffins. *Lemons Collection.*

A 7 ounce jar of Jewel Marshmallow Creme. *Lemons Collection.*

Jewel "hot dog relish" in a 1 lb. glass jar. *Lemons Collection.*

In 1976, two boxes of this Jewel "Imitation Lemonade Mix" sold for $2.22. The five 3-oz. envelopes found within each made 1 quart. This mix came complete with sugar, just add water. *Ferriera Collection.*

A 1 lb. container of "JOYA" Imitation Lemonade Mix. *Lemons Collection.*

In 1975, two packages of twelve 10" x 16" bags and ties of Jewel "Oven Bags" sold for $2.29. They were regularly $1.19 each. A recipe booklet was provided inside. *Vogel Collection.*

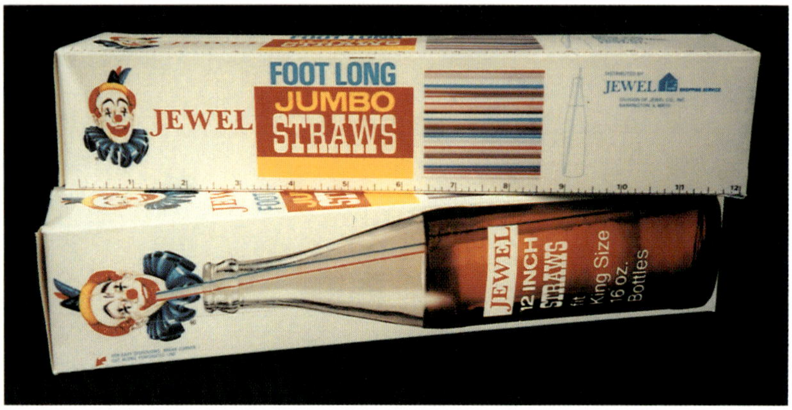

"Jewel In-Home Shopping Service, Division of Jewel Companies Inc.," foot long "Jumbo Straws." The Jewel In-Home Shopping Service dates to the 1970s. *Byerly Collection.*

A 1 lb., 6 ounce Jewel "Beverage Syrup Grape Flavor." "Served Cold — Use No Sugar." Marked "JEWEL TEA CO., INC., JEWEL PARK BARRINGTON, ILL." *Hamilton Collection.*

This carton contained 200 Jewel "Jumbo Sandwich Bags." They were transparent and heavily waxed. *Lemons Collection.*

CHAPTER 7
MACARONI, NOODLES AND SPAGHETTI

Jewel macaroni, noodles, and spaghetti were all made from Durum wheat. Durum wheat was produced in areas that have a rich alkaline soil and where the rainfall is slight.

Jewel pointed out that some of the best Durum wheat was grown in North Dakota, South Dakota, Montana, and Minnesota. Jewel claimed that "The choicest Durum wheat was used in the manufacture of Jewel's macaroni, egg noodles, and spaghetti. Egg noodles offered by Jewel contained only the freshest eggs and each 12 ounce package contained the equivalent of two eggs."

Under expert supervision, each manufacturing and packaging operation for Jewel macaroni was performed by automatic machinery.

This mid-1930s photograph promoted Jewel Egg Noodles, Jewel Macaroni, and Jewel Spaghetti. This photograph appeared in various Jewel publications during that period.

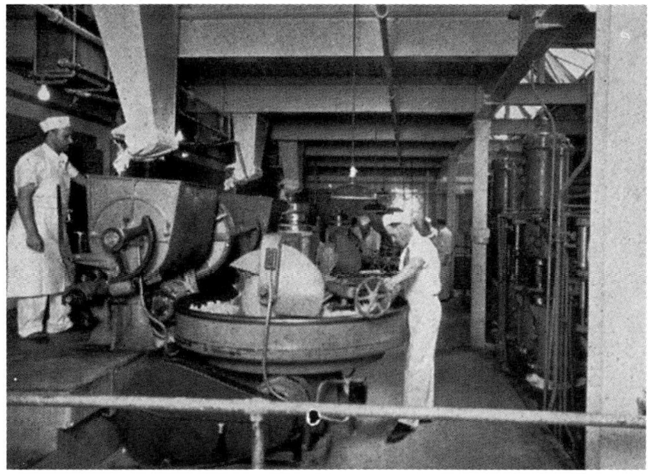

The Kentucky Macaroni Company of Louisville, Kentucky was the only producer of Jewel Macaroni Products. Mixers and kneaders are shown making Jewel Macaroni in the Kentucky plant.

"Long cut" and "short cut" presses were operated in a "clean, bright and ventilated environment."

A section of the bulk packing room is shown in this photograph. To acquire the desired length, a band saw was used to cut macaroni and spaghetti.

In 1938 it was Jewel Macaroni Products that sent one Jewel salesman to the New York World's Fair and to the San Francisco Exposition and established 11 district and branch champions. The sales champions were those Jewel men who proved they knew more about Jewel spaghetti, macaroni, and egg noodles by doing the best job of selling those products between October 24 and November 5, 1938.

Jewel indicated in a survey in the late 1920s that over 500,000,000 pounds of Macaroni products were being sold yearly. The company maintained that Jewel macaroni products held their shape, when prepared, and "provided a tender, light, and palatable, delicious nutty taste."

Jewel Enriched "Elbow Macaroni." Someone has written in the word "Shell." Distributed by "JEWEL TEA CO., INC.,, BARRINGTON, ILL." *Hamilton Collection.*

Purchase two boxes of "Jewel Macaroni 'n Cheddar" for $2.38 and receive 25¢ Free Jewel Money. This promotion appeared in 1977.

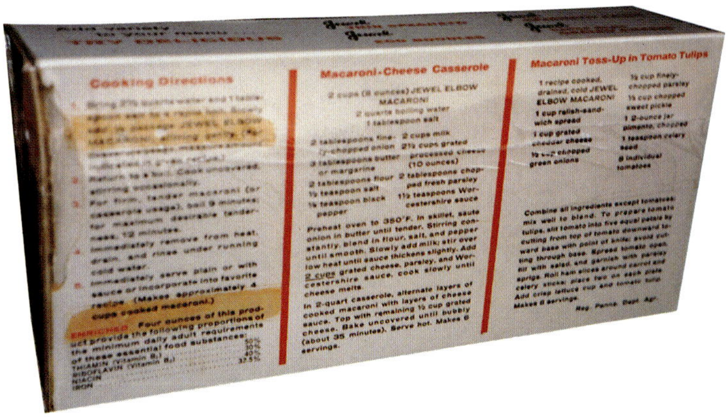

The back panel of "Elbow Macaroni" provided cooking directions and recipes. *Hamilton Collection.*

Jewel egg noodles were manufactured under strict sanitary conditions. Each package contained the equivalent of two eggs, which achieved the natural coloring in the egg noodle.

Jewel Enriched "Elbow Macaroni" and "Spaghetti." *Hamilton Collection.*

The original advertisement for "Jewel Macaroni," "Jewel Spaghetti," and "Jewel Pizza" appeared in a Jewel publication in 1977.

In 1977 Jewel promoted the "MEAL MAKERS CABINET" in the promotional display shown here. In the cabinet were JEWEL Spaghetti, Spaghetti Sauce, Noodles, Macaroni 'N Cheddar, Stuffing Mix, Instant Potatoes, Krazy Salt, Minced Onions, Hot Roll Mix, and Biscuit Mix. This is the original promotional advertisement.

Jewel explained that their spaghetti had a rich flavor because they were made from Durum wheat which contained abundant protein and gluten.

JEWEL Italian Style Pizza Mix came with enough cheese and sauce to make two 12" pizzas. Regularly priced at $1.59. For a limited time Jewel offered them at two for $2.99.

Jewel "Italian Style grated cheese." *Hedges Collection.*

The 1 lb., 5 ounce Jewel "Elbow Macaroni" was distributed by "JEWEL TEA CO., INC., JEWEL PARK BARRINGTON, ILL." *Ferriera Collection.*

The "Spaghetti" was distributed by "JEWEL TEA CO., INC., JEWEL PARK BARRINGTON, ILL." This grocery product appeared on the back page of the "Spring and Summer 1952 Jewel Home Shopping Service" catalog. *Hamilton Collection.*

Jewel "Macaroni" and "Spaghetti" appeared on the back of the "Spring and Summer 1952 Jewel Home Shopping Service" catalog. The back panels provided recipes and the "Mary Dunbar Seal of Approval." Distributed by "JEWEL TEA CO., INC., JEWEL PARK BARRINGTON, ILL." *Hamilton Collection.*

These historical photographs appeared in various Jewel publications promoting a series of recipes using Jewel Macaroni. All Jewel products underwent a series of tests in Jewel's test kitchen. Only those products passing the tests were offered to Mrs. Brown and received the "Mary Dunbar Seal of Approval."

CHAPTER 8
VICTORY PRODUCTS

"V" for Victory was a sign that promoted patriotism and which became an icon, symbolizing support of American troops during World War II.

When a Victory icon appeared on Jewel products, it was designed to save inks and other materials essential to war production. Jewel assured the consumer that the high quality of the product itself was always maintained.

The Jewel Victory Package symbol first appeared on a product in the "Jewel-News," in September of 1942. This single letter from the alphabet became a part of World War II history. There are many items of collectible memorabilia carrying the "V" sign appearing in various color's, patterns, and design. Jewel was not the only organization to understand the importance of this simple letter that was to become an American icon.

After the Japanese attacked Pearl Harbor, Americans throughout the United States plastered the Victory sign everywhere in support of the American troops. As the "V" for Victory sign promoted patriotism, Americans of all ages became involved, many placing banners in windows of their homes that read: "This is a Victory Home." American drivers who took to the roads of the United States often had clipped to a license plate a sticker that read: "Drive for Victory."

The Victory icon appeared everywhere and on everything, from postcards, pins applied to ones clothing, cigarettes, stationery, newspapers and printed literature, to various food products. The list is almost endless.

As Americans focused on the war, the Jewel Tea Company began to conserve materials that were scarce. During this period of history, packaging was affected. This scarcity was not only felt by the Jewel Tea Company, but by many organizations dealing in food products that involved scarce packaging materials.

Jewel's contribution was the appearance of the "Victory Seal" that appeared on a majority of their products. These products are steadily climbing in price and becoming more difficult to locate. Jewel collectors and patriotic collector's both seek them out.

A collection of "Victory Seal" products will take a considerable amount of time. Have patience with these products. "Condition Factor" has no rule here. If it has a "Victory Seal," buy it! *Hamilton Collection.*

"Roasted and Packed By JEWEL TEA CO., INC., JEWEL PARK BARRINGTON, ILL.," this Jewel Blend Coffee box held 1 lb. but has been stamped over in black with an indication of 1-1/2 lb. Note stamp seal in the right-hand corner. This indicated that this package was NOT FULL and reads: "IN ORDER TO HELP DISTRIBUTE COFFEE MORE EQUALLY UNDER GOVERNMENT CONSERVATION PROGRAM, UNTIL PACKAGING MACHINERY CAN BE ALTERED." *Hamilton Collection.*

Note the side panel of the coffee box. Beside the "Victory Seal" it reads: "This 'Victory Package' is designed to save inks and other materials essential to war production. The high quality of the product itself will always be maintained." *Hamilton Collection.*

A 4 ounce cardboard carton of Jewel "Orange Pekoe and Pekoe Black Tea." Packed by "JEWEL TEA CO., INC., JEWEL PARK BARRINGTON, ILL." *Sivils Collection.*

On this Jewel Blend Coffee, only the "Victory Seal" appears. Note that the black stamp indicating NOT FULL does not appear. *Steelman Collection.*

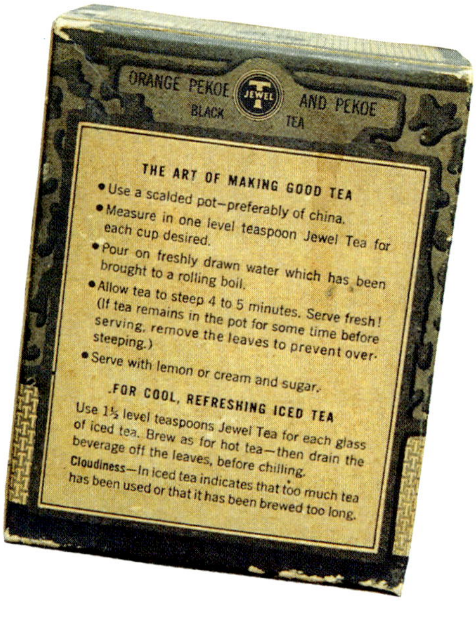

The back panel of the Jewel "Orange Pekoe and Pekoe Black Tea." *Sivils Collection.*

At first you might overlook the "NRA Seal" on this 1 lb. Pure Cocoa tin. It is located in the left hand corner. This tin is marked "JEWEL TEA CO., INC., JEWEL PARK BARRINGTON, ILL." *Hamilton Collection.*

This view of the 1 lb. Pure Cocoa tin gives you a better view of the "NRA Seal." *Hamilton Collection.*

Packed by "JEWEL TEA CO., INC., JEWEL PARK BARRINGTON, ILL.," the exceptional tin held 1 lb. of Jewel Rich Chocolate Cocoa. *Hamilton Collection.*

This 2 lbs., 10 ounce cardboard carton of Jewel "Quick Oats" was distributed by "JEWEL TEA CO., INC., JEWEL PARK BARRINGTON, ILL." *Orr Collection.*

This cardboard cartons held 12 soap filled "Aluminum Cleaner" steel wool pads. Marked "JEWEL TEA CO., INC., JEWEL PARK BARRINGTON, ILL." *Ferriera Collection.*

"Triple Action Cleaners Cleans, Scours, and Polishes." Distributed by "JEWEL TEA CO., INC., JEWEL PARK BARRINGTON, ILL." *Hamilton Collection.*

Distributed by "JEWEL TEA CO., INC., JEWEL PARK BARRINGTON, ILL.," the "Giant Size Drain Cleaner Cleans and Opens Drain Pipes." *Lombard Collection.*

"U-NO-Me" Soap Stretcher. "Makes all soap go farther." *Ferriera Collection.*

A 2 lbs., 5 ounce box of "Pure Gloss Starch," which "Irons to a Satin Smoothness." *Hamilton Collection.*

On the back panel of the "Pure Gloss Starch," directions were provided for use as "Hot or Thin - Quick Starch." *Hamilton Collection.*

The Jewel "French Process Soap" was distributed by "JEWEL TEA CO., INC., JEWEL PARK, BARRINGTON, ILLINOIS." The carton contents list four cakes of soap. *Hamilton Collection.*

This carton contains four cakes of Jewel "Castile Soap" and was distributed by "JEWEL TEA CO., INC., JEWEL PARK BARRINGTON, ILLINOIS." *Hamilton Collection.*

This carton held four cakes of Jewel "Pine Soap" and was distributed by "JEWEL TEA CO., INC., JEWEL PARK BARRINGTON, ILLINOIS." *Hamilton Collection.*

This Jewel "Ginger" has the "Victory Seal." Packed by "JEWEL TEA CO., INC., JEWEL PARK BARRINGTON, ILL." *Lemons Collection.*

Jewel "Baking Powder" was manufactured by "JEWEL TEA CO., INC., JEWEL PARK BARRINGTON, ILL." Holes have been punched into the lid of this container. This was not uncommon! The holes allowed the housewife to use the container as a shaker. *Hamilton Collection.*

The Jewel "Baking Powder" tin has not been damaged. As with any grocery product containing metal, damaged items command lower prices than their counterparts. Many times when lids are missing, another (completely different) lid has been substituted for the original lid. Examine any product before you buy! *Lombard Collection.*

A 2 ounce container of Jewel "Cinnamon" was packed by "JEWEL TEA CO., INC., JEWEL PARK BARRINGTON, ILL." *Hamilton Collection.*

A 5 ounce container of Jewel "Pepper" was "Packed by JEWEL TEA CO., INC., JEWEL PARK BARRINGTON, ILL." *Hamilton Collection.*

During a conversation with her Jewel salesman, in 1943, Myrtle Gutwein, of Dayton, Ohio, mentioned she was looking for employment ... since her husband had gone off to War. Her salesman directed her to the Dayton East 3rd Street headquarters of the Jewel Tea Company, Inc. After completing a special driving test and answering questions, she began a one year career with the Company on June 22, 1943.
Mrs. Gutwein, served the Tipp City and the Vandalia area in old North Dayton. Her first pay check was for $25.50 which surprised her, so she placed a call to the office and learned she had won an award.
Occasionally, Mrs. Gutwein paid, out of her own pocket, the coffee, tea, and rice bill of a single mother and her crippled son, who lived in the country, and she remembered how the War rations effected her supplies, truck, and her customers.
Mrs. Gutwein, who is now 77 years old, enjoys her garden and is an avid bowler, a devoted mother and grandmother. This photograph was taken by a Jewel customer. *Courtesy of Myrtle Gutwein.*

The "NRA" (National Re-Employment Agreement) stamp appeared on various Jewel grocery products during the mid-1930s. It may take time in searching these products out, presently they are hard to locate.

We Do Our Part — Jewel News 1933

"When you by from Jewel you are helping us to do our part. The great wings of the Blue Eagle and the Jewel label protect you from inferior merchandise, cheap products and cut-rate prices for Jewel men and women march with Jewel Quality under the NRA."

20% More Employees

"Jewel is proud of its employment record. During the trying times of the last four years, when hundreds of thousands of men were unemployed, Jewel was actually adding employees. Today (1933) Jewel is employing over 20% more persons than it did at the peak of prosperity in 1929."

We Follow The President — Jewel News 1933

"Jewel is complying with the spirit and the intent of the President's Re-Employment Agreement to the fullest possible extent. By buying from Jewel you also will be aiding business recovery."

Buy More and Buy Now!

"Jewel always strives to save its customers money. Buy NOW and you will save more than you probably could by waiting. The more you buy right now the more quickly will business recover. Order your next premium today. Buy extra Jewel grocery products and you will help largely to speed business recovery."

CHAPTER 9
HISTORICAL MEMORABILIA

Historical Photographs

The selection of historical photographs in this chapter required a lot of time and patience to acquire. Throughout this publication and in both of my previous publications, many historical photographs appeared, courtesy of the Barrington headquarters. The majority of the photographs in this chapter are in the collection of Jewel collectors or private collectors of historical documents and photographs.

Historical photographs and related material are beginning to gain the attention of Jewel collectors. Prepare yourself, these photographs are beginning to escalate in price. Purchase any historical photograph whenever available. In many of these old photographs, Jewel premiums and products can be seen.

Occasionally, I am approached and asked if any of the historical photographs, of the horse/mule and wagon photographs that appeared in both publications, are available for sale. I estimate that 90% of these request are from collectors of historical horse and wagon photographs. I inform them that the majority belonged to Barrington and have been returned to them. I was surprised when an elderly gentleman told me he had, in his own possession, one of the photographs that appeared in my first publication.

First, carefully look the photograph over, with today's high-tech reproduction equipment it is almost impossible to tell the real photograph from a reproduction. Always ask! Most dealers in Jewel Tea are trustworthy ... however, there is always the first time, so prepare yourself.

Most copies that are done through a local camera store are easy to recognize. Most reproduced photographs will have a Kodak™ mark printed on the reverse side. Always look! There is nothing wrong with purchasing a copy or reproduced photograph, many Jewel collectors, having old photographs, have them reproduced for resale. These collectors are trustworthy and will first draw your attention to the fact that the photographs that they are selling are reproductions.

It is not uncommon to find large Jewel photographs that have been professionally framed. Most of these depict events such as Jewel picnics and large business functions conducted by Jewel headquarters in various parts of the United States.

Condition factor is not important. Old photographs provide an abundance of historical information and data. I have seen, and have in my own collection, photographs dated by the photographer of the event. This practice was not uncommon. In this chapter there are a couple of these photographs.

If you should have any old Jewel photograph in your collection, I would like to hear from you. I may be reached through the publisher of this book.

M.H. Karker was Jewel's president until 1942. He was succeeded by Franklin Jerome Lunding, Jewel's president from 1942 until 1950. In 1950 George L. Clements took over the presidency. This photograph was purchased in St. Charles, Illinois along with numerous other historical photographs that appear in this chapter. *Housel Collection.*

Jewel Vice President, C.W. Kaylor, was general chairman of the 1938 convention held in Grand Beach, Michigan. This convention was one of the most successful conventions ever held in the company's history. *Housel Collection.*

Mrs. J.O. Love is shown here, the wife of J.O. "Daddy" Love. Mr. Love began his 20 year career with the Jewel Tea Company, Inc. in 1918 and worked directly out of the Chicago location without help from assistant managers. Later in his career he moved to Great Bend, Kansas and took charge of a one-wagon Jewel branch. When J.O. Love signed his first contract with the Jewel Tea Company, he crossed out the clause stating that he would work for promotion and inserted that he would "work for success." Jewel President Karker paid tribute to Love for his nearly 21 years of Jewel service. J.O. Love spoke highly of his wife and often said: "A wife can make a job, but she can also tear it up. She can be 100% of the job. If a man has cooperation he is apt to succeed, but a few succeed without cooperation." I purchased a box of paper documents and old photographs at an antique show and sale in Atlanta, Georgia. This was one of those photographs. *Author's Collection.*

Dated 1956, this photograph was taken at the corner of State Street and Randolph, in Chicago, Illinois. Note the billboard above the Walgreen Drug Store advertising "Jewel Food Stores" and "JEWEL HOME SERVICE COAST TO COAST." *Author's Collection.*

This photograph represented 160,000,000 cups of coffee that arrived in Barrington by train in 1938. *Housel Collection.*

An eight week supply, totaling 3,531,000 pounds of green coffee, was received at the roasting facilities in Barrington on August 20, 1938. This shipment filled 26,750 bags that were carried from South America via five different steamers, then transferred to 107 freight cars destined for Barrington. Once roasted, ground, and brewed into coffee, this supply of coffee could actually have floated one of the 12,000 ton steamers during its course between South America and the United States.

In 1938, Barrington received a thirteen freight car shipment of brooms from the Merkle Broom Company of Paris, Illinois. This shipment contained enough brooms to supply every man, woman, and child in Alaska.

The Aluminum Goods Manufacturing Company supplied Jewel with 25 carloads of aluminum premiums by the end of 1938. This shipment included 100,000 jelly roll pans, 100,000 handy kitchens sets, and regular requirements of teakettles, double boilers, combination utility cookers, and covered kettles.

Thirty-three carloads, from the Federal Glass Company in Columbus, Ohio, delivered a shipment of seven-piece cereal sets to the Barrington facility.

In 1938, Jewel shipped groceries and premiums from suppliers in more than 20 states to branches in 27 states, aiding in the transportation industry. Jewel owned a fleet of 1,650 automobiles. With the constant operation of those automobiles, thousands of dollars were put into operation for the purchase of gasoline, oil, tires, parts, and maintenance.

This historical photograph is marked "Jewel Tea Company Picnic May 31, 1936 Grand Rapids, Michigan." *Spayde Collection.*

Baskets

The 1950s metal frame/fiberboard Jewel salesman carrier "A Better Place To Trade." There are various Jewel baskets available to collectors. See "JEWEL TEA Sales and Houseware Collectibles." *Hamilton Collection.*

The opposite side of the 1950s carrier, marked "JEWEL TEA CO. INC." This carrier measures 12" wide x 24" long x 7" high. At one end was a section, which is missing, that held salesman's ledgers, catalogs, and various supplies. *Hamilton Collection.*

Jewel Salesman H.M. King with his Jewel basket. *Wilson Collection.*

E.F. Moore of Toledo, Ohio with his Jewel basket and various Jewel products. *Wilson Collection.*

The hammered aluminum salesman's carrier, shown here, measures 15" wide x 24" long x 8-1/2" high. The height with the handle is 13" to the center, at one end was a 2" compartment that held the salesman's supplies. This carrier was purchased from an estate auction of a former Jewel Salesman. *Lombard Collection.*

Wilmington, Delaware's Jewel route salesman Paul Camp with his Jewel basket. Note the coffee maker. *Wilson Collection.*

Note the West Coast Coffee in the Jewel basket of George Spielvogel. *Wilson Collection.*

Route salesman R.W. Baum with his Jewel basket. *Wilson Collection.*

Personnel

Route salesman Bob Hill with a Jewel order for customer Mrs. M.O. Braute of Reynolds, North Dakota. Mrs. Braute's order included six dozen Jewel-Jells, 30 Baking Powders, and 10 Imitation Vanilla Extracts. The order totaled $38.72. *Wilson Collection.*

Jewel Tea salesman J.R. Benson. *Wilson Collection.*

Jewel route salesman J.F. O'Kelley. *Andrews Collection.*

R.E. Bigley of Pittsburgh, Pennsylvania, is seen here with his stack of Jewel Biscuit Flour. *Wilson Collection.*

Waverly, New York route salesman J.L. Wade. *Wilson Collection.*

In 1938, Oswego, New York was served by Jewel route salesman Herb Barnes. *Andrews Collection.*

In 1938, Jewel route salesman C.H. Noll was photographed with a Jewel Blend Coffee and a Modern 9-cup Drip Coffee Maker. The 9-cup Dripper also fit the large Hall China Coffee Server. Jewel also offered a 4-cup Drip Coffee Maker. This Dripper also fits the Hall China Teapot. Both Dripper's are highly sought by collectors. *Housel Collection.*

Jewel route salesman F.P. Scott pictured with his supply of Jewel Blend Coffee. *Wilson Collection.*

Jewel route salesman R.W. Gottshall, shown with a supply of Jewel products. *Wilson Collection.*

No information was available about this historical photograph. *Wilson Collection.*

Jewel Vice President, C.W. Kaylor, is shown on the left with Jewel route salesman Leonard Nease of Pittsburg, Kansas. Vice President Kaylor was, at one time, supervisor of this Kansas route. Photograph dated 1937. *Wilson Collection.*

In 1937 Corbin, Kentucky was served by Jewel route salesman C.C. Lewis. Lewis believed that a clean Jewel car was essential to good advertising and coffee sales. *Wilson Collection.*

H.E. Byram was the "big urn" salesman when he averaged 455 pounds of coffee per week during the 1938 period. Most coffee urns were sold to church societies along with Jewel Coffee. "Church women praised Jewel Coffee as one of the best and most economical coffees used." See "Coffee, Tea and Cocoa Chapter" for "SPECIAL HOTEL AND RESTAURANT COFFEE." *Wilson Collection.*

Special Events

Mrs. W.P. Kay of Cartersville, Georgia had acquired 182 pieces of Hall Autumn Leaf China and Jewel premiums. Mrs. Kay had shopped the Jewel Way since 1927. Shown with her neighbor, Mrs. Stella Strickland and J.M. James. *Private Collection.*

A complete set of Hall Autumn Leaf, together with many Jewel premiums, purchased by Mrs. Marybelle McClelland Rhodes. Where is this collection today? *Private Collection.*

In 1938, one of the popular establishments in Lakeland, Florida was "The Fountainette." The owner, Mr. W.B. Slates, used 6 to 9 pounds of Jewel Coffee per week. Fresh coffee was made hourly until midnight. *Wilson Collection.*

Route salesman, E.W. Price of Iowa Falls, Iowa presents his wife a Universal mixer-beater. *Wilson Collection.*

Jewel salesman R.L. Krump and Mrs. B.H. Gibbons of Des Soto, Missouri. Mrs. Gibbons had been a Jewel customer since 1916. *Wilson Collection.*

Harold and Charles Wortz; no other information is available. *Wilson Collection.*

Shown in the top photograph is: L.E. Burch, T.B. Bly, and W.J. Kelly. Note Jewel Coffee products and Hall Autumn Leaf coffee maker. Lower photograph, front row: R.F. Thiry and G.H. Dyer. Back row, l - r: E.L. Uhler, Sol Lenhart, Erma Oswald, Charles Hopkins, and Paul Mertz. The historical photograph is dated 1938 on the back. *Wilson Collection.*

Miss Jose Bolin, center, with A.B. Romer and R.E. Nagler in this historical photograph. Miss Bolin began her career in 1933 as a stenographer for the Jewel Tea Company. *Wilson Collection.*

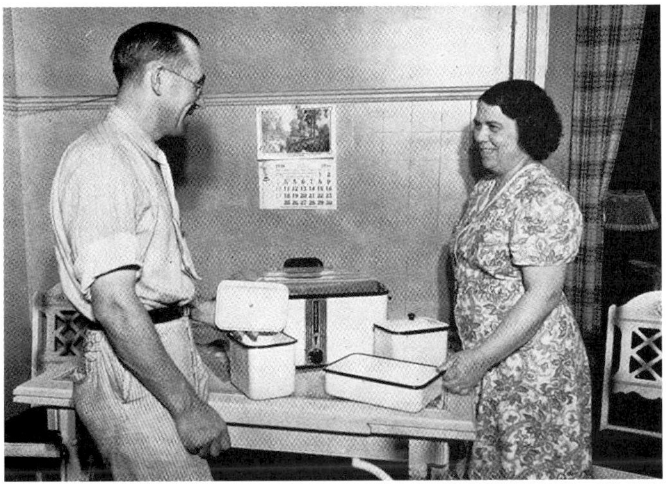

In 1938, route salesman Fred Englemann of Dayton, Ohio won the electric roaster for his wife. *Housel Collection.*

A group of Jewel route salesmen in Dayton, Ohio: R.R. Lunsford, E.F. Smith, W.C. Smith, Donald Gross, E.H. Morlock, G.E. Pendergast, C.M. Britton, G.B. Motley, J.H. Herby, and J.K. Smith. *Wilson Collection.*

Grand Rapids route salesmen C.L. Fisher, B.W. Harris, and R.G. Adams. *Wilson Collection.*

This long historical photograph is marked "Jewel Tea Co. Annual Picnic Danville, Ill 1930." This may have been taken at the Douglas Park. As a child I attended numerous family events held in this park. *Author's Collection.*

Note the logo behind the gentleman on the right. This appeared on numerous Jewel vehicles during the 1930s. This historical photograph is marked Danville, Illinois. No other information appears. *Wilson Collection.*

This 1930s historical photograph was taken in Barrington, Illinois. The men are: W.D. Kilner, H.A. Haeher, F.J. Letzner, Ed Avery, H.J. Starzynski, and W.M. Sweitzer. *Wilson Collection.*

Dated 1937, R.E. McGlaughlin and his father–from Columbus, Ohio–had driven to the Barrington headquarters. During this era a guide would show visitors through the Barrington plant. The 1930 Columbus city directory lists "The Jewel Tea Co., at 1187 Cleveland Avenue Columbus, Ohio." The manager was J.S. Ballentine. *Author's Collection.*

Mrs. Julia Goddard of the Jewel Homemakers' Institute with coffee experts J.A. Moran, J.E. Dawe, Mrs. Goddard, H.W. Powell, F.L. Whatley, and G.G. Williams. *Wilson Collection.*

In 1938, Anna Malmquist was the first woman in the history of Jewel to receive a five star pin. Shown with R.D. Spencer, Carol Larson, Cora Fremming, and Mrs. Malmquist. President Karker said of Mrs. Malmquist, "You have been one of the steadying influences and inspirations in the Twin Cities and many of the men of that branch owe a portion of their success to your patience and encouragement. I hope that your five star pin may be a constant reminder of happy associations during the years which you have made more pleasant and productive for so many others." Mrs. Malmquist retired from Jewel during this period. *Housel Collection.*

Arriving in Barrington, in 1939, were, from left to right: Mrs. J.B. Crockett, J.B. Crockett (Manager), Milbrey Crockett (sister), Mr. T.O. Crockett, Jr., (brother) and Mrs. T.O. Crockett, Jr. J.B. Crockett joined the Jewel family in 1936. *Wilson Collection.*

In 1938, J.G. Miller had an order of $90.58 from the St. Joseph's Hospital, Sioux City, Iowa. The order included 36 biscuit flours, 36 quick oats, 36 spices, 36 desserts, and 40 cartons of rice. Mr. Miller is shown with his family. *Wilson Collection.*

Office and store workers in Washington, D.C., left to right: E.J. Maxwell, W.E. Mills, Mary Alcock, E.P. Broderick, Martha Rothrock, George Julian, Marie Thornton, J.L. Moore, Evelyn Scott, A.E. Shrout, Dorothy Harvey, and F.J. Buncie. *Wilson Collection.*

In 1918, G.B. Jackson joined the Jewel family. Shown here during a visit to Barrington in 1938, Mr. and Mrs. Jackson, with daughters, Marjorie and Mary, traveled from California. *Wilson Collection.*

Sioux City, Iowa route man D.J. Layson with his wife and their children, taken during a visit to Barrington. *Wilson Collection.*

Harrisburg, Illinois route salesman S.V. Marvel, shown here with his son, father, wife, and mother. Taken in Barrington, Illinois in approximately 1937. *Wilson Collection.*

Season's Greetings

Jewel's Season Greetings appeared on the cover of "The New Jewel," December 10, 1938. This photograph was purchased in Kankakee, Illinois. *Andrews Collection.*

These Engraved Christmas Greeting Cards are marked "JEWEL TEA CO., INC. NEW YORK — CHICAGO." Enclosed was a particular selection with envelopes to match. *Hamilton Collection.*

This cardboard carton held "Jewel Assortment Christmas Greeting Cards." Their slogan was, "Scatter Sunshine with Greetings Cards." *Orr Collection.*

CHAPTER 10
CARING FOR YOUR PRODUCTS

Condition Factor

Jewel grocery products in mint condition are those free from rust, scratches, blemishes, and which still retain 100% of the original wrapper, label, and/or carton. Lids must be intact and free of any blemish. Those products in mint condition demand more than those damaged or of poor quality. Full containers are in demand over those that are empty.

Products from the early era of the Jewel Tea Company are highly sought after. Often referred to as rare tin pieces, these items are worth more than common pieces of later years. Designs currently popular are those that bear the "SKI-RO" logo (SKI-RO was an abbreviation of "Skiff-Ross," after the company's founders) or the "Victory" sign from World War II.

Sometimes the condition factor does not play an important part with those early products. I have seen early Jewel products in poor condition demand higher prices than those of later years and better condition.

Price is what you as a collector find necessary to pay or are willing to pay. What is high to one person may be low to another and vice versa. Prices differ in different regions of the country.

Intricate design, shape, labels, and unusual sizes help to increase value and demand. Jewel packaging often underwent changes, but the product remained the same. Remember collecting is an INVESTMENT!

The outward aspect of a Jewel cardboard container is important. Look for containers that are not crushed, torn, ragged in appearance, or on which the cover has faded. Cardboard containers in damaged condition hinder the price in much the same way as damaged metal or tin does.

Examine the product carefully. "Distributed by" means that someone else manufactured the product. "Manufactured by" indicates that the product was produced by Jewel.

Caring For Your Products

It is wise to remember that Jewel products in mint condition demand a higher price in the secondary market than those of poor condition. Purchase only those of mint quality, unless you feel that you can not live without it.

I recently spoke with a dealer of old advertisement tins and products who suggest applying a light coat of good car wax to the surface of a metal tin. Using a cotton ball or Q-tip, apply the wax in small sections, but never apply pressure. Repeat the process until the surface has been covered — this results in a protection against the elements that may damage your products, as the elements can damage your car. Wipe residue off with a soft cloth. Do not apply water or submerge products into water, this will cause rusting to continue. It may be wise to first experiment on a worthless tin. Remember, practice makes prefect!

On severely rusted areas of a metal product, apply a light coat of WD-40, available at most hardware stores. Using a Q-tip, gently apply WD-40 to the effected area of the product. Wipe the residue off with soft cloth. Repeat this process as often as needed.

Keep an eye on your products for the invasion of insects. You may not know what lives or is growing beneath the lid of your product. Never consume an old product and keep old products out of the reach of small children.

Jewel bottles that have a cloudy coating inner or outer surface may be submerged in a product call "LIME-A-WAY"®. Be very careful with this product and keep it away from children and from your eyes. Place the bottle into a shallow pan and cover with "LIME-A-WAY"®; it is wise to leave the bottle submerged for six to eight weeks. Check occasionally and add more liquid if needed. This product can be poured directly into the cloudy bottle, shaken, and placed out of the way for some time. Check the bottle occasionally and, once again, if liquid seems low, add some more. Do NOT submerge bottles or jars with paper labels — this will remove and cause harm to those labels.

In this publication, you have seen numerous products that have been sealed for protection. I am totally against this practice of placing cardboard products inside plastic bags or wrapping them in any of the other various products that are readily available. If moisture gets into this wrap/plastic covering, your product is ill-fated. Seek professional assistance in caring for any products, either metal or cardboard. There are firms that will professionally wrap advertisement articles and products.

Note the dull tarnished appearance of the "Jewel 1 lb. Baking Powder" tin. Purchased at a local antique show, this product was "Manufactured by JEWEL TEA CO., INC., Jewel Park Barrington, Ill." *Private Collection.*

Here is a side view of the Jewel Baking Powder tin. The top and bottom have rusted areas and a mottled pattern of rust spots appears on each side of the container. This container is worth only a fraction compared to those in mint condition. *Private Collection.*

The same Jewel Baking Powder tin after a thorough cleaning. Remember, it is impossible to restore the full luster to an old grocery product. I appreciate the assistance of Ralph and Linda Miller, dealers in tins and advertisement memorabilia, for their assistance in cleaning this tin. *Private Collection.*

Have you ever acquired a tin and noticed holes punched in the lid? It is a known fact that both adults and children often recycled grocery products. With a sharp object, holes were punched in the lids to be used a shakers (see Chapter 8) or to provide fresh air for insects gathered on evening expeditions. In 1932, a Jewel customer sent her original household hint to Mary Dunbar. Read what this Quincy, Illinois customer did with Jewel peanut butter, mayonnaise, and mustard jars.

The discoloration on this 5-oz. Jewel Cinnamon container influences the price. The original brilliant color can never be restored. *Private Collection.*

"THE IDEA EXCHANGE"

Send your original household hints to Mary Dunbar. The best, most practical group from each month's contribution will be published. To win, comply with the rules.

RULES FOR THE CONTEST

1. $1.00 will be paid for each idea published. 2. Recipes are not accepted as ideas. 3. Send only one idea for each contest. 4. A new contest opens with the distribution of each issue of the Jewel News. 5. Do not expect letters of acknowledgment.

I save much time by covering my fruit jars with paper bags after washing and before putting them away. Mrs. Etta Woolslayer, 2527 Lase, Beaver Falls, Pa.

I save the "core" from my Jewel Wax Paper Roll and use it to wrap my doilies around. This keeps them from wrinkling in the drawers. Mrs. B. R. Simions, Lake Zurich, Illinois.

When making either hot or iced tea, I add a little bit of cinnamon for a new delicious flavor. Mrs. Roger N. Hutton, R. No. 2, West Nashville, Tenn.

When putting paint away for future use pour a thin layer of paraffine over the top to prevent a hard crust from forming. Mrs. W. R. Finley, Box 104, Riderwood P. O., Riderwood, Md.

An attractive toy chest may be made by hinging the cover of a box and covering with cretonne to match the draperies. Mrs. W. E. Bolton, Macon Rd., Griffin, Ga.

I start cucumber and tomato plants in paper cups and transplant cup and all in the garden. The cups will rot away by the time the roots need more room. Mrs. B. Andrews, R. R. No. 6, Florence Sta., Omaha, Nebr.

I use paper napkins for shelf covering. It is so easy to remove one, should something be spilled. Mrs. K. E. Bartoo, 104 Edmonston Road, Hyattsville, Md.

I use empty Peanut Butter jars for many things. For instance strips of bandage ready for use can be kept clean and ready in the bathroom by storing in jars. Mrs. B. F. Roberts, 611 So. Virginia Ave., Marion, Ill.

When I want to carry two pies any place I take the rack of my Mary Dunbar cooker and place it in the cake safe and put one pie below the rack and the other on the rack. They can be carried in safety. —Mrs. M. E. Garver, 113 W. Friendship St., Medina, Ohio.

I find a grapefruit knife very handy for removing cup cakes or muffins from tins. Mrs. G. B. Miltenberger, 219 1st N. W. St., Jackson, Missouri.

One of those spongy "kneeling pads" keeps baby from slipping if placed in the high chair. It clings to the chair and is soft to sit on. Mrs. Roy Q. Young, Mandan, N. D.

A convenient bill holder can be made by removing the trigger from an ordinary mouse trap and hanging the trap on the wall. The spring holds the bills in place. Mrs. R. F. Narthey, 668 N. Idlewild St., Memphis, Tenn.

I use pure peroxide to remove fruit, tea or cocoa stains from white table linen or clothes. Dr. Daisy E. Barnhart, 243 W. Main St., Ligonier, Penn.

I find it convenient to make up a large cookie recipe once a week. I divide the dough in portions flavoring one with spice, another with nuts and raisins and leave one portion plain. Then roll the dough into rounds, wrap in wax paper and leave in the ice box until ready to cut and bake on a moment's notice. This saves much time in the long run. Mrs. C. Desmond, 3136 131st St., Toledo, Ohio.

I find that my Jewel Silverware never tarnishes when I store it by wrapping in cloth and putting a few drops of camphor on the roll. It saves much time. Mrs. E. J. Morey, R. No. 5, Pittsburg, Kansas.

A Marion, Illinois customer shared her household hint using empty Jewel Peanut Butter jars in the original "Idea Exchange."

"THE IDEA EXCHANGE"

Send your original household hints to Mary Dunbar. The best, most practical group from each month's contribution will be published. To win, comply with the rules.

RULES FOR THE CONTEST

1. $1.00 will be paid for each idea published. 2. Recipes are not accepted as ideas. 3. Send only one idea for each contest. 4. A new contest opens with the distribution of each issue of the Jewel News. 5. Do not expect letters of acknowledgment.

I paint a Jewel peanut butter, mayonnaise, or mustard jar to harmonize with the bathroom and cut a slit in the top for dropping in used razor blades. Mrs. A. W. Day, 722 North 24th St., Quincy, Ill.

When making children's dresses, fasten a piece of the material to the inside seam so that you will have material later on for mending of the same color as the dress. Mrs. Wm. Shawhan, 321 Vine Street, Leavenworth, Kans.

A metal kitchen stool can be made more comfortable by making a padded seat covered with oil cloth. Mrs. T. J. Dee, 4707 Old York Road, Baltimore, Md.

To remove blood stains soak in cold salt water, wash in warm water and Grano and boil. Mrs. L. D. Pierce, 2509 Ave. L, Fort Madison, Ia.

When making biscuits or short cake, I always roll my dough thin, then fold in half and roll lightly again. When baked they are easy to split. Mrs. W. M. Gierhart, 725 W. 12th Street, Pueblo, Colo.

To make your boiled icing creamy and prevent it from cracking, add a teaspoon of Jewel cornstarch or flour to each cup of sugar before boiling. Mrs. R. Downey, 305 W. Pearl Street, Batesville, Ind.

By using the three inset pans of my Mary Dunbar Cooker in my cake safe, I have an ideal picnic lunch box. There is room left at the top for a pie, small cakes or sandwiches. Mrs. Jas. T. Johnston, Drawer F, Springdale, Ark.

To remove a fresh fruit stain, hold cloth tightly across basin or tub and pour boiling hot water through stain. If stain is old, tie up with a little cream of tartar, put in cold water and bring to a boil. Mrs. J. A. Oberman, 903 Liberty Street, Aurora, Ill.

I find that pastry shells are nicer when baked on the bottom of a layer-cake pan instead of a pie plate. When baked turn right-side-up and fill. Mrs. Hazel Ledley, 1507 De Sota Road, Morrell Park, Md.

Place a piece of cheesecloth under the grating of a cold air register. It saves time in cleaning and many things from becoming lost. Mrs. Dan Powell, 157 Atlantic N. W., Warren, O.

Sheets made with hem the same depth at each end will wear much longer, as one end is not then always in the same position. Mrs. Arthur B. Metcalf, 4302 Leland Street, Chevy Chase, Md.

Covers for gowns and coats made from pillow tubing are inexpensive and easy to launder. Lay a hanger on material and mark shape with pencil for the top. Work a buttonhole for the hook of the hanger to pass through and hem bottom. Mrs. Fred C. McGill, 98 North Oakland Avenue, Sharon, Pa.

To break nut meats quickly, I place them in a paper bag and roll with a rolling pin several times. Ruth E. Stewart, 612 Spring Street, Latrobe, Pa.

When lemons are dry and hard, put them into a hot oven for a few minutes to freshen. Mrs. Howard Johnson, Stambough, Mich.

I apply a little floor wax to the woodwork around the knobs of drawers and cupboards. This restores the luster and protects these areas from soiled fingers. Mrs. Shondell, 1205 Jefferson Avenue, Defiance, O.

"THE IDEA EXCHANGE"

Send your original household hints to Mary Dunbar. The best, most practical group from each month's contribution will be published. To win, comply with the rules.

RULES FOR THE CONTEST

1. $1.00 will be paid for each idea published. 2. Recipes are not accepted as ideas. 3. Send only one idea for each contest. 4. A new contest opens with the distribution of each issue of the Jewel News. 5. Do not expect letters of acknowledgment.

I cut the tops and bottoms out of empty Jewel Baking Powder cans, to use as forms for chilling ice box cookies. It makes a nice, square cookie, and the dough can be easily pushed out for thin slicing when chilled. Mrs. E. H. Starkman, Box 1174, Ely, Minnesota.

For an easy way of making sure that each curtain tie-back is fastened at the same height on the window, I pull the shades down to the point desired and fasten the curtains in line with the bottom of the shade. Miss Mary Stainton, 1303 W. 6th St., Ontario, Calif.

We find an old fashioned nut cracker makes an ideal opener for the bottles that use screw tops instead of corks. Mrs. E. H. Wilson, 312 Shuart Ave., Syracuse, New York.

When clothes lines have become soiled and stained, I make them like new again by taking them down, soaking in a pan of cold water in which Jewel Grano is dissolved, then bring to boil with Jewel Ammonia in the water, and finally rinse in clear water and starching with Jewel Gloss Starch. Mrs. Gritsko, 308 E. Broad St., Nanticoke, Pa.

I find my Mary Dunbar Cooker splendid for frying chickens that are past the frying stage. This cooker gets them nice and tender, and browns them well, too. Mrs. Isaac B. Bell, Alta Vista, Va.

Oil of pennyroyal left uncovered at night in the sleeping room will drive out mosquitoes. Miss Blanche Wright, 125 Church St., Staunton, Va.

I feel that silk things wear longer if rinsed in vinegar water before the final rinse. Miss Florence Smith, Rt. No. 4, Box 1, Fredonia, Kan.

Rag rugs straighten out better if you put starch in the last rinse water. I empty the kettle of starch that I have used for other things into the rinse for rugs at the end of the washing. Mrs. L. H. Eckerman, 5433 43rd Ave., So., Minneapolis, Minn.

To avoid scratching table tops, etc., I glue pieces cut from old felt hats to the vases, bases of lamps, ash trays, etc. Lucille Cowger, Bainbridge, Ind.

A tablespoon of vinegar in hot water removes the onion or fish odor from kettles in which these foods have been cooked. Mrs. T. G. Dayman, 525 Trenton St., Orlando, Fla.

I keep a sheet of sandpaper on hand to use when opening Mason jars. One can get a better grip on the lid. Mrs. A. Wheeler, 1009 Oakland Ave., Mt. Vernon, Ill.

Anything such as a piece of bread or a match, placed between the teeth so as to allow breathing through the mouth instead of the nose, while peeling, dicing, or slicing onions, will prevent the eyes from watering. Mrs. Anthony Cetinske, 312 Walton Ave., Dayton, O.

When making pastry shells for individual pies or for serving vegetables, I make them on the bottoms of jell molds. This furnishes an attractive shape which is nicer for parties. Mrs. Elmer L. Miller, 312 A. Prospect Ave., Amarelto, Tex.

This idea may be old, but is worth repeating occasionally for the young housewife who does not know that a pinch of Jewel Baking Powder added to mashed potatoes makes them white, fluffy and delightful. Mrs. Frank Reber, 1012 Montrose Ave., Nashville, Tenn.

I like to sprinkle Jewel Powdered Ammonia Compound on my carpets before sweeping. It seems to brighten the colors and remove grease spots. Mrs. C. F. Watrous, 1519 Elwood Ave., Glenwood, N. C.

A Ely, Minnesota customer cut the tops and bottoms from empty Jewel Baking Powder cans. Read what she did, in 1932, with those sections in "THE IDEA EXCHANGE."

An oxcoptional "Jowol Brand Coffoo" tin, micsing a small portion of tho original label. The "Diamond" logo that appears on this tin appeared in a Jewel publication in 1916. The missing label particles will not effect the selling price of this tin. *Private Collection.*

The next time you acquire such an item, remember the loving hands that might have held it or the small child trying to punch holes with an ice pick. Every item acquired in such conditions has a story behind it and this story, be it known, may be worth more than what you paid for the item.

This Jewel "COFFEE" carton has been through a great deal. It served its purpose, survived years of being moved, and then ends up in a collection. The "Bulls eye" logo on this colorful carton was introduced in approximately 1921 - 1922. In this condition, I suggest you purchase it, you may never have another opportunity. *Private Collection.*

The opposite side of the Jewel Brand Coffee tin; as you can see most of the original label is intact, except around the lid. This is normal. *Private Collection.*

Beware

The Jewel Tea Company, like many other companies, placed their name before the public as much as possible. Personally, I believe if it says "JEWEL T" it is from this historical company. Jewel was aware that as long as their name was before the public they would be secure as a business. Customers were also aware of the name Jewel when items were imprinted with the famous "JEWEL T" name or a tag bearing a period logo. Jewel made the public notice this name.

It is not uncommon to find products from this historical company marked only "JEWEL T" or "JEWEL TEA" with no other indication marking. Many collectors do not care if it's from the Jewel Tea Company, as long as it says "JEWEL" they are happy! It is your own personal taste when collecting advertisement products.

As in most cases there are exceptions to the rule. You will see both "JEWEL" and "JEWELL." Be careful and make a wise decision!

I suggest that you read any available material on this historical company. Before you purchase a grocery product, examine the product carefully. You may overlook a dent or a defect, not discovering it until you have it home — then it's to late. Remember, many dealers have a no return policy.

Beware of dealers subtracting a 10% restocking fee, which is not uncommon. This fees applies to orders being returned by the purchaser who has purchased through MAIL ORDER. Always inquire before you buy from any newsletter publication listing.

Remember, it is almost impossible to find missing parts, be they lids, caps or labels. Many homemakers reused glass jars for other purposes. When Mrs. Brown thoroughly washed the jar, she also removed the label. Such is the case of the jars shown here.

A milk glass container, missing the paper labels. The only indication of the Jewel Tea Company, Inc. is on the lid. See "Chapter 6." *Private Collection.*

This green glass container is missing its paper labels. The only indication of the Jewel Tea Company, Inc. is on the lid. See "Chapter 6." *Private Collection.*

Carefully examine the following; remember that these items pictured are not from the Jewel Tea Company, but they are still collectible and are found in many collections. Either having one "L" (Jewel) or a double "LL" (Jewell), many collectors search for related items not directly associated with the historical Jewel company — that is their personal taste.

Fruit Jars

It is not uncommon to find three different sizes of fruit jar marked "JEWELL JAR." These jars are machine made of clear glass with glass lid and screw band. Another fruit jar will say "JEWEL JAR MADE IN CANADA." This clear, machine made jar, with glass lid and band, is also available in three sizes. There are four sizes available in "Canadian JEWEL MADE IN CANADA." Like the other fruit jar, these are machine made with glass lids and metal bands. The lids are embossed with the print "MADE IN JEWEL CANADA." These fruit jar has no connection with the historical Jewel Tea Company. They are sought by Jewel collectors and referred to as a "Go-Along."

In 1927, the Jewel Tea Company, Inc. offered "Jewel Fruit Jar Rubbers," listed as Item No. S-1161 and priced at 10¢. See "The Jewel Tea Company. Its History and Products" page 139. In a historical photograph appearing in an issue of the Jewel News, fruit jars can be seen in a section of the photograph.

Jewell Dairy

Most states had or even have a "Jewel" or "Jewell" Dairy. In the Ohio area, products from such a location can be found. Shown here, a 1 quart "Jewell Ice Cream" cardboard carton. Marked "JEWELL ICE CREAM & MILK CO., MT. VERNON, OHIO." Many dairy products from this firm can be found bearing their name. *Edelman Collection.*

Various sizes in "Jewel" and "Jewell" cream bottles can be found. Two variations in size and design, these are marked with the double "LL." Both are still collectible among Jewel Tea and milk bottle collectors, but they are not in big demand. Also available are a variety of milk bottles and cottage cheese containers, both in clear glass and, occasionally, with colored printing on clear glass. *Edelman Collection.*

Pure Distilled Water

From the "JEWELL WATER CO. 555-57 W. Fulton St., Chicago, Ill., PH: Central 6-0947-48." This bottle of "JEWELL PURE DISTILLED WATER" was found in a vacant building in Hoopeston, Illinois. Note carefully the double "LL." This Distilled Water bottle has no connection with the Jewel Tea Company, Inc. *Author's Collection.*

Jewel Collar Tins

In my first book "The Jewel Tea Company, Its History and Products," I assumed this metal container held tea. This is not so!

This 3" x 4-1/2" x 14" metal container held men's collars, that part of a garment that encircles the neck. The paper labels on these tins indicate men's neck sizes. Although not associated with the "Jewel Tea Company, Inc.," they are still collectible. *Hamilton Collection.*

Jewel Buttons

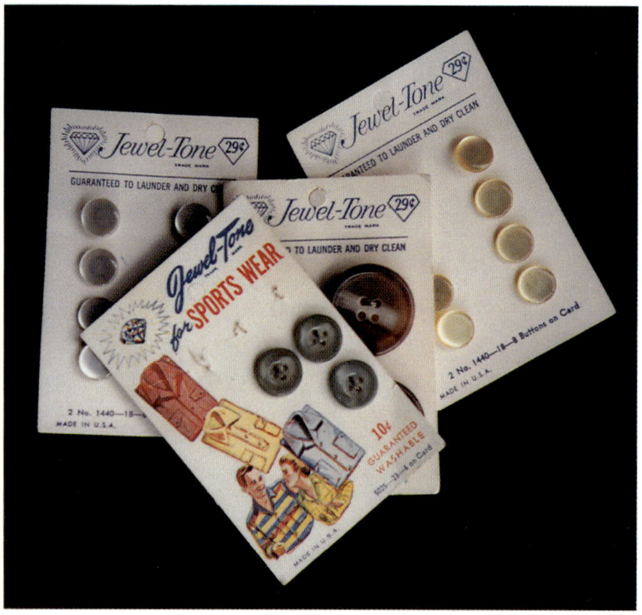

This collection of "Jewel-Tone" buttons is not associated with the Jewel Tea Company, Inc. But they are collectible! *Housel Collection.*

Jewel did provide various sewing items, very few have any indication of this company printed on their surfaces.

The Jewel Food Stores offered an oval cardboard needle case marked "Jewel Food Stores" on the front; on the reverse side is printed "Welcome ... TO YOUR NEW JEWEL ... We Are Happy to Serve You and Are Looking Forward to Serving You Again." Printed inside across the seam is "JAPAN." Another variation of this needle case has the front marked "Jewel Food Stores," and on one section of the back is printed "MADE AND PRINTED IN WEST GERMANY," the center section is printed "WELCOME TO YOUR NEW JEWEL PLEASE ACCEPT THIS IMPORTED GIFT FROM YOUR JEWEL FRIENDS," and on the right section it is printed "FRANK KRAUS, LOS ANGELES 36." Most collectors have examples which are marked "JAPAN."

The Jewel News and Jewel catalogs offered a selection of items. Jewel Patterns could be ordered directly from: "The Jewel Pattern Bureau, P.O. Box 6710, Chicago 80, Illinois."

A Pattern Service By Ruth Rutledge was available by writing "JEWEL PATTERN SERVICE, 160 FIFTH AVE., NEW YORK CITY." This service was handled by other companies, Jewel only offered this service under the famous name.

JEWEL PATTERN SERVICE

By Ruth Rutledge

For Wee Maidens

A cute dress is this little one-piece affair for that important girl of the family of 2, 4 or 6 years. It's a model too that will provide a basis for many variations.

For instance, there's the original model in French blue linen with white yoke and cuffs and tiny blue button trim.

Then too, Jane must have a frock of dimity print. This one is fetching in red and white with tiny dot pattern with plain white dimity trim.

For real honest-to-goodness hardy wear, there's gingham, poplins, pique and cotton broadcloth.

Style No. 3191 takes but 1¾ yards of 35-inch material with ½ yard of 32-inch contrasting for the 4 year size.

Pattern price 15 cents in stamps or coin (coin preferred).

The new Summer Fashion Magazine is 10 cents. Summer Fashion Magazine ready May 10th.

3191

How to Order

To order either the fashion book or the patterns, address Jewel Pattern Service, 200 Fifth Ave., New York City. Give all the information called for in the coupon and enclose coin wrapped in paper.

ORDER BLANK FOR THE JEWEL PATTERNS

JEWEL PATTERN SERVICE, 200 Fifth Avenue, New York City, N. Y.
Enclosed find $....Please send me the Ruth Rutledge Patterns listed below:
Pattern Nos. and sizes:..........
Name..........
Number and Street..........
City..........State..........

SEND ME JEWEL FASHION MAGAZINE

I am enclosing 10c for Summer Fashion Book.
Name..........
Number and Street..........
City..........State..........

An original 1930s advertisement for the "JEWEL PATTERN SERVICE By Ruth Rutledge." Many collectors are having these original Jewel News clippings framed. *Eisnaugle Collection.*

Also see Chapter 16 in "Jewel Tea Sales and Houseware Collectibles" for further details.

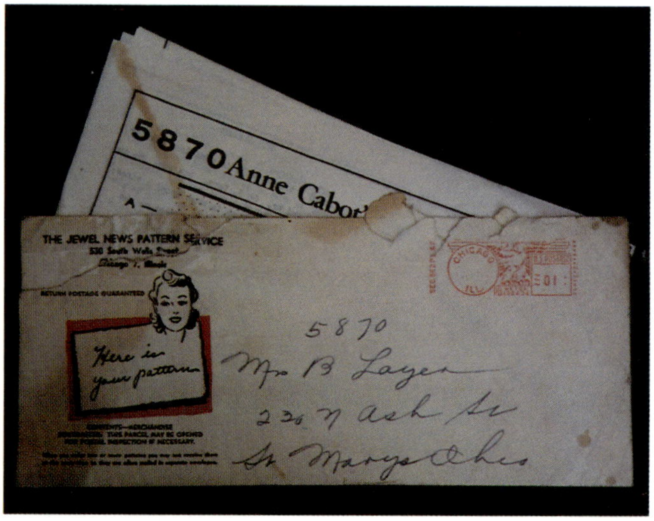

A portion of the pattern from the Jewel News Pattern Service has been removed. *Vogel Collection.*

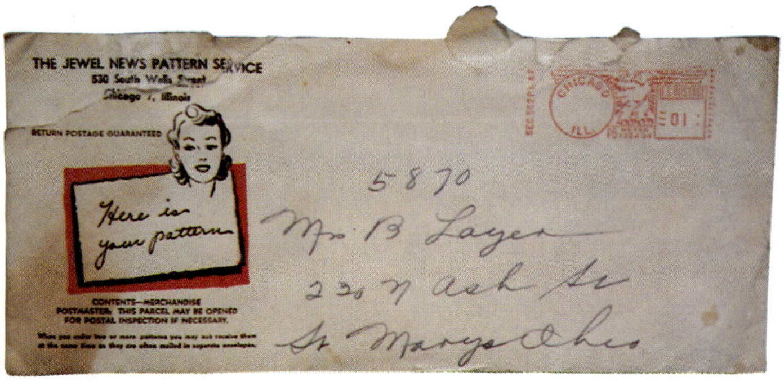

An envelop containing an original pattern. Note the return address: "THE JEWEL NEWS PATTERN SERVICE 530 SOUTH WALLS STREET CHICAGO 7, ILLINOIS." This is from the "JEWEL TEA CO., INC." *Vogel Collection.*

Jewel Sewing Machine

The Jewel "Sewing Machine" had been removed from its original treadle base. It was received as a gift from friends, who are aware that I search for anything marked "JEWEL" or "JEWELL." There is no association between this machine and the Jewel Tea Co. Jewel did offer sewing machines. *Author's Collection.*

The "Jewel" name appeared on various pieces of large furniture and had no association with this historical company.

Light Bulbs

Jewel "Incandescent Lamps" in the original carton. Its association with the Jewel Tea Company, Inc. is unknown at present. *Hamilton Collection.*

The original Incandescent Lamp bulb still enclosed inside the container. *Hamilton Collection.*

Jewel Machine Oil

A metal tin marked "Our Jewel Axle Oil. INDEPENDENT OIL CO., MANSFIELD, O." The same printed paper label appears on the reverse side. *Andrews Collection.*

In the Ohio area, collectors can find a 6-1/2" high bottle with a cork stopper. The bottle is marked "Our Jewel Machine Oil Will Not Gum. Mfd. by INDEPENDENT OIL CO., MANSFIELD, O." These bottles are readily available to collectors and require little searching, most of them are found full. *Edelman Collection.*

Jewel Flour

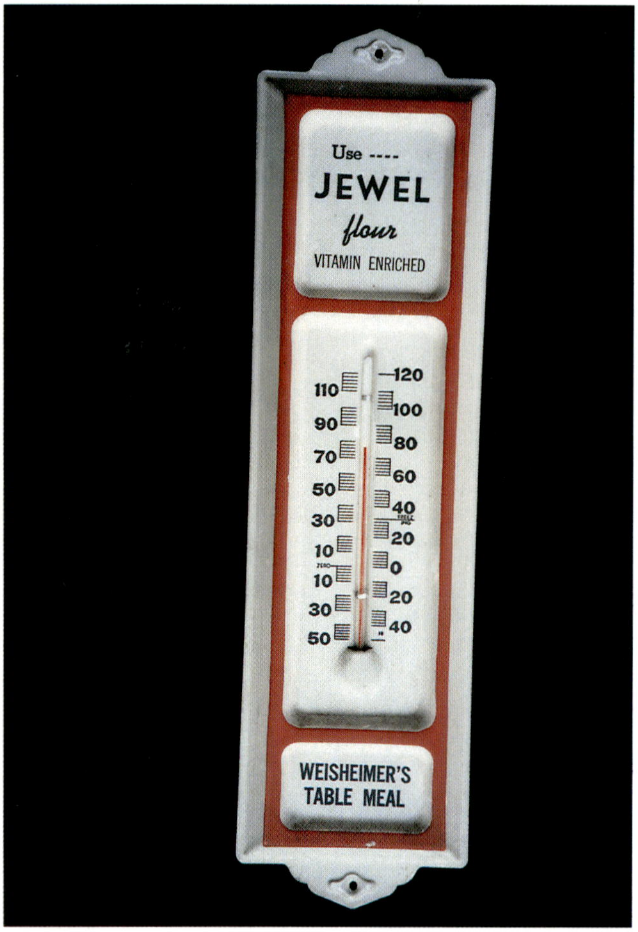

The Jewel Flour "Thermometer," shown here, has no association with the Jewel Tea Company, Inc. This thermometer is approximately 13" long by 3-1/2" wide. A set of playing cards marked "Jewel Flour" can be found. I know of one in a private collection. *Author's Collection.*

On page 53 in "Jewel Tea Sales and Houseware Collectibles," a pair of Jewel Kitchen Tongs appear. These tongs were incorrectly listed as being marked "JEWEL TEA." Only "JEWEL" appears on the handle. I believe these tongs are related to the above Jewel Flour "Thermometer" and "Playing" cards.

The Jewel Box

This two piece plastic container is marked "The Jewel Box" on the lid. A collection of Jewel tea bags are kept inside. The container, and its association, is unknown. I am familiar with the famous "Jewel Box" located in Forest Park in St. Louis. Could this have been a novelty item from this popular location? *Hamilton Collection.*

Jewel Paper Products

The association of these Jewel paper products is unknown, unless stated otherwise. You be the judge! IT'S ALL COLLECTIBLE...

Jewel "Typewriter Paper" with original banding. *Sivils Collection.*

No indication of the Jewel Tea Company, Inc. appears on the Jewel "Order Book." On the cover a list of Numbers with Description, Size and No. of Leaves are provided. Below this listing "Specify by Number When Ordering." This publication is marked WESTAB.® See "Construction Paper" below. *Randall Collection.*

A full package containing Jewel "Construction Paper REG. U.S. PAT. OFF. Excellent for use with water color paints CRAYON OR PENCIL." This "Construction Paper" is marked WESTAB.® *Eisnaugle Collection.*

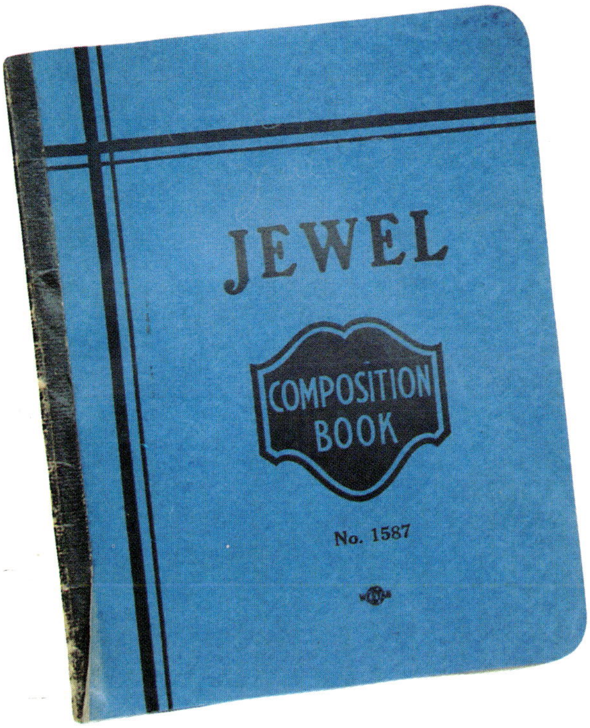

Jewel "Composition Book" No. 1587. *Sivils Collection.*

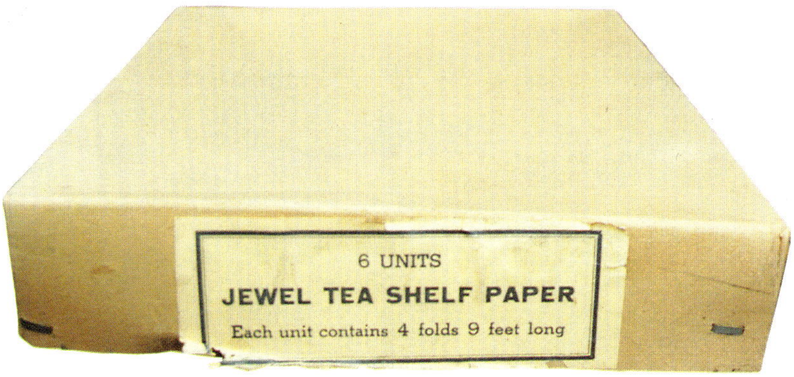

This carton held "6 Units JEWEL TEA SHELF PAPER Each unit contains 4 folds 9 feet long." This shelf paper can be dated to 1945. Original packaging is almost impossible to find. *Sivils Collection.*

Jewel Stove

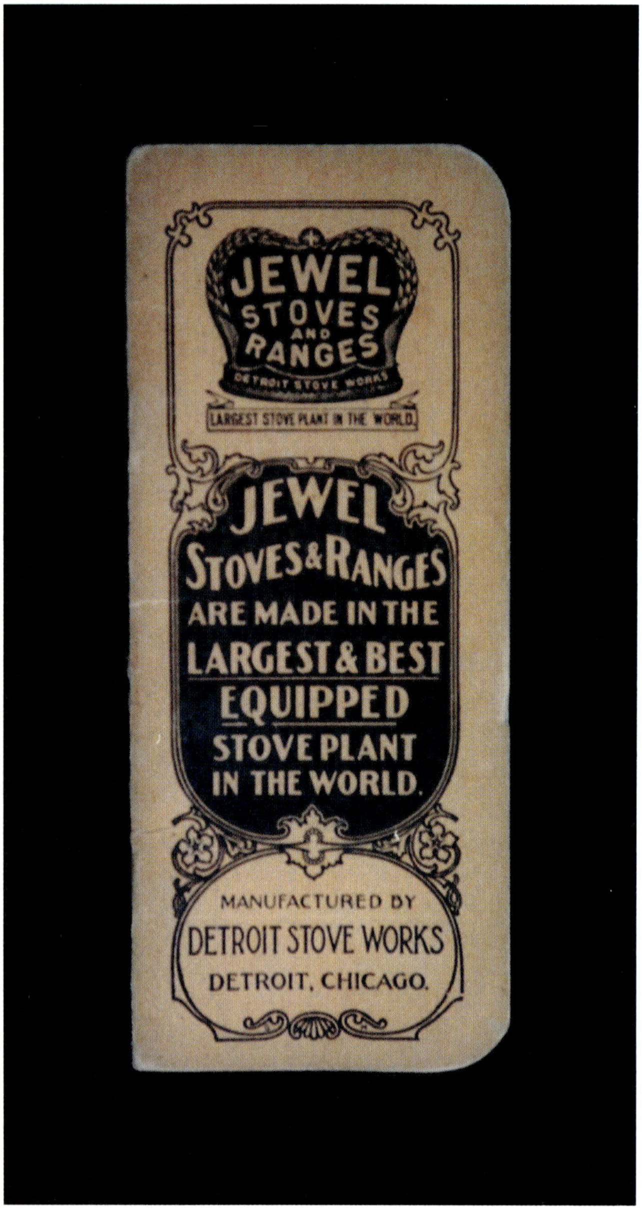

The "Jewel Stoves and Ranges" booklet may have been a give away with the purchase of a stove or range. The cover promoted "JEWEL Stoves & Ranges are made in the LARGEST & BEST EQUIPPED STOVE PLANT IN THE WORLD." Manufactured by "DETROIT STOVE WORKS DETROIT, CHICAGO." This publication is 5-1/2" long x 2-1/2" wide. Pages inside are blank lined pages. Various "Jewel" pokers and related stove items can be found from this company. Beware, this has no association with the Jewel Tea Company, Inc. *Eisnaugle Collection.*

An interesting "WARNING" is printed on the last page next to the "JEWEL Stoves and Range" trademark.

"The use of the name 'Jewel' as applied to stoves, ranges and furnaces was granted for use by UNITED STATES Letters Patent No. 4994, dated July 31st, 1877, and No. 6435, dated August 6th, 1878, renewed as No. 29707 and No. 29708, the name 'Jewel' having been used by us many years before 1877 and continually ever since.

"For many years the Detroit Stove Works has identified its wares by casting upon each of its stoves, ranges and furnaces the well known 'Jewel' trade mark pictured above. It is a mark of quality and economy, and a protection to stove buyers.

"Notwithstanding these facts, and without our sanction, some stove manufacturers have adopted the name 'Jewel', using it generally with prefaces or affixes, thus attempting, we believe, to trade upon our name and reputation. Take warning and do not be deceived. All genuine 'Jewel' stoves, ranges and furnaces have, in addition to the above trade mark, the name 'Detroit Stove Works' upon them. On our Gas Ranges we have prefixed the word 'Detroit' to the name 'Jewel'. Don't accept counterfeits or substitutes, or allow yourself to be convinced that something else is just as good as the genuine 'Jewel', and you will profit by low fuel bills, and have a stove or furnace that is made right in every respect. DETROIT STOVE WORKS."

The famous Jewel Tea Company began in 1899, twenty-two years after the "Jewel Stoves and Ranges — Detroit Stove Works" was granted by the UNITED STATES the use of the name "JEWEL" on stoves, ranges, and furnaces.

In Barrington, Illinois, Mary Dunbar and her staff used a Clark Jewel Oven in their test kitchen. This Jewel oven appeared in a historical photograph in The Jewel News Vol. 11 No. 6 1933.

Jewel Shortening

A four pound bail handle "Swift's Jewel Shortening" container. Marked: "Made From Hardened Vegetable Oil Swift & Company General Office: Chicago, Ill. Reg. U.S. Pat Off." The shortening was excellent for "pastry, for sauteing, and for deep frying." This container is highly collectable, but it is not Jewel Tea. A variety of accessories marked "Swift's Jewel" can be found. *Eisnaugle Collection.*

APPENDICES

APPENDIX 1

Membership Information

When writing to any of the organizations listed below, enclose a stamped, self-addressed, return envelope, otherwise no reply will be mailed to you in return.

Barrington Area Historical Society
Michael Harkins, Executive Director
212 West Main Street
Barrington, Illinois 60010

China Specialties, Inc.
P.O. Box 361280
Strongsville, Ohio 44136
Phone 1 (216) 220-7456 or write.
See Appendix 2.

Hall China Collector Club
P.O. Box 360488
Cleveland, Ohio 44136
Membership $13.00 per year.

Jewel Tea Historical Foundation
212 West Main Street
Barrington, Illinois 60010-3011
Phone 1 (708) 381-1730
One year membership is $30.00.
Five year membership is $100.00.

N.A.L.C.C.
Patti Byerly, Vice President
4514 Errington Rd.
Columbus, Ohio 43227
Membership is $20.00 payable to N.A.L.C.C.
See Appendix 3.

APPENDIX 2

China Specialties, Inc.

In 1990, The Hall China Company of East Liverpool, Ohio agreed to produce an exclusive line of "Limited Edition" Autumn Leaf items for China Specialties, Inc., of Strongsville, Ohio.

These "Limited Edition" Autumn Leaf items are **not reproductions, but new, collectible additions to the Autumn Leaf line.** Hall China utilized only shapes NEVER before offered in the Jewel Tea Company Autumn Leaf pattern.

Many of the decals used to decorate their line of products were original (left over from the Jewel Tea production and in storage at Hall all these years). Their first piece was the classically art decor "AIRFLOW" Teapot with the famous Autumn Leaf decal. Hall produced 1,999 teapots and then the issue was retired.

The popular Hall China Football Teapot was released during the 1995 football season. Each "Football" is numbered and marked "A China Specialties Exclusive Limited Edition of less than 1,399 by HALL.® The Autumn Leaf pattern was first produced by the HALL CHINA COMPANY in 1933. This FOOTBALL Teapot shape was created in 1938 as part of the Novelty Line of teapots. Cast from the original molds and glazed and decorated by hand by the Hall China Craftsmen, the combination of the Autumn Leaf Pattern and this shape is unique and exists for the first time ever in this piece. 1995 China Specialties, P.O. Box 361280, Strongsville, OH 44138." Decorated with the Autumn Leaf decal and gold trim, this piece was a great companion for the 1993 Autumn Leaf Automobile teapot. See page 238, "The Jewel Tea Company, Its History and Products."

APPENDIX 3

N.A.L.C.C.

In 1978, Nancy Brock and Norma Jones Shaughnessey formed the National Autumn Leaf Collectors Club (N.A.L.C.C.).

"The purpose of the Club is to broaden the collectors knowledge of Autumn Leaf Dinnerware and to further the enjoyment and pleasure of collecting through fellowship."

N.A.L.C.C. newsletters are published and mailed to members only during January, March, May, July, September, and November. Club pieces are announced in these publications and produced in limited numbers. All pieces are manufactured by The Hall China Company, East Liverpool, Ohio and were never offered by the historical Jewel Tea Company.

N.A.L.C.C. does not stock additional pieces or have additional pieces offered from past years; occasionally those pieces are available in the secondary market and they can be costly. All club pieces will have a backstamp indicating N.A.L.C.C. and the year.

The "Philadelphia" tea set. This three piece set was offered in 1990.

APPENDIX 4

"THE JEWEL LINE OF PRODUCTS" appeared on the back page of the "1926 - 1927" Jewel Calendar Housecard. This Housecard contained 12 pages of cooking suggestions, recipes, advice on how to make coffee, premiums, historical photographs, and general information. The cover section of this document has a 12 month calendar (July 1926 - June 1927). Using a magnifying glass will help you in studying "THE JEWEL LINE OF PRODUCTS," in this historical document. Note all products are marked "JEWEL TEA CO., INC. NEW YORK — CHICAGO." Use this as a reference in dating your products.

APPENDIX 5

During the period that Jewel products and premiums were sold, logos occasionally overlapped because the packaging was used up rather than destroyed when a new logo was introduced. It is not uncommon to find late 1920s packaging still being sold after Jewel moved into their Barrington headquarters in 1930.

The "Bar 'n Circle" logo is believed to be the oldest logo, dating from 1903 until approximately 1910.

The "Diamond" logo/trademark was used c. 1916, when Jewel redesigned their logo to commemorate the incorporation of the Company. The redesigned logo became "SKI-RO" and was used with the "Diamond" until approximately 1919.

The "Scale" logo appeared for a very short time during the early 1920s.

The "Laurel-Wreath" logo appeared during the mid-1920s and appeared on numerous pieces of Bavarian China. See "Appendix 3, "Jewel Tea, Sales, and Houseware Collectibles."

The "Bulls eye" logo was introduced in the early 1920s and continued in use until Jewel's move into their Barrington headquarters.

In 1933, the "Barrington Circle" logo appeared on many products. In one of the outer circles appears "Reg. U.S. Pat. Off," inside the larger circle "TESTED AND APPROVED BY MARY DUNBAR — JEWEL HOMEMAKERS INSTITUTE." The center section has the 1920s style "Bulls eye" logo. Many products marked with the "Barrington Circle" logo, can be found marked 1933. Jewel moved into their new headquarters in April 1930. Whereafter, we see the words "JEWEL PARK" on many products.

The "Jewel Home Shopping Service" within the Laurel-Wreath was popular during the early 1950s.

The "Mary Dunbar" logo and her famous signature appeared in numerous Jewel Home Shopping Service Catalogs and was the mark of quality. See Appendix 4, "Jewel Tea, Sales, and Houseware Collectibles."

The "Scripted Jewel" logo was popular during the 1950s - 1960s. Also popular was a 1950s slogan "A Better Place to Work, A Better Place to Trade."

The Melior/Helvetica block "JEWEL HOME SHOPPING SERVICE" logo was popular during from 1960 to 1966. No illustration is available. See "The Jewel Tea Company, Its History and Products" page 6.

The "Jewel In-Home Shopping Service" logo dates to the 1970s; it first appeared on the cover of the 1970 Summer Special Catalog. In 1981, Jewel ceased operations under the "JEWEL" name.

APPENDIX 6

Old Mother Hubbard

In 1927, old "Mother Hubbard," shown in this cartoon, was a smart Jewel shopper. Mother Hubbard relied on Jewel for her pantry needs and in the end no cupboard was bare if Jewel was allowed into your home. Why? Ask "Mother Hubbard."

BIBLIOGRAPHY

"Coffee Facts For You," *Jewel Tea Co., Inc.*, New York - Chicago, ©1927.

Drury, George H. *Train Watchers Guide to North America Railroads,* Ref. 2nd Edition. 1992 Kalmbach Books (Reporting Marks p. 255).

"Hall China Collector's Club Newsletter" *Wilson Publication* Four times a year publication.

"How to Get New Customers" *Jewel Tea Co., Inc.*, Jewel Park Barrington, Ill." 1936.

"Jewel Cereal Products," *Jewel Tea Co., Inc.*, New York - Chicago.

"Jewel New Customer Representative," *Jewel Direct Marketing Division,* A Division of Jewel Companies, Inc. Rev. 1972.

"Men of the Year," *Jewel Home Shopping Service*, 1971.

Miller, C.L. *The Jewel Tea Company, Its History and Products*, Schiffer Book for Collectors, 1994.

_____________ *Jewel Tea Sales and Houseware Collectibles*, Schiffer Book for Collectors, 1995.

"N.A.L.C.C. Newsletter," bimonthly publication, *National Autumn Leaf Collectors Club.*

"New Route Builder Sales Training Manual," 1966.

"Other Quality Groceries," *Jewel Tea Co., Inc.*, New York - Chicago, ©1929.

"Sales Course," *Jewel Tea Co., Inc.*, New York.

Stahl, James H. *Key-Wind Coffee Tins*, L-W Book Sales 1991.

"What You Should Know About Tea," *Jewel Tea Co.*, Five North Wabash Ave., Chicago, 1928.

"Why 700,000 Housewives Buy the Jewel Way," ©1925.

INDEX

PRICE GUIDE

Page	Position	Description / Price
		Cookie Jar Cover Photograph $25-30
3	C	Historical photographs vary $1-100
4	B	Historical photographs vary $1-100
5	T	$75-100 complete
	B	$75-100 complete; $8-12 cook book only
7	B	Historical photographs vary $1-100
9	T	Historical photographs vary $1-100
10	B	Historical publications vary $10-30
12	B	Historical publications vary $10-30
13	BL	Historical photographs vary $1-100
15	TR	Historical photographs vary $1-100
15	B	Historical photographs vary $1-100
16	C	Complete Jewel Catalogue's $20-25
17-18		Historical photographs vary $1-100
19	BR	$15-20
20		Historical photographs vary $1-100
21		Historical photographs vary $1-100
21	BR	$100-125 complete
22	TL	$55-75
22	TR	$55-75
22	BL	$55-75
22	BR	$55-75
23	TL	$55-75
23	BL	$60-75
23	BC	$60-75
23	BR	$60-75
24	TL	$50-60
24	TR	$45-55
24	BL	$40-50
24	BR	$45-55
25	TL	$45-55
25	TR	$40-50
25	BL	$45-55
25	CR	$40-50
25	BR	$40-50
26	TL	$15-20 ea.
26	R	$15-20
26	BL	$15-20 ea.
26	BR	$15-20
27	TL	$15-20
27	BL	$20-25 cardboard
27	BR	$20-25 cardboard
28	TL	$7-10
28	TR	$7-10
28	BL	$20-25
28	BR	$20-25
29	L	$50-60
29	TR	$50-60
29	BR	$50-60
30	TL	$50-60
30	CR	$50-60
30	BL	$50-60
31	TL	$50-60
31	TR	$50-60
31	BL	$50-60
31	BR	$50-60
32	TL	$45-50
32	BR	$45-50
32	TR	$75-100
32	CR	$75-100
32	BR	$75-100
33	TR	$45-50 ea.
33	L	$45-50 ea.
33	BR	$45-50 ea.
34	TL	$45-55
34	BL	$45-55
34	TR	$45-55
34	BR	$45-55
35	TL	$25-35 ea. (Fine and Regular Grind)
35	BL	$25-35
35	TR	$25-35
35	BR	$25-35
36	TL	$25-35
36	L	$25-35 ea.
36	R	$25-35
37	TL	$30-40
37	BR	$25-35
38	TL	$75-100 unopen
38	CL	$75-100 unopen
38	BL	$75-100 unopen
38	TR	$35-45
38	CR	$35-45
38	BR	$35-45 ea.
39	TL	$5-8
39	TR	$5-8
39	BR	$10-15 open original carton
40	TL	$125-150
40	TR	$125-150
40	BL	$45-55
40	BR	$45-55
41	BL	l. $20-25 r. $5-10
41	BR	25-30 complete
43	CL	$50-60
43	BL	$50-60
43	R	$50-60 ea.
44	TL	$50-60
44	BL	$35-45
44	R	$40-50 ea.
45	TL	$40-50
45	CR	$60-75
45	BL	$20-25
46	TL	$20-25
46	TR	$20-25
46	BL	$20-25
46	BR	$35-45
47	TL	$35-45
47	BL	$35-45
47	R	$35-45 ea.
48	TL	$35-45 ea.
48	TR	$45-55
48	BR	$45-55
49	TL	$25-35
49	TR	$35-45
49	BL	$1-3 ea. (loose bags)
49	BR	$1-3 ea. (loose bags)
50	T	$50-60 ea.
50	CL	$50-60 ea.
50	BL	$50-60
50	R	$50-60
51	TL	$20-25
51	C	$20-25
51	BR	$20-25
52	TL	$15-20 with original label
52	TR	$15-20 with original label
52	BL	$25-35 with original label
52-53C		$100-125 with original label (Chest)
53	TL	$25-35 with original label
53	TR	$10-15 ea.
53	BR	$6-8
54	C	l - r. top row $50-65 ea.; l - r. bottom row $40-50, $50-65, $50-65, $30-40, $20-30
55	TL	$50-65 ea.
55	BL	$50-65 ea.
55	TR	$40-50 without lid
55	BR	$50-65
56	TL	$50-65 ea.
56	CR	$50-65ea.
56	L	$85-100
56	R	$85-100
57	TL	$50-65
57	L	$30-40 ea.
57	C	$30-40 ea.
57	BR	$30-40 ea.
58	TL	$30-40
58	R	$30-40
58	BL	$10-15 original cardboard cartons
59	R	$30-35 ea.
60	BL	Biscuit Flour $35-45; Cinnamon $30-40; Nutmeg $30-40
60	R	$35-45
61	TR	$30-40 ea.
61	CL	$30-40
61	BR	$30-40 ea.
62	TL	$30-40
62	CL	$30-40
62	BL	$30-40
62	TR	$50-60
62	BR	$50-60
63	TR	$20-25
63	BR	$55-75
63	CR	$55-75 ea.
63	BR	$55-75 ea.
64	TL	$55-75 ea.
64	BL	$55-75 ea.
64	TR	$60-80
64	BR	$60-80
65	L	$50-65
65	TR	$60-80
65	BR	$60-80
66	TL	$20-30
66	BL	$20-30
66	TR	$8-12
66	BR	$25-35
67	TL	$30-40 ea.
67	BL	$30-40 ea.
67	TR	$30-40 ea.
67	BR	$30-40 ea.
68	L	$30-40
68	TR	$30-40
68	BR	$30-40
69	L	$30-40
69	TR	$55-75 ea.
69	BR	$55-75 ea.
70	TL	$30-40 ea.
70	TR	$30-40 ea.
70	BR	$30-40 ea.
71	TL	$30-40
71	BL	$30-40
71	TR	$30-40
71	CR	$30-40 ea.
72	TL	$30-40
72	BL	$35-45
72	TR	$30-40
73	TL	$30-40
73	BR	$30-40
74	T	Historical photographs vary $1-100
75	BL	$25-35
75	TR	$25-35
75	CR	$50-75 with original carton
75	BR	$50-75 with original carton
76	CL	$10-15
76	BL	$50-60
76	CR	$50-60
76	BR	$75-100 with original carton
77	TC	$50-60
77	L	$60-75
77	R	$60-75
77	B	$60-75 ea.
78	TL	$20-25 ea.
78	TR	$30-40
78	BR	$30-40 original carton
79	TL	$35-45
79	TR	$35-45
80	BL	$30-40
80	TR	$30-40
80	BR	Historical photographs vary $1-100; Baking Powder $30-40
81	TC	Historical photographs vary $1-100
81	BL	$35-45 ea.
81	BR	$35-45 ea.
82	TL	$35-45
82	BL	$30-40 without lid
82	TR	$30-40
82	BR	$30-45 ea.
83	TL	$30-40
83	TR	$30-40
83	CL	$35-45 ea.
83	BR	$35-45
84	L	$20-24
84	R	$5-6
85	C	Historical photographs vary $1-100
86	TC	Historical photographs vary $1-100
87	TR	$30-40
87	BR	$30-40
88	R	$55-65
89	TL	$55-65
89	BL	$55-65
89	R	$55-65
90	TL	$55-65
90	TR	$55-65
90	BL	$55-65
90	BR	$55-65
91	TL	Historical photographs vary $1-100
91	TR	$25-35
91	BC	l. - r. $55-65, $25-35, $55-65
92	TL	45-55
92	TR	Historical photographs vary $1-100
92	CR	35-45
92	BR	35-45
93	TL	25-35 unopen
93	BL	25-35 unopen
93	R	50-60
94	T	Historical photographs vary $1-100
94	BR	45-50 unopen
95	L	$40-50
95	R	$40-50
95	B	$20-25 ea.
96	TL	$20-25 ea.
96	BL	$25-30
96	CR	$35-40 unopen
97	TR	$15-20
97	BC	$20-25 ea. unopen
98	TL	$15-20 without lid

98 TR $20-25

98 BL $20-25

98 BR $20-25

99 TL $45-55 complete 2 bottles

99 R $75-85 complete 3 bottles with tag

99 BL $75-85 complete 3 bottles with tag

100 TL $65-75

100 TR $65-75

100 B Historical photographs vary $1-100

101 TL $65-75

101 TR $65-75

101 BL $45-55

101 BR $45-55

102 TL $35-45

102 TR $35-45

102 BL $45-55

102 BR $45-55

103 TL $30-40 ea.

103 BR $30-40 ea.

104 TL $20-30

104 R $20-30

104 BL UND

105 TL Historical photographs vary $1-100

105 TR $25-35

105 BL $25-35

106 L Historical photographs vary $1-100

106 TR Historical photographs vary $1-100

106 BR $40-50 complete

107 L $40-50 complete

107 BL $40-50 complete

107 TR $40-50 complete

107 CL $40-50 complete

107 BR $40-50 complete

108 TL $8-12 with original wrapper

108 TR $40-50 complete

108 L $85-100 complete

108 CR $40-50 complete

108 BR $40-50 complete

109 C $175-200 complete

110 TL $40-50

110 TR $40-50

110 C $40-50

110 B $40-50

111 TL $50-75

111 TR $12-15 single bar

111 CL $40-50

111 BL $55-65 complete

111 CR $55-65 complete

112 TR $60-85 complete

112 C $55-75 complete

112 B $55-75 complete

113 TL $25-30

113 TR $25-35 complete

113 CL $35-45

113 BL $75-85 full

113 BR $75-100 full

114 TL $75-85 full

114 R $20-25 ea.

114 BL $20-25 ea.

115 TL $35-45 complete

115 R $35-45

115 BL $35-45

116 TL $55-75 complete

116 TR $55-75 complete

116 BL $55-75 with original carton

116 BR $25-35

117 TC $35-45 complete

117 R $15-20 complete/unopen

117 BC $15-20 complete/unopen

118 TL $25-35 full

118 TR $25-35 full

118 BL $25-35 full

118 BR $25-35 full

119 TL $20-25 ea.

119 TR $6-8 unopen

119 BL $25-35

119 BR $6-8

120 TL $25-35

120 TR $25-35 ea.

120 CL $25-35

120 BR $50-60 ea.

121 TC $100-125 complete

121 BL $75-85 complete

121 BR $75-85 complete

122 TL $30-40

122 TR $30-40

122 BL $50-60 complete

123 TR $35-45 complete

123 BL $35-45 full

124 TL $15-20

124 TR $5-8

124 CL $25-35 complete

124 CR $15-20

124 B $20-25

125 T $75-100 complete

125 B $75-100 complete

126 C $35-40 ea.

127 T $25-35 ea.
Baby Powder see page 113
$75-100 full

127 R $35-45

127 BL $35-45

128 L&R $20-25 ea.

129 TL $20-25

129 BL $20-25

129 TR $50-75 full

129 BR $50-75 full

130 L&R Historical photographs vary $1-100

130 CL $15-20

130 BR $40-50

131 L $40-50

132 TL Historical photographs vary $1-100

132 TR Historical photographs vary $1-100

132 BL Historical photographs vary $1-100

132 CR $40-50

132 BR $40-50

133 TL $55-60

133 BL $55-60

133 TR $55-60

133 CR $55-60

133 BR $55-60

134 TR $85-100 full

134 L $85-100 full

134 BR $85-100 full

135 TL $50-60

135 BL $50-60

135 TR $30-40

135 BR $30-40

136 TL $40-50

136 BL $40-50

136 TR $45-55 ea.

136 BR $45-55 ea.

137 TL $50-60

137 BL $50-60

137 TR $20-25

137 BR $20-25

138 TL $175-200 full

138 BL $40-60

138 R $15-20 Jewel Grocery Stock Cards Complete

139 TL $20-30

139 BL $40-50

139 BC $40-50

139 R $40-50

140 TL $20-25 ea.

140 BL $20-25 ea.

140 TR $20-25

140 BR $20-25

141 TL $20-25

141 BR $20-25 ea.

141 R $20-25 ea.

142 TL $40-50

142 CL $40-50

142 BL $30-40

142 TR UND

142 CR UND

142 BR $30-40

143 TL $35-45 complete

143 CL $35-45

143 TR $20-25

143 BR $20-25

144 TL $15-20 ea.

144 BL $15-20

144 TR $20-30

144 BR $15-20

145 TL $20-25 ea.

145 BL $15-20 ea.

145 R $10-15

146 TL $15-20

146 TR $20-25 complete

146 BL $25-35

146 BR $40-50 ea.

147 TL $15-20

147 R $15-20

147 BL $15-20

148 TL $35-45

148 CL $35-45

148 BL $35-45

148 CR $35-45

148 BR $35-45

149 T $15-20 Jewel Grocery Stock Card Complete

149 BL $75-100 full

149 BR $75-100 full

150 TL $40-50

150 BL $30-40

150 TR $30-40

150 CR $30-40

150 BR $30-40

151 TL $50-60

151 BL $50-60

151 TR $15-20 ea.

151 CR $20-25 ea.

151 BR $20-25

152 TL $20-25 ea.

152 BL $20-25

152 R $20-25 ea.

153 TR $20-25

153 BL $20-25 ea.

153 BR $20-25 ea. (original Jewel Money1-5)

154 TL $20-25

154 BL $35-45

154 TR $35-45

154 BR $20-25

155 TL $30-35

155 TR $30-35

155 BL $20-25

155 BR $30-35

156 TL $30-35

156 TC $30-35

156 TR $30-35

156 BC $30-35 ea.

157 TL $15-25 ea.

157 BL $35-45 complete

157 TR $20-25

157 CR $15-20

157 BR $20-25 full

158 TL $25-35 full

158 TR $20-25 full

158 BL $25-35 full

158 CR $20-25 full

158 BR $20-25 full

159 TL $20-25

159 TR $20-25 complete

159 BL $20-25 complete

160 TL $20-25

160 TR $20-25

160 CL $125-150 complete

160 BL $20-25

160 BR $20-25

161 TL $20-25

161 TR $20-25

161 CL $20-25

161 BR $20-25 ea.

162 TL $20-25

162 BL $20-25

162 R $20-25

163 L $50-60 complete

164 L $40-50 complete

164 TR $25-30

165 T $45-50 ea.

165 L $45-50

165 BR $45-50

166 TL $55-65 complete

166 BL $55-65 complete

166 TR $55-65

166 BR $55-65

167 TL $25-30

167 BL $25-30

167 TR $30-35

167 BR $30-35

168 TL $50-60

168 CL $50-60

168 BL $50-60

169 TL $45-55

169 R $45-55

169 BC $45-55

170 TL $75-100

170 CL $100-125

170 BC $35-45

170 BL $50-60

171 TR $10-15

171 BR $10-15

172 TL $10-15

172 C $10-15

172 BL $10-15

173 TR $35-45

173 L $35-45

173 CR $35-45

173 BR $35-45

174 TL $55-60

174 BL $25-35 full

174 R $30-35

174 BR $30-35

175 TL $25-35 full

175 CL $5-7

175 R $5-7

175 BC $75-90 complete

176 L $25-30 full

176 TR $10-12

176 CR $10-15

176 B $10-15

177 TL $20-25

177 R $20-25

177 CL $10-15

177 BR $15-20 ea.

178 TR $100-130 complete

178 BC $100-120

178 BR $100-120

179 T $35-45 ea.

179 CR $100-130

179 BL $100-130

179 BR $25-35

180 TL $50-60

180 TR $50-60

180 BC $50-60

180 CR $50-60

180 BR $50-60

181 TL $50-60

181 CL $15-20

181 TR $15-20 ea.

182 L $30-35

182 BL $25-35 ea.

182 TR $25-35

182 CR $25-35

182-183 BC $20-25 ea.

183 TL $25-35

183 CL $25-35

183 TR $75-80 complete/full

183 BR Original Jewel Money $1-5

184 TL $75-80 complete/full

184 TR $75-80 complete/full

184 CL $20-30

184 BR $20-30

185 TL $10-20

185 TR $30-35

185 CL $35-40

185 BL $25-30

185 BR $25-35

186 TL $50-75

186 CR $50-75

186 BL $45-60

187 TR l. $75-100 r. $100-125

187 L $100-125

187 BR $20-35

188 TR $15-20

188 TL $10-15

188 CL $10-15

Page	Position	Value
188	BL	$15-20
188	BR	$20-25
189	T	$30-40 complete
189	BR	$10-15
190	TL	$10-15
190	TR	$10-15
190	BL	$10-15
190	R	$10-15
190	BR	$10-15
191	TL	$10-15
191	R	$5-8 lids only
191	BL	$10-15
192	TL	$15-20
192	BL	$25-35
192	TR	$15-20
192	CR	$20-25
192	BR	$25-35
193	TL	$45-55
193	CL	$30-45
193	TR	$50-65
193	BR	$45-55
194	TL	$20-25
194	L	$5-10 ea.
194	R	$50-75
194	BL	$50-60 full
195		Historical photographs vary $1-100
196	L	$15-25 ea.
196	TR	$15-25
196	CR	$15-25
196	BR	$15-25 ea.
197	T	$15-20 Jewel Grocery Stock Cards Complete
197	B	$15-25 ea.
198	TL	$35-40
198	TR	$35-40
198	CL	$20-25
198	CR	$20-25 ea.
198	B	Historical photographs vary $1-100
199	L	$50-60
199	BR	$65-75
200	TL	$65-75
200	TR	$45-55
200	BL	$65-75
200	BR	$45-55
201	TL	$45-55
201	TR	$45-55
201	BL	$55-65
201	BR	$75-100
202	TL	$45-55
202	TR	$45-55
202	BL	$45-55
202	BR	$45-55
203	TL	$45-55
203	TR	$50-60
203	BL	$45-55
203	BR	$50-60
204	TL	$50-60
204	BL	$45-55
204	TR	$85-100
204	BR	$45-55
205	TL	$85-100
205	TR	$85-100
205	B	UND
207-221		Historical photographs vary $1-100
210	TL	$150-175
210	CL	$150-175
210	BL	$150-175
222	TL	$20-25
222	R	$15-20
222	B	$15-20
223	BR	$25-30 (poor condition)
224	TL	$25-30
224	TR	$25-30
224	L	$25-30
224	R	$5-8 Jewel News clippings
225	TL	$5-8 Jewel News clippings
225	TR	$60-75
225	BL	$50-60
225	BR	$60-75
226	R	$20-25
226	B	$20-25
227	TL	$45-50
227	TR	$8-12 ea.
227	BL	$45-50
227	CR	$25-35 ea.
227	BR	$25-35 ea.
228	TL	$3-5 ea.
228	TR	$5-8 Jewel News clippings
228	CR	$35-45 complete
228	BR	$35-45 complete
229	TL	$20-30
229	TR	$12-18 ea. complete
229	BL	$10-15
229	BR	$25-30
230	TL	$35-45
230	TR	$5-8
230	BR	$20-25
231	TL	$20-25
231	TR	$20-25
231	BL	$20-25
231	BR	$75-125 complete
232	L	$5-10
232	R	$18-20
234	L	$100-130
234	R	$100-130
235	C	$175-225 complete